D0989572

JOURNAL FOR THE STUDY OF THE NEW TESTAMENT
SUPPLEMENT SERIES
91

JSOT Press
Sheffield

Matthew's Narrative Web

Over, and Over, and Over Again

Janice Capel Anderson

Journal for the Study of the New Testament
Supplement Series 91

Published by JSOT Press
JSOT Press is an imprint of
Sheffield Academic Press Ltd
343 Fulwood Road
Sheffield S10 3BP
England

Typeset by Sheffield Academic Press
and
Printed on acid-free paper in Great Britain
by Bookcraft
Midsomer Norton, Somerset

British Library Cataloguing in Publication Data

A catalogue record for this book is available
from the British Library

ISBN 1-85075-450-0

CONTENTS

PREFACE

This book is a slightly revised version of my doctoral dissertation, 'Over and Over and Over Again: Studies in Matthean Repetition' (University of Chicago, March 1985), available from the Regenstein Library, the University of Chicago, Chicago, Illinois, 60637. I have revised, combined and condensed Chapters 1 and 5 of that dissertation. Chapters 2 through 4 have only minor changes, primarily improving typographical errors and clarity of expression. I have eliminated a comparison of repetition in Matthew with one literary critic in Chapter 5 and added a brief discussion of orality and aurality. In the footnotes to each chapter I have given references to important works that have carried the discussion forward since the dissertation was written. I would appreciate hearing from readers who know of additional bibliography.

I was at first reluctant to publish this work, some ten years after I completed it in Advent of 1983. A great deal of water has passed under the bridge since then. For example, then I composed the dissertation by hand and mailed it from Idaho to Chicago to be typed by an approved dissertation office typist, and today I am word processing this preface on a computer. The key method I used then I called rhetorical literary criticism. It was essentially a position lying between what the guild has now settled on calling narrative and reader-response criticisms. In Gospel studies since then the problems as well as the possibilities of these approaches have been revealed. Several criticisms have been particularly telling. One is that the rallying cry of the Gospels as wholes, the Gospels as unified narratives, is just as much an *a priori* presupposition as previous assumptions that they were not. Secondly, narrative critics, influenced by American New Criticism, tended somewhat polemically to overemphasize the separation of text and historical context. Thirdly, the 'implied reader', pretending to be a neutral concept, masks a real reader: the Gospel critic herself (or more often himself) with a very particular social location. Today, literary criticism and social scientific criticism are attempting a *rapprochement.* Cultural criticism reigns, at least currently, in non-biblical literary studies.

Several factors have persuaded me to take the plunge anyway. The first is the strong encouragement I received from Elizabeth Struthers Malbon, whose own work, involving a structuralist approach to Mark, was also published by Sheffield Academic Press. Professor Malbon pointed out to me that readers are at different places in regard to developments in Gospel criticism. While my dissertation may appear to some as an example of an earlier stage of work, to others it will appear as a break with scholarly tradition—a break nonetheless more comprehensible to a redaction critic than a leap directly into post-structuralism. Further, I am convinced by Mieke Bal (*Murder and Difference: Gender, Genre, and Scholarship on Sisera's Death* [Bloomington: Indiana University Press, 1988]) that interpreters should read a text with multiple disciplinary codes in order to see what each code reveals and conceals about the text as well as the interests of the guild that employs it. If not quite a discipline, narrative/reader criticism constitutes one code through which the Gospels can be read along with historical, social scientific, theological and gender codes. What Bal says about the narratological code in relation to Judges 4 and 5 applies equally to narrative/reader criticism of the Gospels: 'Like other codes, it can be used judiciously or injudiciously, to open or close the interpretation, to oppose or support other codes, to impoverish or enrich the thematic universe of a text' (p. 85). Like other codes it can be used in the service of and against various ideological interests.

A second factor that persuaded me to publish was the continuing requests I receive for copies of my dissertation. Scholars who find references to it have difficulty obtaining it. Chapter 2 also essentially contains an unpublished 1981 paper on point of view in Matthew for the Society of Biblical Literature's Literary Analysis of the Gospels and Acts Group. Since it was cited in Jack Kingsbury's widely used *Matthew as Story*, I have received a number of requests for copies of it.

Finally, I have several convictions that remain unchanged. One is that analyzing the gospels with categories familiar to educated readers, such as plot, character, and point of view, makes the work of biblical critics—and the Gospels themselves—more accessible to students and to the public at large. Scholars may debate the exact genre of the

Gospels, but all readers need at least a vague sense of generic expectations to read. This is true whether the text they read is a letter, a chemistry textbook, or a detective story. Reading the Gospels with the basic categories of narrative at least allows readers to take up the Gospels without giving up on them as too alien or nonsensical. Narrative and reader-response criticisms also provide a set of reading conventions that continue to reveal/create new and exciting interpretations. The final conviction that remains unchanged is that the web of verbal repetitions in the Matthean narrative is *a* key to constructing any reading of the gospel.

In the original preface to my dissertation I dedicated the work to my teachers: to my teachers at Macalester College: David H. Hopper, Calvin J. Roetzel, and Lloyd Gaston, who introduced me to biblical studies; to my teachers at the University of Chicago Divinity School: Paul Ricoeur, William G. Thompson, SJ, and Jonathan Z. Smith, who graciously took over when Norman Perrin, my original advisor, died; and to a great scholar and man of faith, Norman Perrin. To this dedication I would like to add my thanks to my friends and colleagues in the Group on the Literary Analysis of the Gospels and Acts of the Society of Biblical Literature. Without their stimulation and encouragement this and subsequent work would have been greatly impoverished. I would also like to thank the staff of Sheffield Academic Press, especially my desk editors, Malcolm Ward and Andrew Kirk, for helping to bring this work to publication.

Janice Capel Anderson
Moscow, Idaho

ABBREVIATIONS

AnBib	Analecta biblica
ATR	*Anglican Theological Review*
BAGD	W. Bauer, W.F. Arndt, F.W. Gingrich and F.W. Danker, *Greek–English Lexicon of the New Testament*
BDF	F. Blass, A. Debrunner and R.W. Funk, *A Greek Grammar of the New Testament*
BDR	F. Blass, A. Debrunner and F. Rehkopf, *Grammatik des neutestamentlichen*
BLS	Bible and Literature Series
BR	*Biblical Research*
BTB	*Biblical Theology Bulletin*
CI	*Critical Inquiry*
CBA	Catholic Biblical Association
CBQ	*Catholic Biblical Quarterly*
FMLS	*Forum for Modern Language Studies*
GBS	Guides to Biblical Scholarship
HSCP	*Harvard Studies in Classical Philology*
ICC	International Critical Commentary
Int	*Interpretation*
IRT	*Issues in Religion and Theology*
JAAC	*Journal of Aesthetics and Art Criticism*
JAAR	*Journal of the American Academy of Religion*
JAF	*Journal of American Folklore*
JBL	*Journal of Biblical Literature*
JR	*Journal of Religion*
JSNT	*Journal for the Study of the New Testament*
JSNTSup	*Journal for the Study of the New Testament* Supplement Series
JTS	*Journal of Theological Studies*
NLH	*New Literary History*
NTS	*New Testament Studies*
PMLA	*Proceedings of the Modern Language Association*
PTMS	Pittsburgh Theological Monograph Series
SBLDS	SBL Dissertation Series
SE	*Studia Evangelica I, II, III*
SNTSMS	Society for New Testament Studies Monograph Series
TAPA	*Transactions of the American Philological Association*
TDNT	G. Kittel and G. Friedrich (eds.), *Theological Dictionary of the New Testament*
USQR	*Union Seminary Quarterly Review*
ZNW	*Zeitschrift für die neutestamentliche Wissenschaft*

Chapter 1

INTRODUCTION AND METHOD

1. *Introduction*

In E.B. White's novel, *Charlotte's Web*, the main characters are Charlotte, a spider, and her dear friend Wilbur, a pig.[1] The one blot that hangs over Wilbur's life is the knowledge that he is being fattened up to be slaughtered at Christmastide. Over the course of the summer and fall, Charlotte spins, in turn, the phrases 'Some Pig', 'Terrific', 'Radiant', and 'Humble' in her web. Her web hangs over Wilbur's pen. Visitors to the barn read the words and spin their own webs of meaning. With each succeeding phrase, Wilbur's fame spreads. Before she comes to the end of her own life and of the tale, Charlotte has saved Wilbur from ever becoming a Christmas ham. The Gospel of Matthew is a complex narrative web spun with numerous verbal repetitions. Like Charlotte's web it contains key words and phrases which readers must interpret to weave their own webs of meaning. Instead of 'Some Pig' or 'Terrific', Matthew's web contains repeated words like 'little-faiths', repeated phrases like 'Repent for the kingdom of heaven is at hand' (3.2 = 4.17), and doublets like the feeding stories or the Sign of Jonah stories. These verbal repetitions weave in and out of the narrative web. They contribute to the rhetoric, character, and plot of the narrative. This study has the dual purpose of examining Matthew as a narrative and the web of verbal repetition that helps to spin the tale. One difficulty that hovers over the project is whether the evangelist, the narrative, or the reader spins the web. Is it Charlotte, her web, the readers of the web, or the context in which all are involved that saves Wilbur's life? I prefer to think that there is a complex process involved which requires them all.

In this chapter I will discuss previous studies of verbal repetition in

1. E.B. White, *Charlotte's Web* (New York: Harper Trophy, 1952).

Matthew and outline the methods of narrative and reader-response criticism. I will also discuss the light that the concept of redundancy sheds on the functions of verbal repetition.

Chapter 2 focuses on narrative rhetoric, particularly direct commentary and point of view. Chapter 3 turns to character, examining the characterization of Peter, John the Baptist, and the Jewish leaders. Chapter 4 discusses plot and structure. Chapter 5 turns to the examination of verbal repetition in Matthew in the light of several literary critical analyses of verbal repetition in other narratives, and in the light of questions about orality, aurality and literacy.

2. *Previous Studies of Verbal Repetition in Matthew*

A review of Matthean studies since the turn of the century shows that scholars have long been aware of the existence of *verbal repetition* in Matthew.[1] Ernst von Dobschütz, for example, writes:

> one of the characteristic peculiarities of Matthew is that he loves parallels. In contrast to the more literarily cultured Luke who strives for the most possible variations, when Matthew has once found a formula he sticks to it as much as possible and uses it repeatedly.[2]

Although not always clearly defined, the phenomenon in question involves the lexical repetition of a series of words, not merely the repetition of similar images, themes, characters, or incidents. Thus, for example, the repeated Matthean phrase 'Repent, for the kingdom of heaven is at hand' (3.2 = 4.17) qualifies. The equally significant repetition of mountain scenes (except where reinforced by verbal repetition) does not.[3] For most of this century scholars have been

1. In recent commentaries the notation of repetition continues. U. Luz (*Matthew 1-7: A Commentary* [trans. W.C. Linss; Minneapolis: Augsburg, 1989]) discusses repetition as an important feature of Matthew's structure (pp. 36-41) and style (p. 49). W.D. Davies and D.C. Allison (*A Critical and Exegetical Commentary on the Gospel According to Matthew* [ICC; Edinburgh: T. & T. Clark, 1988], I, pp. 88-95) note a number of forms of repetition in their discussion of Matthew's literary characteristics.

2. This is my translation from 'Matthäus als Rabbi und Katechet', *ZNW* 27 (1928), p. 339. I consulted and modified, based on the original, R. Morgan's translation in *The Interpretation of Matthew* (ed. G. Stanton; Philadelphia: Fortress Press and London: SPCK, 1983), p. 20.

3. A more detailed definition and the criteria used in this book to chart verbal

interested in verbal repetition primarily for the light it might shed on the Synoptic Problem or the historical situation in which the Gospel was written. The presence of repetition has been used to support various source theories and a theory of orally influenced composition. The focus, except in the analysis of individual cases of repetition, has been on the origin of the phenomenon. Its functions in the Gospel as narrative have not been explored systematically.

a. *J.C. Hawkins*

J.C. Hawkins's *Horae Synopticae: Contributions to the Study of the Synoptic Problem*[1] serves as the basis for most study of verbal repetition in Matthew among modern biblical scholars, especially those in the English-speaking world. What Hawkins provided is a handy catalog of many Matthean repetitions. He produced this catalog as part of an effort to provide statistical data for solving the Synoptic Problem. The repetitions appear in *Horae Synopticae* under several headings. Hawkins lists ninety-five *characteristic Matthean words and phrases* which occur at least four times in Matthew and either are not found in Mark or Luke or are found in Matthew at least twice as often as in Mark and Luke together. He also lists twenty-two *doublets*, defined as fairly long 'repetitions of the same or closely similar sentences',[2] and twenty-five *formulas* peculiar to Matthew. Nineteen of the formulas Matthew uses in common with Mark and/or Luke and also independently in another part of the Gospel. Six are differently placed by Matthew and Mark or Matthew, Mark and Luke.[3] The formulas are 'short sentences or collocations of two or more words, which recur mainly or exclusively in one or other of the Synoptic Gospels, so that they appear to be favorite or habitual expressions of the writer of it'.[4] They are longer than the characteristic words and phrases, but shorter than the doublets.

Since the purpose of Hawkins's study was to provide statistics for the solution of the Synoptic Problem, he saw the doublets as evidence

repetition are discussed later in this chapter.

1. Oxford: Clarendon Press, 1898, 1909, reprint 1968.

2. Hawkins, *Horae Synopticae*, pp. 80-98; quotation, p. 80. He treats the phrase 'He that hath ears' in an appendix, p. 106.

3. Hawkins, *Horae Synopticae*, pp. 168-73.

4. Hawkins, *Horae Synopticae*, p. 168.

primarily of the two-source solution.[1] He saw the formulas as evidence that the evangelists freely supplement their sources with their memory of the tradition:

> A careful examination of such cases certainly leaves the impression that the mind of Matthew was so familiar with these collocations of words that he naturally reproduced them in other parts of his narrative, besides the places in which they occurred in his sources. It is to be observed that these apparent reproductions often occur earlier in the gospel than do the apparently original occurrences of the formulas, which seems to indicate that Matthew drew them from his memory of his sources and not from documents before him. So far as it goes, then, the drift of this section is in favor of some considerable element of the oral theory.[2]

The characteristic editorial words and phrases appeared in both unique and common material. This showed, Hawkins argued, the freedom of the evangelist in slightly modifying his sources.

b. *B.C. Butler*

B.C. Butler took up Hawkins's discussion of Matthean doublets and formulas in *The Originality of St Matthew: A Critique of the Two-Document Hypothesis*[3]. He examined these repetitions in order to prove the priority of Matthew. He argued that the Matthean doublets are not the result of using two sources. They are, rather, 'In some cases due to St. Matthew's habit of repeating himself'; and in others, 'a device for cross-reference, the custom of using footnotes not being found in antiquity'.[4] Unfortunately, he did not explain or develop either suggestion. Instead he concentrates on demonstrating Matthean independence and, in several cases, Markan dependence on Matthew.

One of Butler's major arguments is that close similarity or identity between two members of a doublet precludes the use of diverse sources. Of course, there is no reason an editor could not assimilate the two sources to one another. In seven cases (Hawkins's nos. 1, 2, 3, 9, 10, 13 and 20) Butler suggests that one member is an editorial cross-reference because it is not integral to its context, while the other member is. He attributes eight cases (nos. 4, 5, 6, 7, 8, 11, 21, 22) to Jesus' repeating himself or editorial repetition; two (nos. 12 and 14)

1. Hawkins, *Horae Synopticae*, pp. 81-82.
2. Hawkins, *Horae Synopticae*, pp. 171-72; cf. also p. 173.
3. Cambridge: Cambridge University Press, 1951.
4. Butler, *Originality*, p. 138.

to Semitic *inclusio*; and five (nos. 15–19) to Matthew's 'economical habit of self-repetition'.[1] In three cases where Mark has at least one member of a Matthean cross-reference doublet (nos. 1, 2, 9), Butler sees an argument for Markan dependence because 'Mark has the second member, that is, the reference note, not the original occurrence'.[2] Butler treats *inclusios* and Hawkins's list of formulas in the same manner as the doublets.[3] He argues, for example, that Hawkins's observation that a number of Matthean formulas occur prior to where they appear in Mark or not at all in Mark is evidence of Matthean priority and not the oral theory.[4] Butler, then, begins to ask what the functions of certain repetitions are within the narrative, but concentrates on the question of sources.

c. *G.D. Kilpatrick*

Writing a few years earlier than Butler, G.D. Kilpatrick argued in his *The Origins of the Gospel According to St Matthew*[5] that Matthew was produced in order to be read liturgically. In his argument he also took up Hawkins's list of Matthean doublets and formulas.[6] Like Butler, however, Kilpatrick primarily accounts for them in terms of the Gospel's genesis rather than in terms of their function in the narrative. He argues that the repetition of formulas may have a liturgical purpose. His evidence consists of an analogy to repetition in public worship and the fact that some Matthean repeated formulas cannot be explained as due to more than one source.[7] He also argues that at least half of the Matthean doublets are 'due to the influence of liturgical homily'.[8] Passages were associated with several contexts in the church's homiletic tradition and Matthew preserves these associations.[9] Kilpatrick attributes the other half to the evangelist's

1. Butler, *Originality*, pp. 144-45, quotation, p. 145.
2. Butler, *Originality*, pp. 145-46.
3. Butler, *Originality*, pp. 150ff.
4. Butler, *Originality*, pp. 151-52.
5. Oxford: Clarendon Press, 1946, reprint with corrections, 1950.
6. Kilpatrick's list includes five additional doublets that Hawkins rejected, *Origins*, p. 84 and p. 84 n. 1.
7. Kilpatrick, *Origins*, p. 75.
8. Kilpatrick, *Origins*, pp. 84 and 92.
9. See Hawkins's comments on individual doublets, *Horae Synopticae*, pp. 84-92.

own editorial purposes.[1] Kilpatrick's hypotheses remain in the realm of conjecture. They center on the stages lying behind our present Gospel. He offers no evidence beyond the repetitions themselves and the use of Matthew in later church liturgy. He does not explore what Matthew's editorial purposes might be in using repetition.

d. *M.D. Goulder*

This author also comments on the doublets catalogued by Hawkins in *Midrash and Lection in Matthew*.[2] He sees them as examples of a Matthean midrashic manner. Matthew 'glosses' one context with another in the story, borrowing forward or backward. This method is analogous to that of the Chronicler. Thus, Goulder argues, as it is not 'normal' to account for the Chronicler's repetitions by positing independent traditions; neither is it necessary 'to posit independent traditions behind the twenty-one Matthean doublets'.[3] This supports one of Goulder's central theses: Matthew is a midrash on Mark and not a compilation of Mark and Q. Half of the doublets are cases of borrowing forward where the second member of the doublet appears in its Markan context (nos. 1, 2, 3, and 4, 5, and 6, 7 and 8, 9, 10, 11). Matthew often borrows forward because he is less bound to Mark in the earlier part of the Gospel. Four are Markan 'epigrams' appearing in their Markan context and then filled out and repeated. For example, 'To him who has...' is found in 13.12 = Mk 4.25 and expounded by the Talents and then repeated in 25.29. The rest of the doublets 'are simply explained as repetitions of favorite Matthean phrases—repetitiveness is too common a rabbinic trait to need illustration'.[4] This tendency also explains many other Matthean passages 'which involve repetitions of language, but which are not so exact as to deserve the name of doublets (e.g., 4.24/14.35; 4.25/12.15; 9.27-31/20.29-34)'.[5] As with Butler and Kilpatrick, Goulder is concerned with the origin of the Matthean doublets and their relationship to the Synoptic Problem. He attributes them to midrash on Mark and to a fondness for repetition. He hints at a function for some in the context

1. Kilpatrick, *Origins*, p. 92.
2. (London: SPCK, 1974), pp. 36-38.
3. Goulder, *Midrash*, p. 36.
4. Goulder, *Midrash*, p. 37.
5. Goulder, *Midrash*, p. 37.

of the Gospel as narrative. Since they allow Matthew to gloss one context with another, they show the contexts in a similar light.

e. *C.H. Lohr*

Although still concerned with the genesis of the text, C.H. Lohr's article, 'Oral Techniques in the Gospel of Matthew',[1] was the first to focus on the function of various Matthean repetitions within the Gospel as a whole. Lohr's thesis is that techniques of oral composition 'played a part in Matthew's attempt to bring together the materials he had at hand into a unified and artistic whole'.[2] The techniques are similar to those used in the Homeric poems and ancient Semitic literature.[3] 'They consist,' Lohr writes, 'of devices such as prologue and epilogue, recurring lines, foreshadowing, retrospections, themes and overall structures, whereby the essentially disparate parts are stitched together to form a unity.'[4] Matthew used analogous devices, Lohr argues, to unify in writing disconnected traditional source material. In his analysis Lohr is most heavily influenced by the oral-formulaic theory of Parry and Lord, C.M. Bowra's *Heroic Poetry* (London, 1952), various articles on oral composition in classical literature,[5] and the study of oral tradition lying behind the Hebrew Scriptures.

The first section of Lohr's article, 'Formulaic Language: The Traditional Style', suggests that ancient scribes and poets—even when the tradition became written—used the traditional oral formulaic style to accommodate new or reinterpret old material. This is why Matthew frequently repeats formulas and does not alter them very much. Although Lohr does not define 'formulas' he lists the following examples:

1. *CBQ* 23 (1961), pp. 403-35.

2. Lohr, 'Oral Techniques', p. 404.

3. Lohr, 'Oral Techniques', pp. 404-405. He accepts the thesis that the Homeric poems developed in oral tradition.

4. Lohr, 'Oral Techniques', p. 404.

5. Including J.A. Notopoulos, 'Continuity and Interconnection in Homeric Composition', *TAPA* 82 (1951), pp. 81-101.

> ...word-collocations like 'the Prophets and the Law', 'heirs to the kingdom', 'the lost sheep of Israel's house', 'blind guides', 'brood of snakes'; concluding formulae like 'Let him who has ears to hear listen' and 'At that same time', and 'When Jesus had finished this discourse'.[1]

Matthew's desire to accommodate his sources to the traditional oral style is also why, according to Lohr, he 'tends to omit or condense Mark's subsidiary and pleonastic details'[2] and introduces such popular motifs as the number two (two Gadarene demoniacs, 8.28-34; two blind men, 20.29-34; two false witnesses, 26.60; etc.)

In his second section concerning the use of formulaic devices for the elaboration of unifying themes, Lohr discusses repetitive devices such as '*inclusio*, refrain, foreshadowing, and retrospection'.[3] Lohr identifies two main functions for these devices:

> They enable the author (1) to indicate the divisions of his work, and (2) to build up in it a thematic structure which will focus the various elements of the tradition on his own central interest...Because they can be used to establish formal patterns and to enrich the texture of a composition by repetitive association, the formulae are singularly apt for achieving the integration so necessary in oral literature. They are, moreover, susceptible of considerable artistic effectiveness.[4]

Lohr next treats each of the above-mentioned devices in turn. The first, *inclusio*, or ring composition, is common in Greek literature and in the psalms and prophets of the Hebrew Scriptures. He describes its function in the following way:

> Because *inclusio* forces the attention of the audience back from the conclusion of a passage to its beginning, it can be used to interconnect the parts of a story. Its function at this stage of a tradition is to provide a frame, which will link more or less self-contained passages—episodes, similes, descriptions and digressions—to the web of the narrative.[5]

The second repetitive device for the elaboration of unifying themes is the *refrain*. Lohr argues that it functions to 'mark thought-groups' and 'can easily be adapted by the oral poet to tie together larger units within the traditional material, and so in some way to compensate for

1. Lohr, 'Oral Techniques', p. 407.
2. Lohr, 'Oral Techniques', p. 407.
3. Lohr, 'Oral Techniques', p. 408.
4. Lohr, 'Oral Techniques', p. 408.
5. Lohr, 'Oral Techniques', p. 409.

its inherent parataxis'. In Matthew refrains are used to mark strophes (7.24-27; 5.17-48) and for 'organizational purposes'.[1] The most obvious example is the formula, 'When Jesus had finished this discourse', used to group sayings in five major sermons (7.28; 11.2; 13.53; 19.1; 26.1). In addition to repeated words, it includes repeated ideas such as the various response to Jesus' miracles in chs. 8–9 (8.27; 8.34; 9.3; 9.26; 9.31; 9.33; 9.34). These not only bind the episodes together, 'they involve the hearers . . . in the strong undercurrent which runs beneath the surface of the action demanding their own reaction and response'.[2]

The third repetitive device is *foreshadowing*. Lohr argues that the oral poet had to prepare the hearer for what was to come in order to unify the composition. Foreshadowing was common in Greek and biblical literature. Matthew's use of foreshadowing, Lohr writes, 'is another indication of his indebtedness to oral technique to stamp his materials with a definite meaning'.[3] Examples are the use of the title Son of David, dreams, the 'prologue' to Jesus' public ministry (4.23-25), and 'little scenes' which 'forecast what is to come'.[4] The last type of foreshadowing occurs in 9.33f where the crowds are amazed and the Pharisees believe Jesus exorcises by the power of the prince of demons:

> The opposition of the Pharisees is to be the main theme of the next narrative section (cc. 11–12), and the Evangelist will use this theme—the very words recur in 12.24—as advice to sustain his listener through the recitation by offering him a thread of unity in his loosely connected material.[5]

Lohr feels that evidence of foreshadowing is important because:

> in it we see how the Evangelist coordinates his materials, that is, how, while leaving the elements of the tradition unchanged in themselves, he is able to stamp them with a single significance by preparing in the mind of his listeners through simple repetitions and rearrangements a whole net of expectations and conjectures, so that each new scene and each new collection of sayings is approached with a definite predisposition.[6]

1. Lohr, 'Oral Techniques', p. 411.
2. Lohr, 'Oral Techniques', p. 411.
3. Lohr, 'Oral Techniques', p. 412.
4. Lohr, 'Oral Techniques', p. 413.
5. Lohr, 'Oral Techniques', p. 413.
6. Lohr, 'Oral Techniques', p. 414.

The fourth repetitive device is *retrospection*, 'by which the later stages of a narrative are related to what has gone before'.[1] According to Lohr, there are various forms of retrospection in oral literature: 'summaries for recapitulations and repeated words and phrases used for characterization'.[2] They have a number of functions. Originally, Lohr surmises, summaries connected 'the parts of an extended narrative in which recitation would necessarily be interrupted'.[3] Repeated formulas build up themes which impose unity.[4] Retrospection also:

> highlights the significance of the present by projecting the ongoing life of the past into the action. Skillfully employed, retrospection can create an atmosphere of simultaneity in the narrative, giving it an impact transcending the natural limitations of language which necessarily proceeds in time.[5]

Retrospection appears in Greek literature and the Hebrew Scriptures. In Matthew an example of summaries which unify the narrative are those which focus on Jesus as *iatros*:

	Chapters				
	1-4	8-9	11-12	14-17	19-22
He went all over Galilee, teaching... proclaiming... and curing...	4.23	9.35			
They brought to him all who were suffering.	4.24a	8.16a		14.35b	
And he cured them.	4.24c	8.16c	12.15b	15.30	21.14b
The blind are regaining their sight and the lame can walk.			11.5	15.31	(21.1, 4a)[6]

1. Lohr, 'Oral Techniques', p. 414.
2. Lohr, 'Oral Techniques', p. 414.
3. Lohr, 'Oral Techniques', p. 414. A point presented by Notopoulos, 'Continuity', as well.
4. Lohr, 'Oral Techniques', p. 414.
5. Lohr, 'Oral Techniques', p. 414. These comments are similar to those of Notopoulos, 'Continuity', p. 9.
6. Lohr, 'Oral Techniques', p. 415.

Unfortunately, Lohr does not explain why these should be conceived solely as *retrospective*. It is clear that the summaries are involved in a network of symbolic associations focused on Jesus as the healing savior.

The fifth category Lohr examines is thematic development. Lohr concentrates on repetition itself: 'The oral style readily lends itself to a process of thematic development, because all the devices which go to make it up are essentially of a repetitive nature'.[1] The various types of repeated formulas already discussed 'assume a richness of signification by their recurrence as motifs in the narrative'.[2] Lohr uses a wonderful image to describe how they interact with one another:

> Because of the accumulated images which group about them, they resemble a window pane, through which you can see a landscape, while you are aware at the same time that its surface reflects the face of someone standing behind you. The formulae interanimate one another. They are qualified by the whole context in which they figure, and they bring to that context the images derived from other contexts in which they have figured in the past. They are, therefore, of the greatest importance in what we have distinguished as the third stage of a tradition. Their suppleness and pliability to new contexts, their power to take on a meaning deepened by each repetition, and their ability to establish significances through the limitation and specialization of the contexts in which they are allowed to appear enable the skillful user of them to build up a stable structure of meaning even in the most divergent materials.[3]

Lohr offers several examples of this technique. In Matthew he points to the theme of 'The Kingdom of Heaven' and phrases such as 'Your heavenly Father', the 'Son of God', and 'he came up to him, and fell on his knees before him saying'.[4] These phrases 'when they are scattered like mosaic pieces through the Gospel, then are no longer merely groups of words, but they take on a color adapted to the total pattern and help toward unity'.[5]

The third major section of Lohr's article concerns 'Principles of Structure'. He subdivides this section into 'A. Unity in the Individual Sections' and 'B. Structural Arrangements'.[6] Sub-section B will be

1. Lohr, 'Oral Techniques', p. 416.
2. Lohr, 'Oral Techniques', p. 416.
3. Lohr, 'Oral Techniques', p. 416.
4. Lohr, 'Oral Techniques', p. 417.
5. Lohr, 'Oral Techniques', p. 417.
6. Lohr, 'Oral Techniques', pp. 420-34.

discussed in Chapter 4. Sub-section A will be discussed here. In this sub-section Lohr argues that the conditions of oral performance require concentration on one subject with a single mood or effect in each section of discourse. In Hebrew tradition the two most common methods of focus are 'the habit of grouping like materials and the device of developing a leading idea by stressing certain key words'.[1] At the stage of reducing oral tradition to writing materials are frequently grouped according to subject matter, Lohr states. He sees this principle in the arrangement of Jesus' sayings into five major sermons, each with its own character, 'determined by its place in Matthew's outline'.[2] He also sees it in narrative sections grouped according to 'mighty works' (chs. 8–9), the rejection by 'this generation' (chs. 11–12), etc. In terms of developing a leading idea through the use of key words, Lohr points to chs. 11–12 and 13.53–17.21. The key words provide a 'thread of continuity'.[3] In chs. 11–12, for example, the central idea, 'the rejection of the Son of Man by "this generation" and the judgment which is impending because of their failure to recognize his mighty works',[4] is established by the repetition of several key words: '*genea* (11.16; 12.39, 41, 42, 45), *dynameis* (11.30, 21, 23), *semeion* (12.38, 39 *ter*), *krisis* (11.22, 24; 12.18, 20, 36, 41, 42)'.[5] Synonyms and adjectives reinforce these references.

In conclusion Lohr returns to his thesis that Matthew used techniques of oral style in the composition of the Gospel. He contrasts Matthew's success in arrangement and interconnection with what he sees as Mark's failure. He also reiterates the role of the community in responding to Matthew as a traditional author—they enter into the narrative and supply 'the connections hinted at by him'.[6]

Although tied to a thesis about the genesis of the Gospel, Lohr is the first to look seriously at a variety of types and functions of repetition in the Gospel as a whole. It is a remarkable article because it emphasizes the extent of repetition in Matthew and begins to explore its functions. Much of what Lohr says has merit whether or not his main thesis is correct. Foreshadowing, for example, leads the reader

1. Lohr, 'Oral Techniques', p. 420.
2. Lohr, 'Oral Techniques', p. 421.
3. Lohr, 'Oral Techniques', p. 422.
4. Lohr, 'Oral Techniques', p. 422.
5. Lohr, 'Oral Techniques', p. 422.
6. Lohr, 'Oral Techniques', p. 435.

or hearer to see future events in a certain light whether or not its presence is due to oral influence. Lohr's work serves as an impetus to further examination of the functions of repetition in the Gospel narrative.

f. *Verbal Repetition in this Work*

The task of this book is to explore the narrative functions of the complex web of verbal repetition in Matthew. It differs from previous studies in its concentration on the narrative functions rather than the origins of verbal repetition. While interesting in its own right, the question of whether a verbal repetition is due to the use of several sources in written composition, the influence of oral compositional techniques, liturgical or educational influence is not my concern here.

In previous studies the question of the precise definition of verbal repetition in Matthew has received little attention, being for the most part taken for granted. A definition of verbal repetition as the lexical repetition of a series of words leaves two issues unresolved. These are the treatment of minor variations and the length of the series of words. In this dissertation minor variations such as the addition or subtraction of words, and changes of tense, number, gender or case which do not seriously jeopardize the identification of phrases as verbal repetition are ignored. For example, 4.17 'Ἀπὸ τότε ἤρξατο ὁ 'Ιησοῦς κηρύσσειν καὶ λέγειν· μετανοεῖτε· ἤγγικεν γάρ ἡ Βασιλεία τῶν οὐρανῶν and 10.7: πορευόμενοι δὲ κηρύσσειτε λέγοντες ὅτι ἤγγικεν ἡ Βασιλεια τῶν οὐρανῶν are considered repetitions of 3.1-2: 'Εν δέ ταῖς ἡμέραις ἐκείναις παραγίνεται 'Ιωάννηςν ὁ Βαπτιστὴς κηρύσσων ἐν τῇ ἐρήμῳ τῆς 'Ιουδαίας, λέγων· μετανοεῖτε· ἤγγικεν γὰρ ἡ Βασιλεία τῶν οὐρανῶν.

The issue of the length of the series of words is more difficult to resolve. If verbal repetition is treated as a literary or rhetorical device, can every repetition be counted? Is there any controlled way to ensure that one has located significant repetitions and is not merely compiling word statistics? One way to solve the problem would be to count arbitrarily only those phrases four Greek words in length or longer. This would eliminate a catalog of every word and most short phrases which are a necessary part of using language. However, it would also eliminate such striking and memorable repetitions as 'little-faiths' (6.30 = 8.26 = 14.31 = 16.8, cf. 17.20) and 'Brood of Vipers' (3.7 = 12.34 = 23.33), and even conventions which may have a narrative function. As with the question of minor variations—resolved by ignoring variations which do not seriously jeopardize the 'identification' of phrases as repetitions—a certain degree of subjectivity seems inevitable. Cataloging verbal repetition as a literary device involves the recognition of phrases as repetitions by the reader or hearer of the Gospel. One reader might note two phrases as repeated, another might not. The recognition might be conscious or unconscious. One control exists when a number of hearers/ readers have noted a repetition. Previous interpreters have noted most of the verbal repetition discussed in this book. The catalog of verbal repetition in Matthew compiled for this book (Appendix A) consists for the most part of repetitions at least four words in length. The number of words repeated is indicated in each case. Repetitions of less than four words which may be significant for the narrative rhetoric of the Gospel are included along with the words involved. A separate catalog lists repetitions nine words or more in length (Appendix B). Setting aside other considerations, such as the striking character of certain metaphors, the longer a series of words repeated is, the more likely a reader or hearer would be to identify it as verbal repetition. The second catalog, therefore, represents those cases which by virtue of their length seem incontestable examples of verbal repetition.[1]

Once the phenomenon is defined and repetitions cataloged, it becomes clear just how extensive the use of verbal repetition is in Matthew. Therefore, it has been necessary to limit the discussion of verbal repetition in two ways. First, primarily *extended* repetitions which occur in separate sections of the text will be considered. Concentrated repetition within a section of the text and its stylistic effects have been noted more often by scholars than extended repetition and its functions. Extended repetition is also more likely to have functions in the Gospel as a narrative whole. Since the determination of 'sections' of the text is again subjective, concentrated repetition is generally defined as repetition occurring within forty lines of fifty letters each and extended repetition as repetition separated by more than forty lines.

1. I have striven to be as accurate as possible. My original compilation was done by hand. I have spot-checked my original statistics so far as possible by computer. One difficulty is that the reader or hearer has to recognize a phrase before searching for its repetition. Another is that my current software capability only allows me to search for one word at a time. I would appreciate readers sending me any additions or corrections.

An example of concentrated repetition is the phrase 'and your father who sees in secret will reward you' in 6.4b, 6b, 6c, 18a and b. Examples of extended repetition are given above.

A second limitation is that only a representative sample of extended repetition can be analyzed. There are just too many instances even of extended repetition to be treated in an average-sized monograph. Therefore examples are offered of the contribution of verbal repetition to such rhetorical devices as direct commentary and point of view, characterization, and the plot and structure of the Gospel. This covers three major categories of narrative analysis. Symbol, imagery, theme and setting should also be treated in subsequent studies.

3. *Method*

The primary methods used in this book are narrative and reader-response criticisms.[1] I will briefly describe each in turn, and then I

1. For helpful discussions of narrative criticism see N.R. Petersen, *Literary Criticism for New Testament Critics* (GBS; Philadelphia: Fortress Press, 1978); M.A. Powell, *What is Narrative Criticism?* (GBS; Minneapolis: Fortress Press, 1990); E.S. Malbon, 'Narrative Criticism: How Does the Story Mean?', in J.C. Anderson and S.D. Moore (eds), *Mark and Method: New Approaches in Biblical Studies* (Minneapolis: Fortress Press, 1992). Book-length examples of Gospel narrative criticism are R.A. Culpepper, *Anatomy of the Fourth Gospel: A Study in Literary Design* (Philadelphia: Fortress Press, 1983); J.D. Kingsbury, *Matthew As Story* (Minneapolis: Fortress Press, 2nd edn, 1988); D. Rhoads and D. Michie, *Mark as Story: An Introduction to the Narrative of a Gospel* (Philadelphia: Fortress Press, 1982); R.C. Tannehill, *The Narrative Unity of Luke-Acts* (Minneapolis: Fortress Press, I, 1986; II, 1990); and M.A. Tolbert, *Sowing the Gospel: Mark's World in Literary-Historical Perspective* (Minneapolis: Fortress Press, 1989). J. Dewey treated a section in Mark in terms of its literary structure in *Markan Public Debate, Literary Technique, Concentric Structure and Theology in Mark 2.1-3.6* (SBLDS, 48; Chico, CA: Scholars Press, 1980). For a discussion and examples of Gospel reader-response criticism see R.A. Edwards, *Matthew's Story of Jesus* (Philadelphia: Fortress Press, 1985); R.M. Fowler, 'Reader-Response Criticism: Figuring Mark's Reader', in J.C. Anderson and S.D. Moore (eds.), *Mark and Method: New Approaches in Biblical Studies* (Minneapolis: Fortress Press, 1992); R.M. Fowler, *Let the Reader Understand: Reader-Response Criticism and the Gospel of Mark* (Minneapolis: Fortress Press, 1991); J.L. Resseguie, 'Reader-Response Criticism and the Gospel of Mark', *JAAR* 52 (1984), pp. 307-24; and J. Staley, *The Print's First Kiss* (SBLDS, 82; Atlanta: Scholars Press, 1988). For an excellent review and critique of Gospel narrative and reader-response criticisms see S.D. Moore, *Literary*

will show how they are both related to a communication model in widespread use in many disciplines.

a. *Narrative Criticism*

Narrative criticism of the Gospels emerged in the early 1980s primarily out of the engagement of American critics with non-biblical literary criticism. Although there is no exact counterpart to 'narrative criticism' in the literary world, the school of non-biblical literary criticism which narrative criticism most closely resembles has been variously dubbed narrative poetics or narratology.[1] For Gospel critics Wayne Booth, Seymour Chatman and Gerard Genette were particularly influential. Previous Gospel criticism had focused on the origin and historical circumstances of the Gospels. Source, form, and redaction criticisms focused on individual tessarae of the Gospels or on the seams that connected them. Narrative critics, rebelliously rejecting what they saw as disintegrating methods, began to examine the Gospels as literary wholes. They also turned from a focus on the genesis of the Gospels to the interrelations of elements within the text and how the text creates meaning. Traditional narrative categories such as character, plot, and setting took center stage. To this, in alignment with narratology, they added rhetoric or discourse, how the story is told. Narrative critics saw the Gospel texts as mediums of communication between author and audience in a context. In addition to actual authors and reader/hearers, however, narrative critics also distinguished implied author and readers, narrators and narratees. Some form of the following communication model from Chatman (p. 151) was adopted:

Criticism and the Gospels: The Theoretical Challenge (New Haven: Yale University Press, 1989).

1. The interests and fruits of the loosely connected school can be seen in S. Chatman, *Story and Discourse: Narrative Structure in Fiction and Film* (Ithaca, NY: Cornell University Press, 1978); G. Prince, *Narratology: The Form and Function of Narrative* (Berlin, New York, Amsterdam: Mouton Publishers, 1983); S. Rimmon-Kenan, *Narrative Fiction: Contemporary Poetics* (London and New York: Methuen, 1983); and M. Bal, *Narratology: Introduction to the Theory of Narrative* (Toronto: University of Toronto Press, 1985). Narrative poetics is something of an amalgam of various critical approaches including American New Criticism, Russian Formalism, *explication de texte* and structuralism.

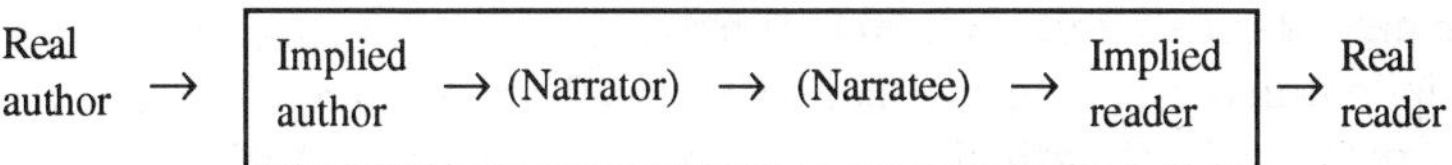

The implied author and implied reader. The *implied author*, a term coined by Wayne Booth, refers to the 'creating person who is implied by the totality of a given work when it is offered to the world'.[1] This voice or persona is the authorial presence the reader experiences in the work.[2] The implied author lives on long after the flesh-and-blood author is dead and buried. Thus the concept of the implied author allows one to focus on the text as a means of communication while avoiding the intentional fallacy, reducing a work to the author's conscious intent and experience of it.[3] It is a textual function, reminding the historian that the text does not provide direct access to the actual author.

The *implied reader* is a term originally coined by W. Iser.[4] He defined the implied reader as a concept which 'incorporates both the

1. The term was originally coined and popularized in *The Rhetoric of Fiction* (Chicago: University of Chicago Press, 1961), especially pp. 70-76 and 151. This definition comes from W. Booth's *Critical Understanding* (Chicago: University of Chicago, 1979), p. 269. There he outlined a typology of five authors: (1) the writer, the flesh-and-blood person who writes; (2) the dramatized author, the narrator or 'dramatized speaker; (3) the implied author; (4) the career author, the 'sustained creative center implied by a sequence of implied authors'; (5) the public 'character', 'the fictionalized hero created and played with by author and public independently of an author's actual works', pp. 268-78.

2. M.H. Abrams, 'Persona, Voice and Tone', in *A Glossary of Literary Terms*, (New York: Holt, Rinehart & Winston, 3rd edn, 1971), p. 126 defines the implied author as a 'convincing authorial presence, whose values, beliefs, and moral vision are the implicit controlling forces throughout a work'.

3. The term 'intentional fallacy' was coined by M.C. Beardsley and W.K. Wimsatt in an essay with that title first published in 1946 and reprinted in W.K. Wimsatt, *The Verbal Icon* (Lexington: University of Kentucky Press, 1954), pp. 3-18. See also E.D. Hirsch, 'Appendix I: Objective Interpretation', in *Validity in Interpretation* (New Haven: Yale University Press, 1967), pp. 209-44, who argues that although textual meaning should not be understood as determined by the author's conscious intent, it is necessary to uncover the 'horizon which defines the author's intention as a whole', p. 221.

4. Iser discusses the term in *The Implied Reader* (Baltimore: Johns Hopkins University Press, 1974 [German orig. 1972]) and *The Act of Reading* (Baltimore: John Hopkins University Press, 1978 [German orig. 1976]).

prestructuring of the potential meaning by the text, and the reader's actualization of this potential through the reading process'.[1] The implied reader is distinguished from the flesh-and blood reader past or present since it includes the textual structure which must be realized as well as the structured act of realization. It is the role that the real reader must play, although tensions may remain between the role and the real reader.[2] This is a slightly different formulation than that of Booth or Chatman who see the implied reader as internal to the text, the counterpart of the implied author. Booth holds that the author creates 'an image of himself and another image of his reader; he makes his reader as he makes his second self'.[3] The difference is due to Iser's phenomenological position.[4] What Iser's definition does is to emphasize the interplay of textual structures and the standpoint outside the text that must be occupied by a real reader. Most often Gospel critics use the term implied author in Booth's sense of the role of the reader in the text.[5] In this book the term implied reader refers for the most part to the reader in the text. However, the interplay with the real reader will also be emphasized. As with the implied author, the concept of the implied reader allows one to focus on the text as a means of communication while avoiding a fallacy. In this case, it is the affective fallacy, reducing a work to a real reader's apprehension of it.[6] It also reminds the historian that the text does not necessarily provide a picture of a work's original readers.

The narrator and the narratee. Two further distinctions are often made in narrative criticism. The implied author is distinguished from the narrator and the implied reader is distinguished from the narratee. The *narrator* is the teller of the tale, 'the imaginary being who speaks to us from the pages of a literary work'.[7] A narrator may be

1. Iser, *The Implied Reader*, p. xii.
2. Iser, *The Act of Reading*, pp. 34-37.
3. Booth, *Rhetoric*, p. 138, quoted in Iser, *The Act of Reading*, p. 37.
4. For a brief explanation and critique see S. Suleiman, 'Introduction', in S. Suleiman and I. Crosman (eds.), *The Reader in the Text* (Princeton: Princeton University Press, 1980), pp. 21-26.
5. Chatman, *Story and Discourse*, pp. 149-51.
6. See the essay with this title by Wimsatt and Beardsley in Wimsatt, *The Verbal Icon*, pp. 21-39 and Hirsch, 'Appendix 1: Objective Interpretation', pp. 209-44.
7. W.C. Dowling, *The Critic's Hornbook* (New York: Thomas Y. Crowell, 1977), p. 25.

undramatized or dramatized to the degree of being a character within the narrative.[1] A narrator may also be reliable or unreliable. A reliable narrator does not shift his or her allegiance from one set of norms to another in the course of a work. Nor does a gulf emerge between the ideology of a reliable narrator and the implied author. A reliable narrator serves as a spokesperson for the implied author. The distinction between the implied author and the narrator is clearest when the narrator is a character and/or unreliable. The implied author is the guiding intelligence who creates the narrator and the other narrative elements and arranges them in order to communicate. The implied author has no *direct* voice. However, an undramatized reliable narrator is virtually indistinguishable from the implied author. He or she becomes the implied author's voice.[2]

A second distinction between the implied reader and the *narratee* parallels the distinction between the implied author and the narrator. The narratee is the reader that the narrator addresses or the internal or inscribed audience.[3] Like the narrator, the narratee may range

1. There are various degrees of dramatization.

2. These categories and other factors in narration are discussed in Chatman, *Story and Discourse*, chs. 4 and 5 and in Booth, *Rhetoric*, chs. 6 and 7. One of Booth's headings is 'Reliable Narrators as Dramatized Spokesmen for the Implied Author', p. 211.

3. The term 'narratee' comes from G. Genette and G. Prince via Chatman, pp. 150-51 and Suleiman, 'Introduction', *The Reader in the Text*, pp. 13-15. I do not want to imply, however, Prince's zero-degree narratee. It identifies something similar to the dramatic reader described by Wimsatt, 'the actual reader of a poem is something like a reader over another reader's shoulder; he reads through the dramatic reader, the person to whom the full tone of the poem is addressed in the fictional situation' (*The Verbal Icon*, p. xv). The choice of the term narratee over Iser's intended or fictitious reader is deliberate. Iser defines the fictitious reader as 'the idea of the reader which the author had in mind' (*The Act of Reading*, pp. 32-33). He views this reader as one of the many textual perspectives, including narrator, characters and plot, that make up the implied reader's role, 'by which the author exposes the disposition of an assumed reader to interaction with the other perspectives in order to bring about modifications' (*The Act of Reading*, p. 35). Iser—whether on his own account or because of E. Wolff's definition of the intended reader—blurs the distinction between the reader addressed by the narrator in the text and the actual audience the actual author had in mind when writing, the public the author wished to address. The reader envisioned by an actual author is also called the virtual reader and distinguished from real and ideal readers by G. Prince, 'Introduction to the Study of the Narratee', in J.P. Tompkins (ed.), *Reader-Response Criticism*

from a fully dramatized character(s) to an undramatized stance. When the implied author and narrator are essentially indistinguishable and the narratee is undramatized, the narratee and the intrinsic aspects of the implied reader are very closely related.[1]

b. *Reader-Response Criticism*

With the introduction of the categories of the narratee and the implied reader, narrative criticism opened the door to a shift of attention for some critics. In terms of the author–text–audience communication model narrative critics tend to emphasize the text and the interrelations of its elements. Reader-response criticism concentrates on the audience, the pragmatic dimension of communication. In non-biblical reader-response criticism the focus has been primarily on readers rather than on hearers, on the silent experience of reading rather than on the aural. Gospel critics have adapted their work and added an emphasis on the aural. The writings of Wolfgang Iser, Stanley Fish and an anthology edited by Jane Tompkins have been key influences on the development of reader-response criticism of the Gospels.

With the shift of attention to the reader, reader-response critics foreground three related questions: (1) What role does the reader or hearer of a text play in creating the meaning of a text (i.e., does the reader find or make meaning)? (2) Who is the reader/hearer? (3) What is the experience of reading or listening to a text like?[2] There is a range of

(Baltimore: Johns Hopkins University Press, 1980), p. 9.

1. Of course subtle distinctions can be made. Some picture of the narratee can almost always be drawn even when the narrator does not seem to be addressing anyone in particular. Prince offers the example of this sentence from *Un coeur simple*: 'His entire person produced in her that confusion into which we are all thrown by the spectacle of extraordinary men.' It 'informs us that the narratee has experienced the same feelings in the presence of extraordinary individuals', 'Introduction to the Study of the Narratee', p. 12; see also pp. 17-18. In the non-narrative context Dowling has offered another example. Wordsworth's 'The World Is Too Much with Us' has a generalized dramatic audience, those middle-class people who 'have allowed themselves to get caught up in the world of commerce and financial enterprise... and who have become dulled and insensitive in the process' (Dowling, *The Critic's Hornbook*, pp. 30-32). In such cases the features of the text which create the role the actual reader must assume are the same features that allow us to paint a picture of the narratee or dramatic audience.

2. E.S. Malbon and J.C. Anderson, 'Literary Critical Methods', in E.S. Fiorenza, *Searching the Scriptures. Volume 1: A Feminist Introduction* (New

answers to the first question. Those closest to narrative criticism tend to speak of the reader finding meaning, of the text guiding or educating the reader. At the opposite extreme are those who speak of the reader creating meaning. They argue that without the reader no text exists. This argument can be most vividly seen in a set of dueling articles by Iser and Fish.[1] In *The Implied Reader* Iser compares the text to stars in the night sky. One reader draws lines between the stars to form the Big Dipper, another to form a plough. Nonetheless there are fixed stars. In 'Who's Afraid of Wolfgang Iser', Fish suggests that without the reader not only are there no constellations, but there are no fixed stars.[2] With Iser the reader and the text dance together. With Fish it sounds like a solo act. Jonathan Culler in *On Deconstruction* argues for a theoretical monism and a practical dualism. Theoretically, the distinction between text and reader always breaks down. However, in interpretation, in telling a *story of reading*, we inevitably must speak dualistically of a text and what it does to a reader, or of a reader and what he or she does with the text.[3]

As with the first question about the role of the reader, there are a number of answers to the second, Who is the reader? The answers range from those who examine the responses of flesh and blood readers to those who construct various hypothetical readers. Some critics examine the written or oral responses of real readers. This ranges from asking students to share their differing responses to the same text to reconstructing the reception history of a text, the history of scholarly and popular interpretations. A particularly useful technique in this regard is to note interpretive cruxes in a text, the points at which real readers most often differ.

For those interested in hypothetical readers, there are a number of options. A hypothetical reader may be internal or external to the text. As noted above, for most narrative critics, the reader is in the text, a counterpart to the implied author. A hypothetical reader may also be external to the text. In addition to critics who examine the responses

York: Crossroad, 1993), pp. 248-51.

1. S. Fish, 'Why No One's Afraid of Wolfgang Iser', *Diacritics* 11 (1981), pp. 2-13 and W. Iser, 'Talk Like Whales', *Diacritics* 11 (1981), pp. 82-87.

2. Fish, 'Who's Afraid', p. 7. For a discussion of the difference between Iser and Fish see Moore, *Literary Criticism and the Gospels*, pp. 101, 127.

3. J. Culler, *On Deconstruction: Theory and Criticism after Structuralism* (Ithaca, NY: Cornell University Press, 1982), pp. 73-78.

of real readers, there are other critics who reconstruct a hypothetical audience from historical information about those who might have been the original audience for the work. This information can be garnered (circularly) from clues in the text itself, from other contemporary texts, and other historical sources. In order to construct such a hypothetical interpretive community, some critics attempt to discover the literary conventions writers and readers/hearers shared in the period the work was written. Scholars also look at reading conventions. Do readers of the period in question read silently alone, aloud to a group, etc.? In addition to those critics who use hypothetical internal or external readers, some, notably Iser, construct a reader who is both internal and external to the text. A note of caution is in order, however. All critics must remember that both internal and external readers are constructs of the reader-critic.

Both the questions about the role of the reader and the identity of the reader raise the question of the reader's knowledge or competence. What does the reader know as he or she reads? Is the hypothetical reader someone who is reading the text for the first time? Is he familiar with similar texts? As she reads does she only know what the text has told her so far? Or, is the reader an ideal reader who knows whatever it is necessary to know to realize fully all the text's potential. This knowledge would include all elements of the text as well as a full repertoire of literary and cultural competence. Suspicious readers might construe this distinction between naive and ideal readers as a distinction between those who belong to the critic's interpretive community—who follow its codes and conventions—and those who do not: the ideal reader is one who reads as I and as those like me read. However, again, both the first time reader and the ideal reader are constructs of the critic.

The question of the reader's competence shades into the third question raised above: What happens when we read? The question of the reading process will be central to examining verbal repetition in Matthew. The linear, temporal dimension of reading is a central element of reader-response criticism. We bring certain competencies and information to a text. As we read we are supplied with other information and may develop additional skills. As we read anticipation and retrospection are key elements of the reading process. Our interpretation changes over time. Our understanding and view of the narrative constantly changes as we read. Expectations are created.

Some are fulfilled, others are frustrated. Readers' expectations or predictions can be focal, relating to the immediate context, or global, extending over larger sections including the whole course of a work.[1] Some expectations we bring to a work. For example, the title may indicate that we are reading a detective novel. This creates certain global expectations associated with this genre. Other expectations are created as we read. These may be global or local, associated in a modern novel with the next word, the next paragraph, or the rest of a chapter. These global and focal expectations or predictions are made simultaneously and influence one another. The predictions we make may turn out as predicted, be modified or rejected as we read. Our interpretation of the narrative varies depending on whether we are at its beginning, middle, or end.

In addition to the linear nature of reading and the necessity of prediction, reader response critics also emphasize the necessity of dealing with 'gaps'. We fill in gaps or supply what the text omits or leaves unsaid. We give determinate interpretations to what the text leaves indeterminate. If we presuppose that what we are reading is a unified narrative, we look for links and connections. We build a coherent and consistent interpretation. If we presuppose the opposite, or if we seek to undermine the notion of a single correct reading, we look for inconsistencies, gaps, and omissions. This linear view of reading is at odds with traditional approaches of Gospel critics who call on and refer to the entire narrative at once.

This latter point brings to the fore the importance of the presuppositions, social location, and even personal experience of each reader. Each actual reader/critic can only read as a unique individual. At the same time each can only read through the learned social, linguistic, and literary conventions of the interpretive communities to which he or she belongs. In the biblical guild reading as a cognitive activity is king. It is usually not considered appropriate to speak too much about emotional, political, or behavioral responses to reading a Gospel. In the history of reception, however, these sort of responses have often been the goal of reading.[2]

1. F. Smith, *Understanding Reading: A Psycholinguistic Analysis of Reading and Learning to Read* (New York: Holt, Rinehart and Winston, 2nd edn, 1978), pp. 168-72.

2. See S.D. Moore, *Literary Criticism and the Gospels*, pp. 106-107 on this point.

c. *The Communication Model, Verbal Repetition and Redundancy*

As we have seen although narrative criticism and reader-response criticism have different emphases, both understand a text to be dynamically involved in a series of relationships between author or sender, text or message, and reader-hearer or receiver. One reason that the two so often shade into one another is that critics treat the text as a medium of communication between sender and receiver. The basic model is fundamental to describing any act of communication. It enjoys widespread use in a variety of disciplines. One of the key concepts used to explain the communication process is redundancy. After giving a general description of the communication model, I will point to the role redundancy, including verbal repetition in narrative, plays in communication.

The communications model. The communication model can be represented as follows:[1]

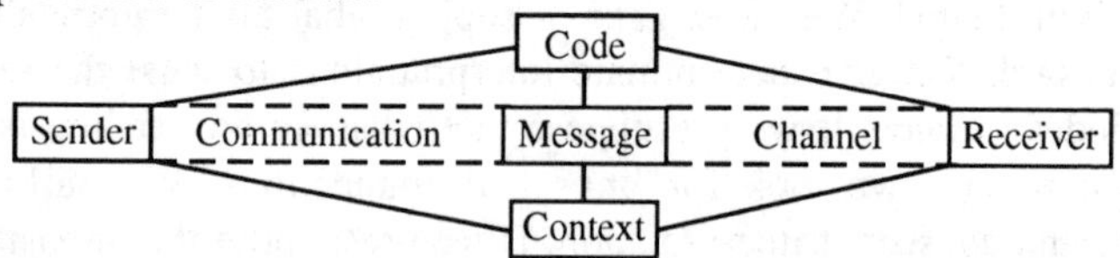

This model is linear rather than transactional. A linear model is sufficient for the Gospel of Matthew since we no longer have the opportunity to affect the sender's behavior.[2] In the basic linear model

1. See descriptions and charts in C. Cherry, *On Human Communication* (Cambridge: MIT Press, 1957), pp. 1ff, 89; U. Eco, *A Theory of Semiotics* (Bloomington: Indiana University Press, 1976), pp. 32-36; Smith, *Understanding Reading*, pp. 1-23; R. Jakobson, 'Closing Statement: Linguistics and Poetics', in T.A. Sebeok, *Style in Language* (Cambridge: MIT Press, 1960), pp. 353-57; P. Ricoeur, *Interpretation Theory* (Fort Worth: TCU Press, 1976), pp. 26-27 and Petersen, *Literary Criticism for New Testament Critics*, pp. 33-48 use Jakobson's model. S. Wittig, 'A Theory of Polyvalent Reading', in *SBL Seminar Papers, 2* (ed. G. MacRae; Missoula, MT: Scholars Press, 1975), pp. 169-84 utilizes Morris, Peirce and Saussure. Literary variants including author, work, and audience include Wimsatt, *The Verbal Icon*, pp. xvii-xviii, and M.H. Abrams, *The Mirror and the Lamp* (London: Oxford University Press, 1953), pp. 6-7. P. Hernandi, 'Literary Theory: A Compass for Critics', *Critical Inquiry* 3 (Winter, 1976), pp. 369-86 creates a helpful elaboration on the basic model.

2. See C.L. Book, T.L. Albrecht *et al.*, *Human Communication: Principles, Contexts and Skills* (New York: St Martin's Press, 1980), pp. 4-68 for an introduction to a more complex transactional model that takes account of verbal and non-

of communication the sender and receiver of a message are connected by a communication channel along which information flows. The message is in a code shared—at least in part—by sender (encoder) and receiver (decoder). Codes may include ordinary language, dots and dashes, literary conventions, customs, gestures, or any other system of signs. If the receiver does not share exactly the same code(s) as the sender, he will be unable to decode the message fully or she will interpret it differently than the sender. For example, a beginning reader, not fully competent in the code used, will have difficulty in completely comprehending a newspaper article. A modern reader may decode 'knave' in a medieval text as 'an unprincipled man, given to dishonorable and deceitful practices' (OED) rather than a boy or boy-servant (OED), its original meaning.

A shared context is also important to an act of communication. Communication takes place within a context and the message refers indirectly to that context. The phrase 'Look at that' combined with a pointed finger is clear when both parties are together in a small room. Uttered over a telephone, its reference is not clear. In either case reference is not direct.

Thus it can be seen that the message refers to the context, it does not re-present it. Messages may designate physical or imaginary objects or beings, abstract concepts, and so on.[1] Narratives create a narrative world or cosmos which is related to the real world, but not identical to it.[2] The context is the world as perceived by sender and receiver. The narrative world may contain a selection of elements from the actual world arranged and represented from a peculiar perspective. It

verbal messages, and the psychological, social and cultural contexts.

1. See Petersen, *Literary Criticism*, pp. 38-40 and Hernandi, 'Literary Theory', p. 378.

2. Petersen points to this fact in *Literary Criticism*, p. 40. The term can be found in Cassirer and Wellek and Warren. Cassirer writes that the literary work is 'a self-contained cosmos with its own center of gravity', quoted by Dowling, *The Critic's Hornbook*, p. 47. Wellek and Warren write:

> But the novelist offers less a case—a character or event—than a world...recognizable as overlapping the empirical world but distinct in its self-coherent intelligibility. The world or cosmos of a novelist—this pattern or structure or organism which includes plot, characters, setting worldview, 'tone'—is what we must scrutinize when we attempt to compare a novel with life or to judge, ethically or socially, a novelist's work. (*Theory of Literature* [New York: Harcourt, Brace & World, 3rd edn, 1962], p. 214).

may also contain elements which do not exist outside the narrative. Often, the structure and relationship of elements in a narrative world are both less complex and more apparent than those we confront in everyday life. This is true of history and fiction alike—of models of the world and of model worlds. All of the elements of the narrative, narrator, characters, plot, and so on, both create and live in this world. It is this world that the author asks the reader to inhabit.

The channel over which communication occurs is also important. The channel, and thus the communication process, can be inhibited by *noise*. In listening to a lecture, for example, noise might be the hum of a radiator which drowns out the lecturer's voice or one's own growling stomach. In silent reading noise can consist of a bad typeface, distracting thoughts, or even the reader's forgetfulness.[1] The classic illustration of overcoming *noise* is Colin Cherry's 'Cocktail Party Problem'. Cherry points to the ability of listeners in crowds to overcome the noise of many voices and concentrate on one speaker.[2] Listeners will concentrate on one message unless the mention of their own name or some other item of interest turns their attention to another speaker. Listeners are able to follow a speaker because they use information about syntax, content, etc. as well as the speaker's voice to decode the message. If the party gets particularly raucous, sometimes noise foils communication until the speaker repeats a comment several times. This adds another layer of redundancy. Redundancy aids in overcoming noise and decoding a message.

Redundancy. Redundancy is the availability of information from more than one source. Information is necessary for a receiver to interpret properly (or decode) any message. He or she must choose from various alternative interpretations. For example, a reader presented with the visual image 'read' must decide whether the meaning is past or present tense. Redundancy increases predictability by decreasing the number of possible alternatives. This reduces uncertainty, facilitating the communication process.[3] One form of redundancy is

1. See Smith, *Understanding Reading*, p. 14 and S.R. Suleiman, 'Redundancy and the "Readable" Text', *Poetics Today* 1 (1980), pp. 119-42.

2. Cherry, *On Human Communication*, pp. 277-78 cited by Smith, *Understanding Reading*, p. 202 and by Wittig, 'Formulaic Style', p. 129.

3. Cherry, *On Human Communication*, p. 18. He defines redundancy as follows: 'Briefly, redundancy is a property of language, codes, and sign systems

the use of both oral and visual cues. In the above example, when presented with oral and visual representations uncertainty is almost entirely eliminated. There are many other types of redundancy, usually involving information the receiver already possesses. Consider the example of redundancy in reading offered by Frank Smith:

> There are frequent examples of redundancy in reading. As an illustration, consider the unfinished sentence (which could possibly appear at the bottom of a right-hand page of a book):
>
> *The captain ordered the mate to drop the an-*
>
> We shall consider four ways of reducing our uncertainty about the remainder of that sentence, four alternative and therefore redundant sources of information. First, we could turn the page and see how the last word finished—we can call this visual information. But we can also make some reasonable predictions about how the sentence will continue without turning the page. For example, we can say that the next letter is unlikely to be *b*, *f*, *h*, *j*, *m*, *p*, *q*, *r*, *w*, or *z* because these letters just do not occur after *an* in common words of the English language: we can therefore attribute the elimination of these alternatives to *orthographic* (or spelling) information. There are also some things that can be said about the entire word before turning the page. We know that it is most likely to be an adjective or a noun, because other types of words such as articles, conjunctions, verbs, and prepositions, for example, are most unlikely to follow the word *the*; the elimination of all these additional alternatives can be attributed to syntactic (or grammatical) information. Finally, we can continue to eliminate alternatives even if we consider as candidates for the last word only nouns or adjectives that begin with *an* plus one of the letters not eliminated by the orthographic information already discussed. We can eliminate words like *answer* and *anagram* and *antibody* because although they are not excluded by our other criteria, our knowledge of the world tells us these are not the kinds of things that captains normally order mates to drop. The elimination of these alternatives can be attributed to *semantic* information. Obviously, the four alternative sources of information about the incomplete word in the above example, *visual*, *orthographic*, *syntactic*, and *semantic*, to some extent provide overlapping information. We do not need as much visual information about the next word as we would if it occurred in isolation because the other sources of information eliminate many alternatives. The four sources of information, therefore, are all to some extent redundant. And the skilled reader who can make use of the three other sources needs much less visual information than the less

which arises from a superfluity of rules, and which facilitates communication in spite of all the factors of uncertainty acting against it', pp. 18-19.

> fluent reader. The more redundancy there is, the less visual information the skilled reader requires. In passages of continuous text, provided that the language is familiar and the content not too difficult, every other letter can be eliminated from most words, or about one word in five omitted altogether, without making the passage too difficult for a reader to comprehend.[1]

Redundant information that the receiver already possesses is acquired through previous experience. Repeated exposure to the English language teaches, for example, that nouns usually follow 'the'. The occurrence of a noun is expected; it is *predictable*. Redundancy may be supplied by a message itself or by the competency of the receiver in linguistic, generic, or other codes—or by some combination of the above. In narrative a character's action may be predictable, for example, because he or she has acted the same way in a similar situation two or three times before in the tale or because that type of character always acts that way in the genre involved.

Verbal repetition and redundancy in narrative. How is verbal repetition in narrative related to redundancy? Verbal repetition is one form of redundancy. With verbal repetition repeated orthographic, semantic and syntactic information is reinforced visually and/or aurally. If the repeated words are read silently, the reinforcement may be entirely visual. If the words are sounded out loud or within the mind of a reader, then the information is reinforced visually and aurally. If one person reads aloud to another, the information is only reinforced aurally for the hearer. Verbal repetition within a single text supplies the reader with this collated information more than once, although variations in the words repeated and variations in context are also involved. Just as repeated experience with reading in English teaches a reader to expect a captain to drop an anchor, so reading the phrase 'Kingdom of Heaven' several times early in the Matthean narrative means the reader will come to expect 'Heaven' to follow 'Kingdom of' as he or she continues to read in Matthew. Verbal repetition of phrases, proverbs, or typical scenes can also be characteristic of a narrative tradition. When we read the phrase 'Once upon a time' certain global expectations that enable reading are set into play. These expectations, however, may be fulfilled, modified, or frustrated.

Verbal repetition works in conjunction with other forms of redun-

1. Smith, *Understanding Reading*, pp. 18-19.

dancy. It can play an important role in increasing the intelligibility and cohesiveness of a narrative. It enhances the speed of transmission of the narrative 'message' and the psychological efficiency of response. It helps to overcome noise in the communication channel. Just as the lecturer repeats points so that the students are sure to get them down in their notes—and hopefully understand them—so in narrative 'points' can be made with verbal repetition. It can help to overcome the reader's or hearer's forgetfulness over the course of a long narrative as well as other distractions. Verbal repetition increases predictability. It has persuasive power.

Several narrative critics have pointed to the importance of verbal repetition and redundancy in ways that illumine the functions of verbal repetition in Matthew. They have particularly emphasized the importance of predictability and persuasion. Susan Wittig makes use of the concept of redundancy in studying repeated formulas, motifs, and scenes in written Middle English verse narratives.[1] She emphasizes the element of predictability:

> The element of predictability demonstrably present in formulaic verse is a feature known to information theorists as *redundancy*; that is some words or groups of words, some syntactical and metrical patterns have a high probability of occurrence in a given context.[2]

She offers the example of the two-verse formula:

> When he awoke and speke myght
> Sore he wept and sore he syght

After having heard or read the formula several times, the Middle English audience could predict (or anticipate) that when the first verse appeared it would be followed by the second.[3]

1. S. Wittig's analyses of redundancy in formulaic narrative appear in 'Formulaic Style and the Problem of Redundancy', *Centrum* 1 (1973), pp. 123-36 and *Stylistic and Narrative Structures in the Middle English Romances* (Austin, TX: University of Texas Press, 1978).

2. Wittig, 'Formulaic Style', p. 126.

3. Wittig, 'Formulaic Style', p. 125. Syntactical and metrical patterns underlie the lexical repetitions. Formulas may vary on the lexical level and remain the same on the other levels as in,

he she he thou	were never so	nobyll a knight fayr ne whyte kene prest

Wittig also notes redundancy on the level of the larger narrative verse formulas of motif and scene:

> many of the narratives will be seen to be structurally redundant in terms of plot as well as verse-form; that is, having heard or read the first scene, made up of a number of obligatory motifs, an audience familiar with several narratives in the same genre can predict the composition of the second scene, and so on, through the course of the narrative.[1]

She is noting both focal expectations relating to the immediate context and global expectations extending over larger sections including the whole course of a work. As noted previously, global and focal predictions are made simultaneously and influence one another. They provide another form of redundancy.

Susan Rubin Suleiman, writing about realistic narrative, specifically the *roman à thèse*, concentrates on global expectations which affect the text as a whole.[2] Suleiman presents the hypothesis that redundancy is highly characteristic of 'readable' texts, especially realistic narratives. Readable (*lisible*) texts are designed to limit meaning.[3] Adopting a schema based on the work of A.J. Greimas and G. Genette, she offers a detailed classification of the types of redundancy possible in realistic narratives on the level of the story, the discourse, and between story and discourse.[4] She goes on to suggest which of these types are prevalent in the *roman à thèse*, the high degree and types of redundancy serving partly to define the genre. While both Wittig and Suleiman are interested in types of redundancy characteristic of genres, many of Suleiman's categories focus on redundancy within a

1. Wittig, 'Formulaic Style', p. 127. They know the generic code.
2. Suleiman, 'Redundancy', pp. 119-42.
3. In employing the term 'readable' she is working with R. Barthes' distinction between readable (*lisible*) and writable (*scriptible*) texts. The former limits meaning, employing traditional grammar, structure and logic. It is analyzable. The latter is modern, extremely open, and plural. The reader becomes the producer of a writable text rather than a consumer. Suleiman, 'Redundancy', p. 119.
4. Story refers to the narrative content, the events and actions (the diegetic level). Discourse refers to the way the story is presented to the reader (the level of *recit*) (Suleiman, 'Redundancy', pp. 123-24). Redundancies on the story level deal with character actions, speeches, and contexts. Those on the discourse level refer to narration, focalization, and time spent on them. Redundancies between story and discourse occur where there is cross-category activity, for example, when a narrator and a character repeat the same words about another character.

text. For example, on the level of the story, 'A1.1 The same event or same sequence of events happens to a single C (character) *n* times', or on the level of the discourse, 'B.2 The narrator pronounces *n* times the same commentary about a character, an event or a context'. For Suleiman the presence of repeated commentary may be characteristic of a genre, but the content which is repeated may vary. Most of Suleiman's types appear in Matthew. Many involve verbal repetitions. Below is a list of those types with Matthean examples in parentheses:

A1.1 'The same event or same sequence of events happens to more than one C (character).'
(The healings involving the pairs of blind men 9.27-31 = 20.29-34)

A.1.2 'The same event or sequence of events happens to a single C *n* times.'
(The two requests for a sign, 12.38-42 = 16.1-4)

A.2.1 'Several C's have the same qualities or accomplish the same qualifying functions.'
(The similarities between John and Jesus.)

A.3.2 'A single C accomplishes the same F's (functions) several times.'
(The actions of Jesus or various character groups in the doublets mentioned above or Peter's role as spokesman for the disciples.)

A.5.1 'Several C's pronounce the same interpretative commentary (judgment, analysis, prognosis) concerning an event, a context, a character, etc.'
(Jesus and John's comments on the Jewish leaders.)

A.5.2 'A single C pronounces *n* times the same commentary concerning an event, a context, a character (who can be the C himself, etc).'
(Jesus' passion–resurrection predictions.)

A.7 'An event is redundant with the interpretive commentary made by a C (or several C's) concerning it.'
(Jesus' prediction of Peter's denial and the denial.)

B.2 'The narrator pronounces *n* times the same commentary about a character, an event or a context.'
(The formula for fulfillment quotations when applied to Jesus.)[1]

1. Suleiman, 'Redundancy', pp. 127-29. A similar typology, also influenced somewhat by Genette, is presented by I.J.F. de Jong, 'Narratology and Oral Poetry: The Case of Homer', *Poetics Today* 12 (1991), p. 414, with reference to Homer. She identifies the following types of verbatim repetition of at least two verses:

a. The same text is used (more than once) by the same narrator-focalizer (the person who speaks and perceives) to refer to the same event.
b. The same text is used by different narrator-focalizers to refer to the same event.

In addition to predictability, the creation of expectations, both Wittig and Suleiman emphasize the power of redundancy to persuade. In relation to formulaic narratives Wittig writes:

> The creation (either consciously and deliberately or unconsciously and unintentionally) of a multi-level set of expectancies not only allows the audience to predict the occurrence of successive items (whether 'the next word in a linear sequence of words, or the next stanzaic sequence, or the next motif or scene in a plot sequence'),[1] but also provides for the audience's *assent* to the sequence, for if the listener can predict the next item (perhaps he may repeat it silently before it occurs) he will be more likely to accept it and agree to it... The persuasive effect of such familiar lexical–syntactical–metrical patterns has been recognized by rhetoricians for centuries, and is the basis of much current advertising theory.[2]

Suleiman makes a similar point about redundancy in the *roman à thèse*:

> it is by means of redundancy that plural meanings and ambiguities are eliminated and a single 'correct' reading imposed.[3]

c. The same text is used (more than once) by the same narrator-focalizer to refer to different events.
d. The same text is used by different narrator-focalizers to refer to different events.

In *Narrators and Focalizers: The Presentation of the Story in the Iliad* (Amsterdam: Grüner, 1987), pp. 179-80 de Jong distinguishes between verbatim repetition of verse clusters in the narrator's speech, a character's speech, and between the first two. She emphasizes that she is interested not in the probable oral origins of the repetitions, but rather in their narrative functions.

1. Wittig, 'Formulaic Style', p. 130.

2. Wittig, 'Formulaic Style', p. 131. Wittig goes on to argue that formulaic narrative verse is a form of mass communication designed to maintain the *status quo*. The formulas on all levels are redundant because they are part of a culture's *langue, Stylistic and Narrative Structures*, pp. 41-46. Formulaic verse narratives such as the Middle English romances embody and support the culture's social norms and ideal world. The persuasive force of the repeated formulas is to preserve rather than produce change.

One should be cautious in extending the implications of these two points. Not all repetition persuades. The context in which it occurs will have an important effect on its persuasive power. Second, not all repetitive narrative (verse or prose) supports the *status quo*, for example, the *roman à thèse*. Even all traditional narrative requires innovation and change if it is to survive. If it does not take on the challenge of reinterpreting the tradition to meet the needs of changing times, it will die.

3. Suleiman, 'Redundancy', p. 120.

In the *roman à thèse* interpretive commentaries by the narrator and privileged characters are frequent and redundant, establishing a 'correct' interpretive line. Characters' functions, such as helping, are redundant with their qualities, such as courage, that is, the characters are redundantly stereotyped. We will also find in subsequent chapters that this is true of Matthew. The *roman à thèse* and Matthew both use redundancy to persuade the reader to adopt a particular ideological viewpoint.

Both Wittig and Suleiman point out that redundancy leads to the creation of expectations that increase predictability, persuade, and reduce the number of possible interpretations.

4. *The Matthean Narrative, Verbal Repetition, and Redundancy*

In the rest of the book I will intertwine the study of Matthew as narrative with a primary focus on the functions of extended verbal repetition in the Matthean narrative. From one point of view I am asking what verbal repetition does to readers (or hearers). From another I am asking how the reader creates—or what the reader does—with verbal repetition. To answer these questions I will draw from the related toolboxes of narrative criticism, reader response criticism, and communication theory. From narrative criticism I will take the categories of narrative rhetoric, character, and plot with an emphasis on the interrelationship of textual elements. From reader-response criticism I will draw on discussions of the reading process. From communication theory I will draw on the concept of redundancy.

Although there are specific functions of verbal repetition that relate to each of the narrative categories, I will show that the temporal dimension of narrative, context. and repetition with variation are important throughout. The temporal dimension of narrative is important because repetition necessarily requires several occurrences of a phrase or episode at various points in the course of the narrative. The reader's memory, expectations, and the building up of associations over time all play a role. Context is important because as each repetition occurs at a different point in the narrative, it occurs in a different context. The context shapes the way in which each repetition is interpreted. Variation is important because, for a reader to recognize verbal repetition, he or she must be able to recognize (or constitute) similarity, but also difference. Even the exact same words are recognized as repetition rather than identity because they occur in a different context. Frequently repetitions are not exact, however. There can be variation in the words themselves or in who utters them, for example. Differences move the reader to draw comparisons and contrasts in order to account for them. The role of the temporal dimension of narrative, of context, and variation in a reader's construal of verbal repetition is illumined by the concept of redundancy prominent in information theory, but also used as we have seen by some narrative theorists.[1]

Although the functions of extended verbal repetition vary depending on whether we view them in the light of the categories of rhetoric, character, or plot, there are a number of general functions which occur again and again. Any given repetition may have any or all of these functions. The functions are:

1. to highlight or draw attention;
2. to establish or fix in the mind of the implied reader;
3. to emphasize the importance of something;
4. to create expectations, increasing predictability and assent (Anticipation);
5. to cause review and reassessment (Retrospection);
6. to unify disparate elements, sometimes creating a background pattern against which other elements can be understood;
7. to build patterns of association or draw contrasts.

1. For subsequent discussions that draw out the importance of repetition with variation, context, and the temporal dimension of narrative see R.D. Witherup, 'Cornelius Over and Over and Over Again: "Functional Redundancy" in the Acts of the Apostles', *JSNT* 49 (1993), pp. 44-66 and 'Functional Redundancy in the Acts of the Apostles: A Case Study', *JSNT* 48 (1992), pp. 67-86. Witherup draws on the work of Meier Sternberg, *The Poetics of Biblical Narrative: Ideological Literature and the Drama of Reading* (Bloomington: Indiana University Press, 1988). Sternberg describes the use of repetition in the Hebrew Scriptures in a way that is very similar to my analysis of Matthew. He has a particularly helpful typology of repetition with variation which includes: expansion or addition, truncation or ellipsis, change of order, grammatical transformation and substitution, pp. 391-92. Sternberg also classifies the structure of repetition with reference to combinations that entail the object of presentation (verbal, i.e. speech, or non-verbal), first source of presentation (narrator or character), source of retelling (narrator or character), mode of retelling (from verbatim to greater variation) and the motivation for mode of retelling (deliberately or non-deliberately), pp. 430-36.

As we examine the threads of Matthew's narrative, we will see how verbal repetition helps to spin the Matthean web *and* how the threads of the Matthean narrative web turn into the strings of a harp playing an intricate progression of verbal echoes.

Chapter 2

NARRATIVE RHETORIC: NARRATOR AND NARRATEE, DIRECT COMMENTARY AND POINT OF VIEW

1. *Introduction*

The implied author of the Gospel of Matthew uses all the elements of the narrative to guide the implied reader's response. The entire text is rhetorical. This involves (1) the sequence and motivation of events or the plot, (2) the development and use of characters, and (3) more overtly rhetorical aspects associated with the narrator and narratee. This chapter focuses on two of the elements most closely associated with the narrator and narratee, direct commentary and point of view. It has two purposes. First, it introduces terms and concepts and provides a context for the discussion of character in Chapter 3 and plot in Chapter 4. Second, it examines the role of verbal repetition in the direct commentary and points of view employed in Matthew.

2. *The Narrator and Narratee*

The narrator of the Gospel of Matthew is reliable and almost completely undramatized. He or she serves as the voice of the implied author. The narrator's reliability is assumed as in most ancient narrative.[1] This can be seen from the very beginning of the Gospel. In the birth story, for example, the narrator reports the contents of Joseph's dream and tells the implied reader directly that Joseph was a 'just man' who 'resolved to divorce Mary quietly' because he was 'unwilling to put her to shame' (1.18-22). There is no attempt to justify either the omniscience or the moral judgment of the narrator.

1. See R. Scholes and R. Kellogg, *The Nature of Narrative* (London/New York: Oxford University, paper 1968, original, 1966), p. 264 and Booth, *Rhetoric*, p. 5 who uses the example of Job.

The implied reader is simply expected to accept them. At first glance the appearance of God (in the baptism and transfiguration) and of God's angels may seem to buttress the narrator's reliability. But even the reliability of God and God's messengers ultimately depends on the reliability of the narrator. It is the narrator who identifies them and recounts what they say.

In addition to being reliable, the narrator, as noted above, is almost completely undramatized. The only clues to his or her 'identity' beyond the general ideological stance are supplied by direct comments to the narratee. For example, the narrator translates several Hebrew or Aramaic expressions for the narratee (1.23; 27.33 and 27.46). This indicates he or she is competent in both linguistic codes. Since the narrator is, in effect, the voice of the implied author, any characteristics attributed to the voice help to create, along with the other narrative elements and their arrangement, the persona of the implied author.

The narratee of the Gospel of Matthew is not a character in the story. Beyond possessing competencies in certain linguistic and cultural codes only generalizations can be made about the narratee. The narratee and intrinsic aspects of the implied reader are so closely related that the ideological stance implied is almost the only means of characterization. A few specific details can be drawn primarily from direct narratorial comments. For example, the narratee does not speak Aramaic or Hebrew since the narrator provides explanatory glosses in 1.23, 27.33 and 27.46. The narratee is also someone who might not realize the significance of the desolating sacrilege mentioned in 24.15. The narrator calls attention to it with the famous 'wink' to the reader: 'Let the reader understand.' Etiological comments in 27.8 and 28.15b also seem to assume that the narratee is aware of the location and the rumor explained. They also place the narratee, along with the past tense used throughout the Gospel, in a time contemporary with the narrator subsequent to the narrative. Further discussion of direct commentary is found below.

3. *Direct or Explicit Commentary*

One way that the implied author communicates with the implied reader of the Gospel of Matthew is through the direct or explicit comments of the narrator to the narratee. Since the relationships between implied author and narrator and implied reader and narratee are so close, direct or explicit commentary almost becomes a direct communication between implied author and implied reader.[1] It provides an efficient and authoritative means of guiding the implied reader's response.

Direct or explicit commentary has various purposes: explanation of the import of a story element, normative evaluation, generalizations relating something in the story world to external facts or established norms, self-conscious comments on the work itself, and so on.[2] Various direct comments in Matthew fulfill one or more of these purposes. A catalogue of direct commentary in Matthew would include at least the following entries:

a. the heading (1.1)
b. the genealogy (1.2-17)
c. fulfillment quotations (1.22-23; 2.15, 17-18, 23; 4.15-16; 8.17; 12.17-21; 13.35; 21.4-5; 27.9-10 and 3.3 without the strict formula introduction)
d. explanatory glosses.
    1. translation of Aramaic or Hebrew (1.23; 27.33, 46)
    2. cultural explanations (22.23; 27.15-16)
    3. etiological comments (27.8; 28.15b)
    4. parenthetical comments (7.29; 10.2-3, names of the Twelve; and 12.8)
e. wink to the reader (24.15)
f. labels such as 'the one called Peter' or 'the betraying one'.

1. Of course, it is actually never *direct* since the voice that speaks is the narrator's. The narrator's voice is but one of the means along with arrangement of episodes, etc., through which the implied author communicates with the implied reader.

2. Booth lists and discusses seven uses of reliable commentary which can be explicit or implicit in ch. 7 of *Rhetoric*:

1. Providing the Facts, 'Picture', or Summary
2. Molding Beliefs
3. Relating Particulars to Established Norms
4. Heightening the Significance of Events
5. Generalizing the Significance of the Whole Work
6. Manipulating Mood
7. Commenting Directly on the Work Itself.

Some of these, such as summary, will be discussed in other chapters of this book. Chatman lists four variables of explicit commentary: interpretation, judgment, generalization and 'self-conscious' narration (*Story and Discourse*, p. 228).

a. *Direct Commentary and Verbal Repetition*
Several of these direct comments involve verbal repetition. The heading. 'The *biblos geneséos* of Jesus Christ, the Son of David, the Son of Abraham' (1.1), contains two striking titles and a name that will recur repeatedly throughout the Gospel, especially in chs. 1–2.[1] Whether the heading is understood as the heading of the whole Gospel, the genealogy, or the infancy narrative,[2] it alerts the implied reader to search for the meaning and significance of the names it highlights. When the names are repeated, the implied reader will know they are a key to unlocking the narrator's message.[3] Actual readers may come to the text with expectations and associations of their own. These will be tested and confirmed, narrowed or expanded with each repetition.[4]

The second item in the catalog of direct commentary also involves verbal repetition. There is extended repetition between the genealogy (1.2-17) and the rest of the Gospel[5] and internal, concentrated repetition within the genealogy itself.

1. Christ appears in 1.7; 2.4; 11.2; 16.16, 20; 22.42; 23.10; 24.5, 23; 26.63, 68. Jesus Christ or Jesus the one called Christ in 1.16, 18; 16.21; 27.17, 22. The Son of David occurs in 1.20; 9.27; 12.23; 15.22; 20.30, 31; 21.9, 15; David in 1.6, 17 (twice); 12.3; 22.42, 43, 45. Abraham occurs in 1.2, 17; 3.9 (twice); 8.11; 22.32.

2. See J.D. Kingsbury, *Matthew: Structure, Christology, Kingdom* (Philadelphia: Fortress Press, 1975), pp. 9-11 and R.E. Brown, *The Birth of the Messiah* (Garden City, NY: Doubleday, 1977), pp. 66-69 for the arguments.

3. As R.E. Brown remarks in relation to the infancy narrative: 'Matt. 1.1 with its emphasis on "Jesus Christ" and on "Son of David" and "Son of Abraham" calls the reader's attention to the basic themes of the infancy narrative' (*Birth of the Messiah*, p. 67).

4. The author may also be guiding the reader's response by means of allusion. The phrase *biblos geneséos* is used in the Septuagint of Gen. 2.4a and 5.1a (MT *sepher toledot*). This, along with the references to David and Abraham, alerts the implied reader to read the Gospel with the rich Jewish scriptural tradition as a ready frame of reference. This inference is immediately confirmed by what follows, the genealogy and an infancy narrative laden with fulfillment quotations.

5. For information on the genealogy see Brown, *Birth of the Messiah*; W.D. Davies, *The Setting of the Sermon on the Mount* (London/New York: Cambridge University Press, 1963), pp. 72-77; M.D. Johnson, *The Purpose of the Biblical Genealogies* (SNTSMS, 8; London/New York: Cambridge University Press, 1969); H.C. Waetjen, 'The Genealogy as the Key to the Gospel According to Matthew', *JBL* 95 (1976), pp. 205-30. See n. 1 above for a list of verses where the names and titles—Jesus Christ, Christ, Son of David, David and Abraham—are repeated.

The genealogy serves as a sort of epigraph for the Gospel. It firmly places Jesus in the context of the sweep of Jewish history from Abraham to David, from David to the Babylonian exile, and from the exile to the point where the narrative begins, Jesus' birth. It repeats the important Christological titles, Christ, Son of David, and Son of Abraham and confirms possible allusions in 1.1. The genealogy also provides a backdrop against which the birth story, in particular, and the entire Gospel, in general, can be read. The implied reader alerted by reading the genealogy will attend to each repeated reference to Christ, David, Son of David, and Son of Abraham. He or she will also understand these repetitions in the light of the genealogy.

Within the genealogy there is a uniform pattern of concentrated verbal repetition: *name* δὲ ἐγέννησεν τὸν *name(s)*.[1] It is repeated thirty-nine times. Major exceptions to the repeated pattern are highlighted by their variation from the pattern. Several variations mark temporal divisions. These include the label 'the king' added to David's name in 1.6, the label 'the one called Christ' to Jesus' name in 1.16, and the reference to the Babylonian deportation in 1.11 and 1.12. The importance of these as dividing points is confirmed in 1.17 which summarizes the generational divisions. The addition 'and his brothers' in 1.2 and 1.11 is another variation. The text offers no interpretation of this break. One actual reader, R.E. Brown, reads these breaks as possibly accenting points at which God exercised selectivity in carrying forward the messianic line.[2] Other variations in the repeated pattern are the inclusion of five women: Tamar, Rahab, Ruth, the wife of Uriah (Bathsheba), and Mary. The women themselves are included in repeated patterns varied with Mary.

ἐκ τῆς Θαμάρ	(1.3)
ἐκ τῆς 'Ραχαβ	(1.5a)
ἐκ τῆς 'Ρούθ	(1.5b)
ἐκ τῆς τοῦ Οὐρίου	(1.6)
Μαρίας εξ ἧς ἐγέννήθη 'Ιησοῦς	(1.16)

The implied reader's attention is drawn to the five women since their inclusion interrupts a repeated pattern. It is drawn to Mary among the five for the same reason. The break in the expected pattern forces him

1. The genealogy begins 'Αββρααμ ἐγέννησεν τὸν 'Ισαακ, lacking for obvious reasons the δὲ.

2. Brown, *Birth of the Messiah*, p. 71.

or her to ask why these five women are included. No answer is provided in the text. This teases the mind of the reader into active thought, to borrow a phrase from C.H. Dodd. In *The Birth of the Messiah*, Raymond E. Brown discusses the three explanations, offered by actual readers, which have won wide acceptance over the centuries. These are.

1. '...the four Old Testament women were regarded as sinners and their inclusion for Matthew's readers foreshadowed the role of Jesus as the savior of sinful men. (p. 71)'
2. '...the women were regarded as foreigners and were included by Matthew to show that Jesus, the Jewish Messiah, was related by ancestry to the Gentiles. (p. 72)' (This would not apply to Mary.)
3. The four women and Mary share two things in common. '(a) there is something extraordinary or irregular in their union with their partners—a union which, though it may have been scandalous to outsiders, continued the blessed lineage of the Messiah; (b) the women showed initiative or played an important role in God's plan and so came to be considered the instrument of God's providence or of His Holy Spirit. (p. 73)'[1]

The first interpretation links the genealogy with the Gospel's portrayal of Jesus as the savior of sinners. It relates gender, sexuality and sin. The second interpretation takes its cue from the phrase ἐκ τῆς τοῦ Οὐρίου in 1.6. The Jewish Bathsheba 'is named by reference to her Gentile husband'. It also takes into account the theme of the mission to the Gentiles in the Gospel as a whole. The third interpretation asks what all of the women, including Mary, have in common. Since Mary is neither a sinner nor a Gentile, the first two interpretations are rejected. The initiative of the women, the role of the Spirit and the irregularity in the production of an heir all link the five

1. Brown, *Birth of the Messiah*, pp. 71-73. For feminist discussions of Mt. 1–2 see J. Schaberg, *The Illegitimacy of Jesus* (San Francisco: Harper & Row, 1987); A.-J. Levine, *The Social and Ethnic Dimensions of Matthean Salvation History* (New York: Edwin Mellen, 1988), pp. 59-88; E.M. Wainwright, *Towards a Feminist Critical Reading of the Gospel According to Matthew* (Berlin: de Gruyter, 1991), pp. 59-75, 155-76 and J.C. Anderson, 'Matthew: Gender and Reading', *Semeia* 28 (1983), pp. 7-10.

women together. Thus the appearance of the four women in the genealogy prepares for the strange circumstances surrounding Jesus' birth described in chs. 1 and 2. The difference between Mary and the other four women is also consistent with the third interpretation. The shift of the repeated verbal pattern 'male begot child "out of" woman's name' to 'Mary, *of whom* was born Jesus' indicates this difference. Jesus has no father. Thus the genealogy raises questions concerning Jesus' birth and identity which will be answered in the birth story. How was Jesus conceived? How can he lay claim to descent from Abraham and David? Jesus was conceived ἐκ πνεύματος ʻαγίου (1.18, 20) and becomes Joseph's legal heir when Joseph names him.

Whatever the actual reader makes of the presence of the women will affect how he or she reads the rest of the narrative, especially chs. 1 and 2. Likewise, his or her reading of the rest of the Gospel will affect in retrospect the interpretation of the women's presence in the genealogy. Given that the narrator is offering direct commentary, the variety of interpretations indicates the importance of the role of actual readers in creating textual meaning.

The next item in the catalog of explicit commentary also involves verbal repetition. The fulfillment quotation is one of the most frequent forms of direct commentary. Ten times the narrator tells the narratee (and thus the implied reader) that an event occurred to fulfill prophecy.[1] Each time the quotation cited is introduced by the formula ἵνα (ὅπως) πληρνθῇ τὸ ρηθὲν (1.22; 2.15, 23; 4.14; 8.17; 12.17; 13.35; 21.4) or the closely related τότε ἐπληρώθη τὸ ρηθὲν (2.17, 27.9). Once the narrator introduces a scriptural citation addressed to the narratee without a formula (3.3).

The nature of these quotations as a means of communication between implied author and implied reader has been observed tangentially in the past. The German term for the quotations, *Reflexionszitate*, 'emphasizes that the citations have been added to the common gospel material as a personal *reflection*'.[2] Raymond E. Brown calls attention to 'Matthew's *nota bene* technique of formula citation'.[3] However, this function has never really been central to the discussion of the formula citations. Interpreters have been more concerned with the origin and

1. Excluded from consideration are fulfillment citations found in the mouths of characters. These are discussed below on pp. 59-61.

2. Brown, *Birth of the Messiah*, p. 96 n. 1.

3. Brown, *Birth of the Messiah*, p. 99.

historical purpose of the citations and the stage the citations appeared in the process of composition, ante- or postcedent to the narrative materials.

The fulfillment quotations play an important role in the Gospel's rhetoric. The repetition of the fulfillment formula along with the sheer number of citations establishes an overall pattern or view, a backdrop for interpretation. Jesus' life is a fulfillment of Scripture. Individual quotations serve specific functions as well. Some evoke particular scriptural references as a context for interpreting the events of Jesus' life and as an aid in establishing Jesus' identity and character (1.22-23; 2.15, 17-18; 8.17; 12.17-21; 13.35; 21.4-5). Some provide a meaning for geographical sites, turning places into symbols (2.23b; 1.14-16; 27.9-10). All, highlighted, united, and reinforced by repetition, guide the implied reader's evaluation of events and persons, leading the implied reader to adopt the narrator's ideological perspective. They perform these functions economically and effectively. They force the implied reader to share in the application of the quotation to the narrative action as he or she searches for the relationship between quotation and context. The implied reader's assent to the narrator's view is likely to be increased. Thus, we see the importance of three elements pointed out in the first chapter, the temporal dimension of narrative, the importance of context, and repetition with variation.

The other direct comments which involve repetition are the etiological comments, 27.8 and 28.15b. They will be discussed below in the section on point of view.

4. *Point Of View*[1]

Traditionally, point of view is defined as the perspective or perspectives from which the narrative is presented. It is classified

1. This chapter relies heavily on a paper entitled 'Point of View in Matthew—Evidence' that I presented to the Society of Biblical Literature Symposium on Literary Analysis of the Gospels and Acts at the 1981 annual meeting. The question of point of view in Matthew has since been taken up by J.D. Kingsbury, *Matthew As Story* (Minneapolis: Fortress Press, 2nd edn, 1988 [1986]), pp. 31-37; D.J. Weaver, *Matthew's Missionary Discourse: A Literary Critical Analysis* (JSNTSup, 38; Sheffield: JSOT Press, 1990), pp. 31-57; D.B. Howell, *Matthew's Inclusive Story: A Study in the Narrative Rhetoric of the First Gospel* (JSNTSup, 42; Sheffield: JSOT Press, 1990), pp. 161-203; and M.A. Powell, 'Direct and Indirect Phraseology in the Gospel of Matthew', in *SBL 1991 Seminar Papers* (Atlanta: Scholars Press,

according to person (first or third), degree of narrator omniscience, degree of narrator intrusiveness, and reliability.[1] Recently scholars have devoted renewed attention to the various narrative phenomena approached under the rubric of point of view. Seymour Chatman, for example, has distinguished between three senses often referred to by the term point of view.

a. literal: through someone's eyes (perception)
b. figurative: through someone's world view (ideology, conceptual system, *Weltanschauung*, etc.)
c. transferred: from someone's interest-vantage (characterizing his general interest, profit, welfare, well-being, etc.)[2]

He calls these senses the perceptual, conceptual, and interest points of view and offers the following sentences as illustrations.

a. From John's point of view, at the top of Coit Tower, the panorama of the San Francisco Bay was breathtaking.
b. John said that from his point of view, Nixon's position, though praised by his supporters, was somewhat less than noble.
c. Though he didn't realize it at the time, the divorce was a disaster from John's point of view.[3]

Chatman also notes that it is not only the narrator who has one or more of these points of view in a narrative. The characters, the narrator, and the implied author (and one might add the narratee and implied reader) may have various points of view. Thus Chatman argues it is important to distinguish between point of view and narrative voice. '*The perspective and the expression need not be lodged in the same person.*'[4] The narrator may describe a scene, for

1991), pp. 405-17. Works from the literary field which I did not draw on, but which I think make further fruitful contributions are S.S. Lanser, *The Narrative Act: Point of View in Prose Fiction* (Princeton: Princeton University Press, 1981) and Bal, *Narratology*. Bal emphasizes the difference between narration, who speaks, and focalization, who sees or perceives. In Homeric studies, de Jong *Narrators*, has very successfully applied Bal's categories.

1. For a traditional definition and classification see Abrams, *Glossary*, pp. 133-36.
2. Chatman, *Story and Discourse*, pp. 151-52.
3. Chatman, *Story and Discourse*, p. 152.
4. Chatman, *Story and Discourse*, p. 153.

example, from the perceptual point of view of a character.

Chatman's concerns are also expressed in the typology of points of view offered in Boris Uspensky's *A Poetics of Composition*.[1] Uspensky distinguishes between point of view on five planes: the ideological, the phraseological, the temporal, the spatial, and the psychological. The ideological or evaluative plane is roughly equivalent to Chatman's conceptual point of view. The phraseological plane is the plane of speech characteristics. The phraseological point of view of the narrator may be revealed, for example, by whose diction he or she uses to describe a character, his or her own, that of another character, etc. The temporal plane has two aspects, view of time and tense. The first concerns whose perspective the narrator uses to divide and count time. The second, tense, is where the narrator is in time at a given moment in relation to characters, narratee, etc. The spatial plane is the plane concerned with geographical location. The psychological plane has essentially to do with whether the narrator describes characters and events internally and subjectively through the consciousness of one or more characters or externally and objectively from a position outside of any character.[2] The internal perspective or psychological point of view roughly corresponds to what Wayne Booth describes as a privileged inside view, one of the author's rhetorical devices.[3] Points of view on all of these planes may shift. Points of view on different planes may also concur or not concur.

5. *Point of View in Matthew*

The undramatized reliable narrator of the Gospel of Matthew tells the story from what one would traditionally call the third-person omniscient point of view. The narrator is an 'intrusive' or overt narrator. He or she frequently makes direct comments to the narratee and

1. B. Uspensky, *A Poetics of Composition* (trans. V. Zavarin and S. Wittig; Berkeley: University of California Press, 1973), p. 8.

2. Uspensky, *Poetics*, pp. 81, 83. He also wishes to use the internal/external opposition on other planes as well.

3. Booth notes that inside views are associated with point of view: 'the author's presence will be obvious on every occasion when he moves into or out of a character's mind—when he "shifts his point of view", as we have come to put it' (*Rhetoric*, p. 17). He also points to the presence of inside views in the Gospels (pp. 17-18 n. 10).

comments on the motivation and moral condition of the characters.

In terms of the recent discussion of various senses of point of view, the most significant factor in the Gospel's rhetoric is the alignment and non-alignment of the points of view of the narrator and the protagonist on Uspensky's five planes.[1] The points of view of the narrator and the character Jesus are aligned on the ideological plane. They are partially aligned on the phraseological, temporal, spatial, and psychological planes. These partial alignments support the ideological alignment. The choice of the term 'alignment' is deliberate. The narrator never simply assumes the point of view of Jesus or vice versa.[2]

a. *The Ideological and Phraseological Planes*

The most important alignment of Jesus and the narrator occurs on the ideological or evaluative plane, 'the system of ideas which shape the work'.[3] This is Chatman's conceptual point of view.[4] Ideological evaluation in Matthew 'is carried out from a single dominating point of view' to which all other points of view are subordinate.[5] The narrator is the implied author's voice and represents the implied author's ideological point of view. For all practical purposes the point of view of the narrator is equivalent to that of the implied author.

How does the ideological viewpoint of Jesus become identified with that of the narrator? First, Jesus is not only the protagonist, he is consistently the most reliable character. A reliable character serves like a reliable narrator as a voice for the implied author. Jesus receives the 'badge of reliability'[6] early in the narrative by means of

1. Norman Petersen has noted the importance of the alignment of the points of view of the narrator and the character Jesus in the Gospel of Mark. See '"Point of View" in Mark's Narrative', *Semeia* 12 (1978), especially pp. 102, 107. He uses Uspensky's categories.

2. The narrator's assumption of the point of view of a character in all the possible aspects is a compositional possibility discussed by Uspensky, *Poetics*, pp. 101-102.

3. Uspensky, *Poetics*, p. 8.

4. The conceptual and interest points of view of Jesus are closely related to Matthew.

5. Uspensky, *Poetics*, pp. 8-9.

6. The term comes from Booth, *Rhetoric*, p. 18. 'The author is present in every speech given by any character who has had confirmed upon him, in whatever manner, the badge of reliability. Once we know that God is God in Job, once we know that Monna speaks only truth in "The Falcon" in Boccaccio's *Decameron*, the

the genealogy, the birth story (including angelic appearances and fulfillment quotations), and the baptismal scene. Second, like the narrator, Jesus can read the minds of other characters and predict the future, including the future actions of other characters. These abilities further substantiate Jesus's reliability and the ideological alignment of Jesus and the narrator. Third, the narrator provides sympathetic and frequent inside views into Jesus, while providing brief, unflattering inside views of Jesus' opponents.[1] The distance between the narrator and Jesus, and thus the implied reader, is small.[2] Fourth, the ideological alignment of Jesus and the narrator can be seen in speech characteristics, that is, on the phraseological plane.[3] There are several important examples of the alignment of the ideological and phraseological points of view of the narrator and Jesus which involve verbal repetition. These include the repeated phrase 'their synagogues', repeated appeals to Scripture, and the repeated use of the historical present.

Their synagogues. The phrase 'in their synagogues' appears repeatedly in the voices of both Jesus and the narrator (4.23, 9.35, 10.17, 12.9 [into], 13.54, and 23.34 [in your synagogues]).[4] The repetition of the phrase in both voices reinforces an 'us' versus 'them' mentality.[5] The

authors speak whenever God and Monna speak'. See also R.C. Tannehill, 'The Disciples in Mark', *JR* 57 (1977), who notes that the badge of reliability has been conferred on Jesus, in Mark (p. 391).

1. The questions of Jesus' omniscience and inside views will be discussed further in the section on the psychological plane below.

2. For a discussion of distance see Booth, *Rhetoric*, pp. 157-59, 243-56.

3. Uspensky is not crystal clear on the distinction between 'the expression of a definite ideological position (point of view) by means of phraseological characteristics' and 'the expression of phraseological points of view'. See his section entitled, 'The Relationships between the Ideological and Phraseological Levels', pp. 15-16. The examples offered here seem to me to indicate ideological as well as phraseological alignment of the points of view of the narrator and Jesus.

4. See also 'their cities' (11.11) and 'their scribes' (7.29).

5. See J.M. Lotman, 'Point of View in a Text', *New Literary History* 6 (1975), pp. 342-43, who makes an interesting comment on traditional narratives:

> The nature of the text as something 'unwrought' induces the author to introduce a great number of pieces of direct speech, to adopt the role of recording clerk rather than creative artist. Yet this does not produce a multiplicity of points of view. All the speeches add up to one of two views: the 'correct' (coinciding with that of the text as a whole) and the 'incorrect' (opposed to it).

narrator and Jesus see those who oppose Jesus as 'them'.

The narrator first uses the phrase in almost identical summary passages, 4.23 and 9.35. There is no precise indication of the identity of 'them' in either passage. In 4.23 there may be an indirect indication, if the label ὁ λαός, 'the people', is taken to refer to the Jewish people. In Matthew the narrator associates this label with the Pharisees. It takes on very negative connotations when the people Jesus was born to save (1.21) take his blood upon themselves (27.25).[1] In 9.35 the summary follows the Pharisee's condemnations of Jesus as exorcising by the ruler of demons. Thus 'their synagogues' in 9.35 might be taken to refer to Pharisaic synagogues. In 10.17, part of the missionary discourse, Jesus speaks in direct discourse of 'the men' who will deliver the disciples to councils and scourge them 'in the synagogues of them'.[2] The 'men' in question appear to be the Pharisees and the Jewish people (ὁ λαός) as in 15.8-9 since the disciples will be persecuted as a testimony to 'them' and to the Gentiles (10.18).[3] The next instance of the phrase, 'their synagogues', is the narrator's description of Jesus' entry into a synagogue in 12.9. There the synagogue seems to belong to the Pharisees whom Jesus has just castigated in 12.1-8 and who plot to destroy him after he heals on the Sabbath (12.14) in 'their synagogue'. In 13.54 the narrator describes entry into Jesus' native town where he teaches 'them' in 'their synagogue'. The townsfolk can be considered 'them' because they are 'offended in him (13.57)' and exhibit their lack of faith (ἀπιστίαν αὐτῶν, 13.58). In 23.34, the last reference to any synagogue in the text, Jesus refers to 'your synagogues'. He is speaking in direct discourse to the scribes and Pharisees.[4] Jesus predicts in words that echo 10.17, 23 that the Pharisees and scribes 'will kill, and will crucify, and will scourge in your synagogues and will persecute from

He gives the Gospel of John as an example. Of course New Testament literary critics would not accept the characterization of the evangelist as 'recording clerk'.

1. See J.M. Gibbs, 'Purpose and Pattern in Matthew's Use of the Title "Son of David"', *NTS* 10 (1963/64), p. 451.

2. For example, 6.1-18; 15.9 and 16.23.

3. Concerning the translation Gentiles for ἔθνη see D.R.A. Hare and D.J. Harrington, 'Make Disciples of All Gentiles', *CBQ* 37 (1975), p. 363.

4. Chapter 23 is labelled as an address in its entirety to the crowds and disciples (23.1). However, following 23.11 Jesus shifts from warning about the Pharisees to condemning them with woes in the second person.

city to city' the prophets, wise ones, and scribes he sends to them. Here the identity of the 'men' in 10.17 is made explicit. The repetitions of the phrase 'their synagogues' build to this dramatic variation, a condemnation in direct discourse.

Narrator and protagonist are aligned in viewing those who oppose Jesus, primarily the Jewish leaders, as 'them' and this is manifested on the phraseological level. In Uspensky's terminology one might ask whether the speech of the narrator has 'contaminated' that of Jesus or vice versa.[1] There are only two passages in which the word synagogue appears with no possessive pronoun. 6.2, 5 and 23.6. In both Jesus addresses the disciples and crowds in direct discourse. The narrator always uses 'of them'. Thus, it seems that the speech of the narrator has 'contaminated' that of Jesus.[2]

Appeal to Scripture. Another example of the identification of the ideological viewpoint of the narrator and the central character expressed on the phraseological plane also involves repetition. It is the appeal that both make to Scripture. There is even one occasion on which it is difficult to tell who is speaking, Jesus or the narrator. Mt. 26.56a: 'But this all has come to pass that the Scriptures of the prophets may be fulfilled' could be a part of the speech Jesus begins in 26.55, especially given his words in 26.54. It could also be a direct comment of the narrator concluding the arrest scene along with the flight of the disciples in 26.56b.

The narrator employs both fulfillment quotations and biblical allusions in his or her own speech. As noted above, the repeated fulfillment quotations are a significant form of direct commentary to the implied reader.[3] Among other things, they establish through repetition the overall ideological view that Jesus' life is a fulfillment of Scripture. In addition to the fulfillment quotations the narrator includes biblical allusions, such as the clothing of John the Baptist and

1. Uspensky, *Poetics*, pp. 32-56.

2. In 6.2, 5 on the one hand Jesus may be judged to be addressing people who go to synagogue and thus not use 'their' synagogues. On the other hand, there seems to be no reason to avoid 'their' since he is speaking about the hypocrites. The same arguments would apply to 23.6 where Jesus is openly condemning the scribes and Pharisees in a similar vein. He also speaks of 'your synagogues' in the same section.

3. See pp. 52-53.

the casting of lots for Jesus' garments.[1] Although these allusions are not direct commentary, they function in much the same way as the fulfillment quotations. The narrator and the implied reader relate the events of the narrative to and evaluate them from the perspective of Scripture.[2]

This scriptural perspective is shared by Jesus, again aligning the narrator and Jesus on the ideological plane. Indeed, Jesus quotes Scripture more times than the narrator. Verbal repetition reinforces this ideological perspective. In 4.4, 7, 10; 11.10; 21.13; and 26.31 Jesus introduces quotations with the word γέγραπται, 'It has been written...'. In 12.3, 5; 19.4; 21.42; and 22.31 he introduces quotations or summaries of Scripture with the phrase οὐκ (οὐδέποτε) ανέγνωτε, 'Did you not (never) read.' As with the narrator's repeated use of the fulfillment formula, Jesus' repeated use of these formulas highlights the scriptural quotations. It also establishes Scripture as a backdrop and validator. Jesus also quotes or refers to Scripture without such repeated introductions numerous times.[3] In one case Jesus' speech is even the speech of Scripture. In 27.46a Jesus cries out the introduction of Psalm 22.[4]

Both the narrator and Jesus share the view of Scripture as an arbiter of truth and value. Both appeal to it in speech.[5] Their points of view

1. John's clothing resembles that of Elijah. Mt. 3.4 is an almost exact repetition of 2 Kgs 1.8. The casting of lots parallel occurs in Mt. 27.35 = Ps. 22.18. See also Hawkins, *Horae Synopticae*, p. 158 who notes three places where Matthew 'without expressly quoting prophecies, seems to be influenced by their language'. Two are in the narrator's speech: 27.34 influenced by Ps. 68(69).22 and 27.57 by Isa. 53.9. One is in the speech of the chief priests: 27.43 where words from Ps. 22.8 appear.

2. See Uspensky's comments on two levels singled out in the '*Life of Avvakam*: The Biblical and the Everyday', *Poetics*, p. 16.

3. Other quotations include the antithesis of 5.21-48; 19.18-19; 22.37-40; 22.43-44; 24.15; 19.18 where Jesus refers to Moses permitting divorce although he does not directly quote and 9.13 and 12.7 where Jesus introduces Hos. 6.6 with the phrase τί ἐστιν. Jesus also refers to Scripture without directly quoting in many places including 5.17-19; 8.4; 22.24, 54 and possibly 56.

4. The phrase is presented first in Hebraicized Aramaic and then translated in a direct narratorial comment (27.46b).

5. The narrator uses Scripture most often to interpret Jesus and the events of his life. Jesus uses it to respond to the devil (4.4, 7, 10); to radicalize it (the antitheses 5.21-48); to identify and value John the Baptist (11.10); to explain his own actions, to explain and predict the disciples' actions (26.31); to predict the future (24.15); in disputes with the Jewish leaders (9.13; 19.4, 8; 21.42; 22.31-32; 22.37-40; 22.43-

concur on the ideological and phraseological planes. The implied reader is invited to share this point of view. Repetition helps by drawing attention to the extensive use of Scripture and its importance to the ideological positions of narrator and protagonist. Since Jesus and the narrator use Scripture to validate their perspective, the implicit assumption is that the use of Scripture will persuade the implied reader to adopt their ideological perspective. Repetition, then, aids in this process.

There are only four other direct quotations of Scripture in Matthew. All are offered by Jesus' enemies: 2.5-6 by the chief priests and scribes of the people; 4.6 by the devil; 19.3-9 by the Pharisees; and 22.24 by the Sadducees. In the first case the chief priests and scribes of the people end up ironically testifying that Jesus is the Christ. This irony occurs because they express their own view on the phraseological plane and the narrator's view on the ideological. In the other three cases enemies tempt and question Jesus using Scripture. Jesus replies with an authoritative interpretation and more Scripture. From the ideological perspective of the implied author only Jesus can properly appeal to Scripture. Only Jesus and the narrator can correctly interpret it. Their ideological opponents cannot have the correct understanding.

The historical present. A fourth example of the alignment of the points of view of the narrator and Jesus on the phraseological plane involving verbal repetition is their use of the historical present. The repeated phrases will be discussed in terms of alignment of temporal perspectives. Here it is important to note that Jesus and the narrator are the only ones in the Gospel to use the historical present.[1] This may or may not have ideological significance. On the one hand, this concurrence is due to the fact that with rare exception[2] only Jesus and the narrator ever narrate. On the other hand, the fact that the narrator and Jesus are the only storytellers is important. To tell a story is to

44); to answer a question concerning the good (19.18-19).

1. For a list of historical presents used in Matthew see Hawkins, *Horae Synopticae*, pp. 148-49. To which add by narrator 2.22, βασιλεύει and 21.45 and 26.25b, λέγει; and by Jesus 11.17, 18, 19; 12.44, 45 (four times) and 26.18, λέγουσιν, λέγει.

2. The Sadducees come close in 22.23-27 with the hypothetical case of the woman with seven husbands.

have the opportunity to affect and perhaps persuade an audience to adopt a particular ideological point of view—at least while assuming the role of the reader or hearer in the text. If the Jewish leaders told as many powerful parables as Jesus does in Matthew, the implied reader would view them differently. Indeed, the reader would be reading a different text.

b. *The Temporal and Spatial Planes*

In addition to the ideological and phraseological planes, the points of view of the narrator and Jesus are frequently aligned on the temporal and spatial planes; that is, their positions in time and space are often identical.[1] However, they are not completely aligned on these planes. Their temporal alignments will be discussed first; the spatial, second; and the interplay of the spatial and temporal planes in a narrative frame, third.

The temporal plane. Uspensky's discussion of the temporal plane can be divided into two parts. view of time and tense. The first concerns whose perspective the narrator uses to divide and count time. Uspensky offers the example of Pushkin's *The Queen of Spades.* Initially the narrator counts time with the old countess from the day she receives Hermann's letter. When she dies, the narrator counts time with Hermann from the day he first heard about the three lucky cards.[2] Of course, the narrator may view time from his or her own perspective entirely or alternate his or her own with those of characters. In Matthew, the narrator has the broad perspective on time represented in the diagram below.

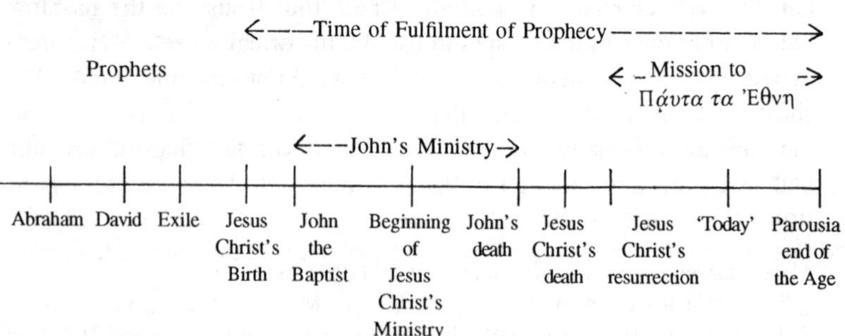

1. Uspensky speaks, for example, of the fixing of the narrating observer's temporal position, *Poetics*, p. 65.

2. Uspensky, *Poetics*, p. 66.

Jesus shares roughly the same broad perspective. He mentions Abraham, Moses, the prophets, David, John, and his own passion, resurrection, and parousia. His view of time also encompasses creation (19.4-5, 8) and Noah (24.37-38). Except for the passion, resurrection, parousia, and Gentile mission, the narrator usually does the actual counting of time. Examples are 3.1, 'And in those days…'; 4.12, 'Now hearing that John was delivered up, he departed…'; 12.1, 'At that time…; and the phrase repeated in 4.17 and 16.21, 'From then Jesus began…' Nonetheless, after the baptism the narrator almost always counts time from an action or reaction of Jesus. Examples include all those above except 3.1.

Of course, the temporal perspectives of Jesus and the narrator are not completely aligned. The 'today' of the narrator is clearly separated from the time of the events narrated by the use of the past tense and the direct authorial comments of 27.8, 'This is why that field was called the field of blood until today' (σήμερον), and 28.15b, 'And this saying was spread about by Jews until today' (σήμερον [ἡμέρας]). The slight verbal repetition involved tends to emphasize, towards the end of the narrative, the distinction between the events of the narrative and 'today'. At the very end, however, the narrator, Jesus, the disciples, and the implied reader are all generally in the same temporal position: the mission period between the resurrection and the parousia.

The second aspect of the temporal plane Uspensky discusses is tense, that is, where the narrator is in time at any given moment. One example Uspensky gives is the shifting from past to present to past tense in N.S. Leskov's *A Lady Macbeth of the Mtensk District*. When the present tense appears, he argues, the author's temporal position is synchronic with that of the characters. The past tense provides the shifts between scenes.

In Matthew there are also shifts of tense and thus point of view. The narrator speaks most often in the past tense. However, from time to time the narrator shifts to the historical present. He or she uses the historical present eighty times.[1] What is the function of the historical

1. For a list of historical presents see p. 61 n. 1. Matthew uses the historical present less than Mark (151) and more than Luke–Acts (22) (Hawkins, *Horae Synopticae*, pp. 144-49). According to Hawkins there are twenty-one cases in which Matthew agrees with Mk in using the historical present (p. 149). See also M.J. Lagrange, *L'Evangile selon S. Matthieu* (Paris: Gabalda, 1948), p. xcii. In

present? Blass–Debrunner–Funk write. '*The historical present* can replace the aorist indicative in a vivid narrative at the events of which the narrator imagines himself to be present'.[1] This is similar to what Uspensky writes concerning the shift from the past tense in ordinary storytelling with a phrase such as, 'And then he says to me. . . '; or at the climax of a story: 'The purpose of this device is to take the listener directly into the action of the narrative, and to put him into the same position as that occupied by the characters of the story'.[2] In the midst of past tenses, the historical present synchronizes briefly the temporal positions of the narrator, characters, and implied reader.

A typical example is Mt. 22.41-46:

> When the Pharisees were assembled, Jesus questioned them saying. 'What does it seem to you concerning the Christ? Whose son is he?' *They say* to him: 'of David.' *He says* to them: 'How then does David call him Lord in the spirit saying: "The lord said to my lord. Sit on my right until I put thy enemies underneath thy feet?" If then, David calls him lord, how is he his son?' And no one was able to answer him a word nor dared anyone from that day to question him any more.

The introduction and conclusion form a past tense frame for the episode. Once conversation has begun the narrator shifts to the present tense. The temporal points of view of the narrator, characters, and narratee/implied reader are aligned during the interchange. This is important because the words that Jesus and the Pharisees speak are addressed to the implied reader as well as to each other. The reader is required to make a judgment.

examining the historical present in Matthew, one should also make use of Wolfgang Schenk, 'Das Präsens Historicum als makrosyntaktische Gliederungssignal im Matthäusevangelium', *NTS* 22 (1976), pp. 464-75 which I had not read when I composed this chapter.

1. In *A Greek Grammar of the New Testament and Other Early Christian Literature* (Chicago: University of Chicago Press, 1961), N. 321.

2. Uspensky, *Poetics*, p. 71. See also W.G. Thompson who writes, 'The historical present (legei) draws the reader into the narrative' (*Matthew's Advice to a Divided Community* [Anbib, 44; Rome: Pontifical Biblical Institute, 1970], p. 219). He also quotes Lagrange, *L'Evangile*, as explaining Matthew's tendency to use historical presents with verbs of saying as 'bien dans sa manière de poser la parole comme une chose importante et pour ainsi dire actuelle (Matthieu, p. xcii)', in n. 17, p. 207. A.A. Mendilow also comments on the vivifying effects, sense of reality and the contemporaneity of the reader accomplished by the historical present in *Time and the Novel* (New York: Humanities Press, 1965 [1952]), p. 98.

This example is typical because out of the narrator's eighty uses of the historical present: λέγει (he or she says), is repeated forty-six times; λέγουσιν (they say), is repeated fourteen times; and φησίν (she says), once. The narrator often uses the historical present to highlight direct speech, especially the words of Jesus. This is reinforced by repetition. In all but nine cases Jesus is the subject of λέγει.[1] After several instances of the phrase καὶ λέγει (αὐτῷ or αὐτοῖς) ὁ Ἰησοῦς or simply λέγει (αὐτῷ or αὐτοῖς) the implied reader is conditioned to shift temporal perspective whenever the phrases occur. The implied reader is repeatedly invited to listen directly to Jesus. When the narrator uses λέγουσιν the subjects are blind men, twice; the crowds, once; the Jewish leaders, five times; and the disciples including James and John, six times. In all but one case, someone speaks to Jesus.[2] In fact the phrase λέγουσιν αὐτῷ (= Jesus) is repeated eleven out of fourteen times the narrator uses λέγουσιν.[3] Repetition again encourages the implied reader to assume the same temporal position as Jesus and the narrator. Thus, the temporal positions of the narrator and Jesus—and implied reader—are usually aligned when the narrator uses the historical present.

Other devices which synchronize the temporal perspectives of narrator, characters, and implied reader are the long sections of uninterrupted direct discourse and the repeated introduction of direct discourse with the present participles of λέγειν.[4] The five major discourses are obvious examples of the first. Without interruption there is little to remind the implied reader that Jesus speaks in the past. For the duration of the speech the implied reader's perspective is contemporary with that of Jesus. A.A. Mendilow speaks of the use of dialogue as 'perhaps the most obvious means of producing the illusion of immediacy and presentness in the reader'.[5] This is essentially true

1. 4.6; 17.25; 19.18; 19.20; 20.21; 26.35; 26.71; 27.13; 27.22a.

2. 27.22 (crowds to Pilate).

3. Of the narrator's nineteen historical presents which are not verbs of saying Jesus is the subject of seven and the accusative of dative object of nine if 27.38 is included.

4. λέγων is used forty-nine times; λέγοντες, forty-seven—not all by the narrator. Other forms of the present participle appear as well.

5. Mendilow, *Time and the Novel*, p. 112. See also pp. 111-12 where he compares the effect produced to that 'felt in the theatre where the spectator is indeed present, though so far as the play is concerned, he is assumed not to be there at all'.

where there are no interruptions to dispel that illusion.

The sense of contemporaneity is enhanced in three of the five major discourses by the use of the second device, the repeated introduction of direct discourse by the present participle of 'to say' (5.2; 10.5; 13.3; and the long discourse of woes in 23.1-2 as well). This is true of shorter sections of direct discourse as well.[1] The action denoted by the present participle occurs at the same time as the action denoted by the main verb.[2] The main verb freezes the moment of action and the participle indicates synchronically what was said at that moment as if it was being said in the present. Perhaps this is why λέγων is often translated as 'saying' instead of 'while (or as) he said' even though the leading verb is an aorist.[3]

The repeated temporal synchronizations of the perspectives of the narrator, Jesus, and the implied reader associated with Jesus' speech are significant. Jesus' speech becomes speech addressed to the implied reader as well as to the characters. This allows the narrator to present his or her ideological position as directly from a temporal perspective as a direct comment spoken into the present moment of hearing or reading. Naturally, the ideological position is still presented indirectly through the medium of the character Jesus.

The spatial plane. The spatial positions of the narrator and Jesus are aligned from the time of Jesus' baptism (3.13-17) until his death (27.50).[4] During this time the narrator and thus the implied reader travel with Jesus even when he is alone. However, they remain observers. The narrator does not describe physical surroundings through Jesus' eyes. The narrator and implied reader are present in

1. The first speech of Jesus in the pericope above (22.41-42) is an example.

2. See J.G. Machen, *New Testament Greek for Beginners* (New York: Macmillan, 1923), pp. 105-106.

3. The RSV often translates 'saying'; in 22.42 for example. The same is true of R. Lattimore in *The Four Gospels and Revelation* (New York: Farrar, Straus & Giroux, 1962). The whole issue of participles is extremely difficult, especially since our concept of past, present, and future does not really correspond with the Greek *Aktionsart.* I suspect Matthew's running style (making frequent use of *kai*, *tote* and introductory participles including the genitive absolute) is another device related to temporal perspective. The participial forms of *proserchesthai* are common, frequently associated with verbs of saying. See Thompson, *Matthew's Advice*, pp. 51, 204.

4. Major exceptions are Herod and John (14.1-12) and Peter's Denial (26.69-75). Minor ones include 12.14 and 14.24.

the same way that a camera might be present if it followed the character Jesus wherever he went. The ideological significance of this spatial alignment, especially when considered with alignment on other planes, is great. The colloquial expression, 'Walk a mile in my shoes' summarizes it best. When combined with sympathetic inside views the spatial alignment of the point of view of an implied author-narrator and a character is powerful. It can even lead the implied reader to adopt the ideological viewpoint of a murderer rather than a victim.[1] If the reader views a murder scene through the eyes of the murderer, he or she is more likely to identify with the murderer than the victim. The camera angles through the eyes of the murderer or victim in film are an analog. Recent horror films have been criticized for causing the identification of the viewer with the murderer when shot through his eyes. Although actual readers may or may not perceive the Matthean Jesus' actions as equivalent to murder, the spatial alignment of Jesus and the narrator contributes to their alignment on the ideological plane and leads the implied reader to adopt their aligned points of view.

The frame. The lack of spatial alignment of the points of view of the narrator and Jesus before the baptism and after Jesus' death is interesting because it is one indication of the literary frame of the narrative.[2] Prior to the baptism the story is appropriately told from a viewpoint external to Jesus since this forms an introduction to Jesus and his ministry.[3] Even within the birth story no character appears until the narrator has placed Jesus spatially, temporally, and ideologically through the heading and genealogy. When characters appear, the narrator follows each one in order to view Jesus from their subordinate perspectives as well as his or her own. With John's appearance, the narrator establishes both John's identity and reliability and a negative view of the Jewish leaders who become Jesus' chief antagonists. The narrator provides the introductory portion of the frame in order

1. For a similar point see Booth's discussion of distance in Jane Austen's *Emma*, *Rhetoric*, pp. 243-49.

2. See Uspensky, *Poetics*, pp. 137-51 on framing. See also N. Perrin, *The New Testament: An Introduction* (New York: Harcourt, Brace, Jovanovich, 1974), pp. 190-91. He argued that Matthew's birth story and Great Commission set off the time of Jesus as a 'sacred time, the time of fulfillment and revelation', p. 191.

3. In addition, some of the events occur before Jesus is born.

to lead the implied reader to adopt the narrator's ideological perspective. This is clear not only from the separation of the perspectives of the narrator and Jesus on the spatial and other planes so often aligned in the rest of the narrative, but also because no one in the story refers to or knows of the birth events after Jesus' ministry begins, including Mary.[1]

The other portion of the narrative frame, from death to resurrection, is also told from a point of view external to Jesus.[2] Death forms a typical ending, and it is not surprising that the narrator begins to follow other characters at this juncture. The narrator focuses on various reactions to Jesus's death. He or she steps back and surveys the immediate effects of the death in 27.51-54. The narrator then introduces the women in 27.55-56. They are followed to the tomb in 27.61 and 28.1-8. Through the women the narrator (and the implied reader) is spatially reunited with Jesus in 28.9-10. However, he or she continues to follow the women as they leave Jesus in 28.11. The only time the narrator leaves the women prior to this point is in order to observe Joseph of Arimathea's recovery and burial of the body in 27.57-60 along with the Pharisees' calumny, sealing of the grave, and setting of a guard in 27.62-66. The narrator takes leave of the women finally only in 28.11. There, through the women, the narrator is connected spatially with the guards and through them with the chief priests and elders. This forms an interlude between Jesus' instructions for the disciples in 28.10 and their arrival in 28.16. The disciples, Jesus, the narrator, and the implied reader are the only ones present for the Gospel's final scene. The Great Commission places all four temporally in the same position: the period of mission following the resurrection and prior to the close of the age. This convergence of spatial and temporal points of view accompanied by the convergence of the ideological points of view of narrator and implied reader was probably ideal from the point of view of the actual author. If one may be permitted a historical inference, the actual author wanted the actual readers or hearers to carry over the ideological viewpoint adopted in assuming the role of the reader or hearer in the text into real life and

1. Brown makes this point in *Birth of the Messiah*, pp. 31-32. There is one highly questionable exception. The slave in Peter's denial refers to Jesus as the Nazorean (26.71). The same word appears in 2.23.

2. The function of the repeated prediction that Jesus will go before the disciples to Galilee which occurs in this section is discussed in Chapter 4.

obey the final commission.[1] The story world seems to intersect with the real world of the author.[2] At any rate, the closing portion of the frame provides a transition between the story world and the real world of the actual reader.

c. *The Psychological Plane*

On the psychological plane, the omniscient narrator of the Gospel of Matthew describes characters sometimes from an external and sometimes from an internal point of view. This is Case Four: 'Changing of authorial position; the Simultaneous Use of Different Positions' of Uspensky's typology of the compositional use of different points of view on the psychological plane.[3] The narrator frequently relies on an individual consciousness or perspective, that is, he or she frequently provides privileged inside views of characters.[4] The narrator sometimes indicates an inside view with verbs of feeling and sometimes he or she does not.[5] One *repeated* marker of an inside view is the use of the phrases ἐν ἑαυτοῖς or ἐν ἑαυτῇ (among or in themselves or himself, 9.3; 9.21; 16.7 and 21.25).

The narrator's psychological point of view is frequently aligned with that of Jesus. He or she offers eight simple inside views of Jesus: 3.16; 4.2(?); 8.10; 9.36; 14.14; 20.34; 21.18(?); 26.37, 39, 42, 44 (these four verses are related).[6] There are also approximately twenty-

1. I am aware of the risks in jumping from the implied author to the actual author.

2. M.A. Tolbert suggests something similar in '1978 Markan Seminar: Response to Robert Tannehill' (paper discussed at the 1978 Annual Meeting of the Society of Biblical Literature, private circulation), pp. 13-14.

3. Uspensky, *Poetics*, pp. 95-97.

4. Uspensky writes, 'In those cases where the authorial point of view relies on an individual consciousness (or perception) we will speak about the psychological point of view...' (*Poetics*, p. 81).

5. Indicators of an inside view offered by an omniscient narrator, according to Uspensky, are verbs of feeling such as: '"he thought", "he felt", "it seemed to him", "he knew", "he recognized", and so on' (*Poetics*, p. 85). However, if modified by words of estrangement such as 'apparently' or 'as if' there is external description. An inside view may also be provided without markers.

6. When a verb of feeling is absent the enumeration of inside views is somewhat subjective. I attempted here and in other lists below to make conservative judgments. Where I was uncertain, but on balance saw an inside view, question marks are used. Statements including verbs of seeing or hearing were particularly difficult. When a passage read, for example, 'Jesus saw two brothers (4.18)' it was excluded. When it read, 'Jesus seeing their faith...' it was included.

one instances of what may be called complex inside views. These are cases where the narrator implies or tells the implied reader that Jesus has an inside view of a third party. The narrator knows that Jesus knows. The narrator explicitly states that Jesus knows (γνοὺς) the thoughts or secret actions of the Jewish leaders in 12.15b, 22.18, and of the disciples in 16.8 and 26.10. In 12.25 he states that Jesus knows (εἰδὼς) the thoughts of the Jewish leaders. In other cases Jesus' insight is introduced with ἰδών (9.2b, 9.4 [εἰδὼς alt. reading], 9.22, 9.36) or implied (12.7[?]; 13.13[?]; 13.16[?]; 13.57b-58; 17.7; 17.20; 20.25[?]; 26.21; 26.23-24; and 28.10; see also ch. 23 where Jesus seems to know the inner workings of the scribes and Pharisees' hearts.) Jesus' ability to read the minds of others is emphasized and highlighted by verbal repetition. Twice Jesus 'knows the thoughts' of the Jewish leaders (9.4 = 12.25, five words in common including the alternate reading).

καὶ ἰδὼν [εἰδως] ὁ Ἰσοῦς τὰς ἐνθυμήσεις αὐτῶν εἶπεν (9.4)
εἰδως δὲ τὰς ἐνθυμήσεις αὐτῶν εἶπεν αὐτοῖς (12.25)

The use of γνοὺς also follows a repetitive pattern: γνοὺς δὲ ὁ Ἰσοῦς (εἶπεν). Jesus 'knows' of the Jewish leaders evil plans twice:

Ὁ δὲ Ἰσοῦς γνοὺς ἀνεχώρησεν ἐκεῖθεν (12.15)
γνοὺς δὲ ὁ Ἰσοῦς τὴν πονηρίαν αὐτῶν εἶπεν (22.18)

He 'knows' the thoughts or words of the disciples twice, as well:

γνοὺς δὲ ὁ Ἰσοῦς εἶπεν (16.8)
γνοὺς δὲ ὁ Ἰσοῦς εἶπεν αὐτοῖς (26.10)

Jesus also repeatedly knows what others think or say in themselves (ἐν ἑαυτοῖς, 9.3-4; 9.21 [ἐν ἑαυτῇ]; 16.7-8; and possibly 21.25). These repetitions call attention to the presence of complex inside views.

A third kind of psychological insight which aligns the narrator's psychological perspective with that of Jesus is provided whenever Jesus speaks at length—whenever he becomes, in a sense, a dramatized narrator. This insight is equivalent to a sustained inside view.[1]

1. Even though Jesus is not a dramatized narrator in the strict sense, he has some of the characteristics and performs some of the functions of one. As noted above, sections of Jesus' direct discourse are often addressed to the reader from a temporal perspective. When he tells a story he uses the historical present in the same way as the narrator. He has also been given the badge of reliability. Concerning the act of narration by a dramatized narrator, Booth has said: 'the act of narration

The frequent alignment of the psychological positions of Jesus and the narrator is important because it reduces the distance[1] between the implied reader and Jesus. This is especially true since the inside views are sympathetic.[2] Indeed, three simple inside views focus on and emphasize by means of repetition Jesus' compassion (σπλαγχνίζομαι): 9.36 = 14.14, four words in common, and 9.36 = 14.14 = 20.34, aorist forms of σπλαγχνίζομαι.[3] In Matthew the ideological and psychological points of view of Jesus and the narrator often concur. This affects the implied reader.

The psychological points of view of Jesus and the narrator are not completely identified, however. The narrator also provides simple and complex inside views into other characters.[4] These are presented in the following chart:

performed by even the most highly dramatized narrator is itself the author's presentation of a prolonged "inside view" of a character' (*Rhetoric*, p. 18). He argues that the presence of the author can be found in such narration as well as in direct commentary, privileged view, etc.

1. Distance may also be called 'involvement', 'sympathy', or 'identification' (Booth, *Rhetoric*, p. 158). Distance is discussed by Booth on pages 155-59 and 245-56 and by Dowling, *A Critic's Hornbook*, pp. 104-13. The distance between the implied reader and a character is governed by the double perspective of detachment and involvement of the narrator (Dowling, *A Critic's Hornbook*, p. 105). Inside views are one means of controlling distance. The subjectivity and empathy created by first person narration can be approximated by reporting the thoughts, motives, and values of certain characters with a greater degree of omniscience than others.

2. It is often argued that the more the reader is given an inside view into a character the less distance and greater sympathy there will be (Booth, *Rhetoric*, pp. 245-46 and Dowling, *A Critic's Hornbook*, pp. 105-13). After noting characters described internally are usually sympathetic and vice versa, Uspensky makes the point that there can be unsympathetic inside views. The ideological and psychological points of view do not have to concur (p. 105).

3. Jesus also declares his 'compassion' on the crowds in direct discourse in 15.32 (= 14.14 = 9.36, three words; = 20.34, aorist forms of σπλαγχνίζομαι). Jesus uses the same verb to describe a master in a parable in 18.27. According to Moulton-Geden the verb appears in Matthew and four times in Mark and three times in Luke and nowhere else in the New Testament.

4. One might also wish to examine the simple and complex inside views in the light of Bal's system in *Narratology*. In some cases the views could be explained as the external narrator narrating what is focalized by a character, for example, 'And Jesus seeing the faith of them...', 9.2b. In this example, the focalized object is the faith of them. What is significant for my case is that Jesus and the narrator both often focalize the internal states of characters.

Simple	
Centurion and/or guards	27.54; 28.4
City	21.10
Crowds	7.28-29; 9.8; 9.33b; 12.23; 14.20; 15.31; 22.33
Disciples	12.1b(?); 14.26; 16.7; 16.12; 17.13; 17.23b; 19.25; 20.24 (the Ten); 21.20; 26.8; 26.22; 28.17; Peter 14.30; 26.75; and Peter, James, and John 17.6
Gadarenes	8.34
Herod	14.3-5, 6, 9
Herod the Great	2.3; 2.7(?); 2.16
Jesus' native town	13.54; 13.57a
Jewish leaders	9.3; 12.10d; 12.14; 16.1; 19.3; 21.15; 21.25b-26; 21.45; 21.46; 22.15; 22.22; 22.35; 22.46; 26.4-5; 26.59(?); 27.1(?); 27.7(?); 28.12(?)
Jews seeking healing	9.21; 20.30
Joseph	1.19; 1.20-23; 2.13f; 2.22
Magi	2.12
Judas	26.16; 27.3
Magi	2.12
Men	8.27
Pilate	27.14; 27.24
Women followers	28.8
Young man	19.22 might be counted as Jewish leader
Complex	
Crowds by Jesus	9.36; crowds and other outsiders 13.13(?)
Disciples by Jesus	13.16; 14.27; 16.8; 17.7 (Peter, James and John); 17.20; 19.25 (the Ten); 26.10; 26.21; 26.23-24
Jewish leaders by Jesus	9.4; 12.7(?); 12.15; 12.25; 22.18; Chapter 23
Native town by Jesus	13.57b-58
Woman by Jesus	9.2b; 9.22
Women followers by Jesus	28.10
Jewish leaders by Pilate	27.18

In addition, at least one other person has the same mind-reading power as Jesus. 'For he [Pilate] knew that they delivered him [Jesus] because of envy' (27.18).[1] Pilate becomes a vehicle for the narrator's

1. 21.45 may be another example: 'And when the chief priests and the Pharisees heard his parables they knew that he speaks concerning them'. However, what they know is deduced from Jesus' spoken words.

point of view, knowing as the narrator does the evil motives of the Jewish leaders.

The mind-reading abilities of the narrator and those of Jesus emphasized by repetition raise interesting questions when posed in the traditional category of omniscience. Not only is the narrator omniscient, Jesus is omniscient. Jesus has privileged access to inside views. He is also able to predict the future, including the future actions of other characters.[1] How is his omniscience to be understood in the light of the narrator's omniscience? What is the degree of his omniscience?

So far as I can determine there is no place in the narrative where Jesus' omniscience is questioned. One possible exception is 24.36: 'But concerning that day and hour no one knows, neither the angels of the heavens nor the Son, except the Father only.' The phrase 'nor the Son', however, is included in the UBS Third Edition text with a 'considerable degree of doubt (C)'.[2] Nonetheless, Jesus is still a creature of the narrator. The narrator 'knows' that Jesus 'knows'. There are complex inside views. Jesus' inside views serve as vehicles for the ideological point of view of the narrator in the same way that Jesus' comments on other characters do. Four of the six times it is explicitly stated that Jesus knows the thoughts or secret actions of others, Jesus reads the minds of the Jewish leaders (9.4; 12.15; 12.25; and 22.18). Jesus' knowledge of their thoughts and motives allows him to confront them verbally in 9.4b, 12.25b and 22.18b, and to escape in 12.15. It also allows the implied reader to see their wickedness. It prepares the reader for their part in Jesus' death. On the other two occasions that it is explicitly stated that Jesus knows the thoughts of others, he knows the thoughts of the disciples (16.2 and 26.10). In 16.7 they reason ἐν ἑαυτοῖς when they do not understand Jesus' warning about the leaven of the Pharisees and Sadducees. In 26.8-9 they are angry with the woman who anoints Jesus with oil. In both cases Jesus' knowledge allows him to chastise and instruct the disciples. It also displays the disciples' lack of understanding to the

1. Examples include the passion-resurrection predictions: 16.21, 27-28; 17.9, 12, 22-23; 19.28-30; 20.18-19; 26.2, 29, 64; the apocalyptic discourse (24–25); large parts of 13; 20.28; 21.2-3; 23.34-36; 26.13, 18, 21-25, 31.

2. Kim Dewey pointed out to me in private conversation two instances in Mark where Jesus' omniscience is questioned, Mk 13.32 = 24.36 and Mk 5.25-34 = Mt. 9.20-22. In Matthew Jesus' question, 'Who touched my garments?' (Mk. 5.30b) is absent.

implied reader.[1] On the occasions Jesus' omniscience is implied—not highlighted by the repeated phrases—he has insight into the Jewish leaders, six times; the crowds, twice; the disciples including Peter, James, John, and the women, ten times; women who need healing, twice; and his native town, once. Very few of these inside views appear so extraordinary that a perceptive person might not have surmised the thoughts or mental state of the persons involved.[2] The possible exceptions are: Jesus' statements about the 'sight' of those outside and that of the disciples in 13.13 and 16; Jesus' knowledge of the motives of the scribes and Pharisees in ch. 23, especially 23.5-7, 25, 27, 28, 30; and Jesus' predictions of betrayal in 26.21, 23-24. The explicitly indicated inside views and Jesus' predictions are on the whole more remarkable. His omniscience allows him to respond appropriately to others. It aligns him ideologically with the narrator who also possesses omniscience. In all cases the implied author is able to reveal something about each character or group through Jesus' insight.

6. *Conclusion*

We have seen in this chapter how direct commentary of the narrator to the narratee and the degree of alignment of the points of view of the narrator and Jesus guide the response of the implied reader in important ways. Several of these will be particularly significant in the following chapters. One is the way in which direct commentary and point of view shape the reader's view of Jesus' identity and nature. A second is the way in which Jesus becomes an arbiter of value along with the narrator.

In Matthew the narrator leads the implied reader to adopt the narrator's point of view. The whole narrative is told from a single, unified perspective.[3] However, since the viewpoints of the narrator and Jesus

1. Although not portrayed as negatively as the 'no faith' disciples in Mark, the Matthean disciples are portrayed as 'little-faiths' who sometimes misunderstand Jesus.

2. In fact Jesus' knowledge of persons' faith, fear or distress (9.2b; 9.22; 9.36; 17.7; 28.10) might be considered reasonable inferences and not examples of inside views.

3. Since the narrator serves as the implied author's voice in Matthew, their ideological point of view is virtually identical.

are aligned, the implied reader also adopts Jesus' perspective. An example of the significance of this alignment is the way that Jesus' reactions to and evaluations of characters and events guide the response of the implied reader. A few comments which foreshadow material covered in Chapters 3 and 4 illustrate this point.

There are five major groups of characters in Matthew: the crowds, the disciples, the Jewish leaders, the supplicants, and the Gentiles.[1] The nature and motivations of each group are revealed in their interactions with and responses to Jesus. They are also revealed in Jesus' responses to them. Since each group must both react to and be judged by Jesus, the implied reader compares them. They serve as foils. Indeed, episodes are arranged in order to heighten the comparison and contrast between groups. Thus, these groups serve as vehicles of various ideological viewpoints the implied author wants the implied reader to evaluate from the implied author's own ideological perspective. The primary means of accomplishing this is for the implied reader to share the ideological perspective of Jesus. He or she is guided by Jesus' responses to the various groups. While the evaluation of the Jewish leaders is always negative and the evaluation of the Gentiles and persons seeking help is almost always positive, the crowds are a pivotal group. The implied reader does not ultimately know how to evaluate them until the end of the narrative. Will they side with Jesus or the Jewish leaders? Since Jesus' reactions to the disciples (and vice versa) are not always uniform, there is a shifting ideological evaluation of them as well.

Verbal repetition plays an important role in direct commentary and the alignment of points of view. It has various functions. One or more can be involved in any given repetition. They are often related. The functions include drawing the reader's attention, highlighting, establishing a pattern or overview, creating expectations, and increasing predictability. The temporal dimension of the narrative involving anticipation and retrospection, context, and repetition with variation all play a role.

The repetition of the phrase γνοὺς δὲ ὁ Ἰσοῦς (εἶπεν) is an example of repetition which draws the implied reader's attention and focuses it. It draws the implied reader's attention to Jesus' ability to read the minds of others. This ability partially aligns Jesus with the

1. For further discussion of the character groups see the chapters on character and plot below, especially the introduction to Chapter 3.

narrator on the psychological and ideological planes. The implied reader is thus invited to share their perspective.

The fulfillment quotations and the phrase 'their synagogues' are examples of repetitions which establish a pattern or overview. The repeated fulfillment formula establishes that Jesus' life is a fulfillment of Scripture. The repetition of the phrase 'their synagogues' establishes an 'us-versus-them' mentality. Both overall aspects of the narrator's ideology guide the implied reader's response to the narrative. The latter phrase is an example of how repetition helps to align the narrator and Jesus on the phraseological and ideological planes. The alignment of narrator and characters on the phraseological plane often involves the use of verbal repetition since the repetition of phrases is one way the same speech characteristics may appear in more than one voice. In Chapter 3 the partial phraseological and ideological alignments of Jesus and John the Baptist achieved by their use of the same phrases will be seen.

The examples given above also show how repetition creates expectations and increases predictability. After several repetitions the implied reader is not surprised to find that Jesus 'knows' the thoughts of others. He or she also comes to expect and look for the ways in which Jesus' life fulfills Scripture. The repetition and concentration of fulfillment quotations in the birth story leads the implied reader to read the rest of the narrative in that light. The later repetitions of the fulfillment formula confirm and reinforce the expectations initially established. The fact that these aspects of the narrative are predictable—are expected by the implied reader—makes them more easily assimilated and accepted. Verbal repetition can have a persuasive power.

The fact that verbal repetition creates certain patterns also means that breaks in those patterns or variations become significant. In this chapter the breaks in the concentrated repetitions of the genealogy are examples. The differences as well as the similarities between instances of verbal repetition will be important to note in subsequent chapters.

The point in the narrative continuum at which repetitions occur and the contexts in which they occur are also important. This is true of the predictions noted above. It is also true of the repeated use of the phrase 'their (your) synagogues' which builds over the course of the narrative to its final use in Jesus' direct address to the scribes and Pharisees. Another example is the narrator's repeated reference to 'today' (27.8 and 28.15) towards the end of the narrative. This repetition moves the reader outward from the narrated events to a temporal position which aligns the narrator, the risen Jesus, the disciples, and the implied reader.

Chapter 3

CHARACTER

This chapter will begin with a general introduction to the analysis of character in the Gospel of Matthew. It will then offer three studies of how repetition is used in characterization. Two characters, John the Baptist and Peter, and one character group, the Jewish leaders, will be considered.

1. *Introduction*

Characters are the persons in a narrative, the participants in its action or plot. The nature and motivations of characters can be revealed in a number of ways. A broad distinction has often been made between two methods of characterization: showing and telling.[1] The narrator may 'show' a character through the character's words and deeds. The narrator may also 'tell' the reader about the character, that is, describe and evaluate directly. Naturally, as noted in the previous chapter, the point of view from which the story is told will affect this process.

A narrator can dramatize or describe a character in several ways. From the perspective of the implied reader these are clues to the character of each of the actors. They include the illustration or description of social identity (gender, marital status, nationality, occupation, etc.); physical or personality traits; emotional state; habits of speech and mannerisms; settings associated with a character; names, labels or allusions; a character's past; thoughts or actions in specific situations; interactions with other characters and the responses evoked; a character's attitude toward him or herself; and the use of foils.[2] Any

1. Abrams's discussion ('Character and Characterization', *Glossary* [3rd edn], pp. 20-22) is typical. See Booth, *Rhetoric*, pp. 3-16 for a critique of valuing showing above telling.

2. For lists of conventional methods of characterization see the lists in

and all of these means of characterization or clues can involve repetition. The use of verbal repetition in this fashion in the Gospel of Matthew will be discussed in this chapter. At this point it will suffice to note that repetition develops, reinforces, and enhances the picture created in the mind of the implied reader as he or she reads. It can establish a character trait as typical or of the essence of a character. It aids in producing a consistent portrait and establishing motivation.

In the Gospel of Matthew, the narrator uses both 'showing' and 'telling' to create the characters. In the feeding stories, for example, Jesus' nature is revealed in his actions—healing and miraculously providing bread—and in his words: 'I have compassion on the crowd' (15.32). It is also described directly: 'and he had great compassion on them' (14.14).

The narrator makes use of the typical means of characterization, although he or she tends to rely on some methods more than others. The implied reader rarely learns of the physical appearance of a character.[1] However, he or she may learn a great deal from a gesture, such as 'doing obeisance' (προσκυνεῖν),[2] or sitting at Jesus' feet. Characters are almost always given a social niche. People are identified as Jews or Gentiles, priests, Pharisees, disciples, daughters, fishermen, and centurions. Names, allusions and labels are important, especially in characterizing Jesus.[3] Jesus' identity cannot be fully understood apart from his name, given because 'he will save his

R. Macauley and G. Lanning, *Technique in Fiction* (New York: Harper & Row, 1961), p. 63 and Wellek and Warren, *Theory of Literature*, p. 219.

1. John the Baptist is described in 3.4, but the description seems primarily designed as a scriptural allusion. Persons to be cured are described as blind or deaf, but this might be considered a description of social status.

2. προσκυνεῖν appears in Mt. 2.2, 8, 11; 4.9, 10; 8.2; 9.18; 14.33; 15.25; 18.26; 20.20; 28.9, 17. BAGD lists 'Mt. 2.2, 8, 11; 8.2; 9.18; 14.33; 15.25; 19.38—Mt. 20.20' as examples of its use where Jesus is 'revered and worshipped as Messianic King and Divine Helper'. It lists Mt. 28.9, 17 as examples of worship of the risen Lord. Thompson (*Matthew's Advice to a Divided Community*, pp. 214-25 n. 62) follows J. Horst in distinguishing Matthew's use of προσκυνεῖν in the imperfect as supplication (8.2; 9.18; 15.25; 18.26) and in the aorist as worship/adoration (2.11; 14.33; 28.9, 17).

3. The notion of labels in Matthew is taken up from a social scientific perspective by B.J. Malina and J.H. Neyrey, *Calling Jesus Names: The Social Value of Labels in Matthew* (Sonoma, CA: Polebridge Press, 1988).

people from their sins' (1.21),[1] and the Christological titles which serve as alternate names. Fulfillment quotations and scriptural allusions are also important means of characterizing Jesus. The past is also particularly relevant. The genealogy and birth story establish the identity and mission of Jesus and provide the background against which the rest of the story may be understood.

The primary means of developing character, however, is the portrayal of interactions between various characters and Jesus. As noted in Chapter 2, there are five major groups of characters: the crowds, the disciples, the Jewish leaders, those who seek healing, and the Gentiles.[2] The nature and motivations of each group are revealed in their interactions with and responses to Jesus, the protagonist. Since Jesus wears the badge of reliability and his ideological point of view is aligned with that of the narrator, they are also revealed authoritatively in Jesus' responses to each group. Because each group interacts with Jesus, the groups also serve as foils for one another. Episodes are arranged so that comparisons and contrasts are heightened. Thus, in addition to Jesus' reactions, the implied reader's response is guided by this arrangement.

Before examining the use of verbal repetition in characterization, it is necessary to explore two additional distinctions often used in

1. Redundancies associated with the name Jesus are discussed by F.W. Burnett, 'Prolegomenon to Reading Matthew's Eschatological Discourse: Redundancy and the Education of the Reader in Matthew', *Semeia* 31 (1985), pp. 95-98.

2. Although various sub-groups of the Jewish leaders are named, there are no sharp distinctions made and all function together as Jesus' opponents. See S. Van Tilborg, *The Jewish Leaders in Matthew* (Leiden: Brill, 1972), pp. 1-7. For recent articles on the disciples in Matthew see M. Sheridan, 'Disciples and Discipleship in Matthew and Luke', *BTB* 3 (1973), pp. 235-55; U. Luz, 'Die Junger im Matthäus-evangelium', *ZNW* 62 (1971), pp. 141-71. See also P.S. Minear, 'The Disciples and the Crowds in the Gospel of Matthew', *ATR*, supp. series 3 (1974), pp. 28-44. Minear, however, treats the supplicants and the Gentiles as members of the crowds. My view is that Jesus and the Jewish leaders vie for the loyalty of the crowds until the crucial shift to ὁ λαὸς in 27.25. J.D. Kingsbury, 'The Title Son of David in Matthew's Gospel', *JBL* 95 (1976), pp. 599-600 differentiates as I do between the crowds and the 'no-accounts'. Although the supplicants appear as individuals, the similarity between them, especially in relationship to Jesus, justifies treating them as a group. The same is true of the Gentiles, although not to the same extent. There is some overlap between the supplicant group and the Gentiles. The Gentiles also can be considered a group because of the important role they play in the development of the theme of the justification of mission to the Gentiles.

character analysis. One is E.M. Forster's distinction between round and flat characters. The second is the related distinction between dynamic and static characters, that is, characters who do or do not develop in the course of a narrative.[1]

'Flat characters,' according to Forster, 'were called "humours" in the seventeenth century, and are sometimes called types, and sometimes caricatures.'[2] He defines flat characters as follows:

> In their purest form, they are constructed round a single idea or quality: when there is more than one factor in them, we get the beginning of the curve towards the round. The really flat character can be expressed in one sentence such as 'I will never desert Mr. Micawber.' There is Mrs. Micawber—she says she won't desert Mr. Micawber, she doesn't and there she is.[3]

Flat characters are easily recognized and so never need to be reintroduced. They are easily remembered because they are static. They are not changed by circumstances. Instead, they move *through* circumstances. In the hands of a master like Dickens, however, flat characters may have vitality and depth.[4] Occasionally they may expand to round for a moment and then return to flat. The genius of Jane Austen's characterization, according to Forster, is that all her characters have this potential.[5]

Round characters are the reverse of flat characters. They cannot be summed up in a single sentence. A round character 'waxes and wanes and has facets like a human being'.[6] 'The test of a round character,' for Forster, 'is whether it is capable of surprising in a convincing way.'[7]

Forster's definitions of flat and round characters take for granted

1. E.M. Forster, *Aspects of the Novel* (New York: Harcourt Brace, 1927), pp. 108-18. I follow Forster's discussion below.

2. Forster, *Aspects*, p. 103.

3. Forster, *Aspects*, pp. 103-104. Similar to Uspensky's characters who never function as vehicles for the psychological point of view, never described from within, *Poetics*, p. 97.

4. Forster, *Aspects*, pp. 105-106. See also J. Souvage, *An Introduction to the Study of the Novel* (Gent: E. Story-Scientia PVBA, 1965), p. 84 n. 179.

5. Forster, *Aspects*, pp. 113-18.

6. Forster, *Aspects*, p. 106.

7. Forster, *Aspects*, p. 118. This is similar to Uspensky's types 2 and 3, *Poetics*, pp. 97-98.

that flat characters are static and round ones dynamic. Some analysts, however, prefer to distinguish between the degree of complexity of a character and development. Scholes and Kellogg distinguish

> between two kinds of dynamic characterization: the developmental, in which the character's personal traits are attenuated so as to clarify his progress along a plot line which has an ethical basis... ; and the *chronological*, in which the character's personal traits are ramified so as to make more significant the gradual shifts worked in the character during a plot which has a temporal basis.[1]

These distinctions between flat and round and static and dynamic characterization are relevant to the Gospel of Matthew. However, they cannot be applied to the Gospel in precisely the same way as they are applied to modern novels. This is primarily due to three factors: (1) the degree to which characters are individualized and particularized; (2) the degree to which the inner life is exposed; and (3) the importance of character to the whole in modern novels. All of these factors are related to one another. They are also related to the length of the modern novel which affords a novelist the space for detail if he or she is so inclined.

In modern novels, round characters are frequently very complex. The reader is often given extended insight into the inner life of these characters. Indeed, in some novels, such as those of Virginia Woolf, the inner life is *the* focus. Character rather than plot takes center stage.[2] So, too, the development of a round character takes on great importance and the reader is made privy *in detail* to the internal processes involved in this development.[3] Very often the development is *chronological* rather than *developmental*. The effects of time are explored.[4]

The characters in the Gospel of Matthew, in comparison to those in a modern novel such as *War and Peace* or *Mrs Dalloway*, are less

1. Scholes and Kellogg, *Nature*, p. 169.

2. A vast change from Aristotle's view in the *Poetics* that plot is central.

3. Scholes and Kellogg suggest that the developing character whose inner life is depicted in some detail only begins in Western culture 'when Christian concepts are blended with the late Celtic romances', *Nature*, p. 167.

4. Of increasing concern from the eighteenth century onward and a 'distinguishing characteristic of such realistic fictions as the novel'. As Forster says 'life by time' in modern narrative and 'life by values' in ancient (Scholes and Kellogg, *Nature*, pp. 169-70).

detailed and more opaque. As noted in Chapter 2, inside views are present, but not sustained. Plot is as important as character. Development is along the axis of value. The characters and character groups change in the course of the Gospel, primarily in their degree of understanding and acceptance of Jesus and his mission. Jesus changes in the way he responds to them and perhaps in his openness to the Gentile mission. Time is an important factor, but in terms of eras which embrace all characters, rather than in terms of the effect the years have on an individual. Indeed, one of the major differences between the Gospel and many forms of narrative, including the novel, is the emphasis on groups with a corporate identity. Only a few individuals are characterized in any depth or play an important role in the development of the plot. Further, many individuals function as representatives of a group. Peter, for example, is the most fully developed of the disciples, but he often serves as spokesman or prototypical disciple.[1] The Roman centurion in 8.5-13 and the Canaanite woman in 15.21-28 are individuals, but it is primarily as members of a class, Gentiles of faith, that Jesus responds to them. While the characters in Matthew are realistic, what is of interest first and foremost is their stance in relation to Jesus and the kingdom of heaven, not individual particularities.

2. *John the Baptist*[2]

The central function of most of the verbal repetition associated with John the Baptist is to establish parallels between John and Jesus.[3] The question of John's identity and character is closely related to the question of Jesus' identity and character. As John's character is developed, so directly and indirectly is Jesus'. Many of the repetitions associated with John are also related to the development of the plot. John is the foreshadower as well as the forerunner of Jesus, and to a lesser extent, of the disciples. Below, repetitions which primarily develop John's character will be discussed first; then repetitions which primarily

1. This will be discussed below.

2. Passages in which John appears or is mentioned: 3.1-17; 4.12; 9.14; 11.2-11; 14.1-13; 16.13-20; 17.10-13; 21.23-32.

3. J.P. Meier independently noted a number of the features that I discuss here in 'John the Baptist in Matthew's Gospel', *JBL* 99 (1980), pp. 383-405. He approaches the Baptist from a theological and redaction critical perspective.

establish parallels between Jesus and John. Discussion of the way repetitions associated with John contribute to the movement of the plot will be reserved for the chapter on plot.

a. *Establishing John's Identity: Labeling, Scriptural Citation, Identification with Elijah*

Repetitions which establish John's identity include the apposition, 'the Baptist' (ὁ Βαπτιστής), scriptural citation, and identifications of John with Elijah. The label 'the Baptist' first appears in 3.1 when John is introduced. It is repeated in 11.11, 12; 14.2, 8; 16.15; and 17.13. It serves to distinguish this John from others, such as John the son of Zebedee. More importantly, it distinguishes John with reference to his characteristic activity. Finally, a label performs a limiting function.[1] This repeated identification tends to limit John's role, almost as much as John's explicit statements that he is inferior to Jesus. The label economically fixes John and his central role in the mind of the reader.

Another important repetition also occurs when John first appears: 'For this is the one spoken of by the prophet Isaiah saying: "A voice of one crying in the wilderness: prepare the way of the Lord, make his paths straight"' (3.3 = Isa. 40.3). Although not an exact fulfillment quotation, this introduction is a direct narratorial comment echoing 1.22, 2.15, 2.17-18, and 2.23b, the fulfillment quotations of the birth story. It also precedes the fulfillment quotations of 4.14, 12.17-21, 13.35, 21.4-5, and 27.9-10. The repetition involves the introductions of the quotations.[2] This repeated introduction, as noted in the second chapter, guides the implied reader to apply the quotation to the narrative situation. It increases the reader's assent to the narrator's view. In each case it also enables the implied reader to see an event or person as part of a pattern, the life of Jesus as a fulfillment of Scripture. Since John is introduced rather abruptly and appears only briefly, the direct comment of 3.3 serves as another economical

1. This was pointed out to me by Kim Dewey in private conversation.

2. For example, compare 3.3: οὗτος γάρ ἐστιν ὁ ῥηθεὶς διὰ Ἠσαΐου τοῦ προφήτου λέγοντος to 2.17: τότε ἐπληρώθη τὸ ῥηθὲν διὰ Ἰερεμίου τοῦ προφήτου λέγοντος. 3.3 = 1.22, 6 words in common = 2.15, 6 words in common = 2.17, 6 words in common = 2.23, 5 words in common = 4.14, 7 words in common = 8.17, 7 words in common = 12.17, 7 words in common = 13.35, 6 words in common = 21.4, 6 words in common = 26.56, 2 words in common = 27.9, 6 words in common.

means (along with the label and allusion to Elijah in v. 4) of characterizing John. It establishes the role he is to play, his relationship to Jesus, and his reliability. This direct comment on John is echoed, although not exactly, by Jesus in 11.10 where he explains John's identity to the crowds: 'This is he concerning whom it has been written: Behold, I send forth my messenger before your face, who will prepare your way before you.'[1] Thus, both the narrator and the most reliable character establish John's identity with reference to Scriptures which echo one another. In the first case the implied reader learns of John's role through direct comment. In the second he or she 'overhears' Jesus' explanation to the crowds, who may not understand what the implied reader, armed with the original comment, does: John is the forerunner of Jesus who is Lord. A similar situation occurs with reference to the identification of John with Elijah.

When John is introduced in 3.1-6, he is identified as Elijah, the forerunner of the messiah by means of allusion. John's clothing and wilderness habitat are those of Elijah. Mt. 3.4 is an almost exact repetition of 2 Kgs 1.8, a passage which deals with how Elijah can be identified.[2] The narrator's allusion to Elijah is confirmed later in 11.14 and 17.13 by Jesus. Elijah becomes another repeated name or label for John. What the implied reader knows from the start is revealed mysteriously to the crowds in 11.14, and then to the disciples who do understand in 17.13. In both instances Jesus speaks of Elijah's *coming*.[3]

1. 3.3: οὗτος γάρ ἐστιν ὁ ρηθεὶς διὰ Ἠσαΐου τοῦ προσφήτου λέγοντος· φωνὴ βοῶντος ἐν τῇ ἐρήμῳ· ἑτοιμὰσατε τὴν ὁδὸν κυρίου, εὐθείας ποιεῖτε τὰς τρίβους αὐτοῦ. 11.10: οὗτός ἐστιν περὶ οὗ γέγραπται· ἰδοὺ ἐγὼ ἀποστέλλω τὸν ἄγγελόν μου πρὸ προσώπου σου, ὃς κατασκευάσει τὴν ὁδόν σου ἔμπροσθέν σου. In 3.3 John is introduced as one crying in the wilderness and in 11.7-8 Jesus asks what the crowds went out in the wilderness to see.

2. 2 Kgs 1.8 (LXX) is not as close as the MT, but has seven identical words in the same order as Matthew, counting περὶ (Matthew) and περιξνσμένος (LXX).

3. Although in different forms θέλω Ἠλιας, ἔρχομαι, and μέλλω appear both in 11.14 and 17.11-12. The significance of the shifting tenses of ἔρχομαι, however, is puzzling. In 11.14 one learns that Elijah is the one about to come (μέλλων ἔρχεσθαι) which Bauer–Arndt–Gingrich identify as simply a paraphrase for the future participle. In 17.10-13, following the Transfiguration where disciples have seen Elijah, one learns first that Elijah indeed is coming or is come (ἔρχεται) and *will* restore all things (17.11) and that Elijah already came (ἤδη ἦλθεν, 17.12). Is there a future role for John-Elijah as well as his past role ending with his death

In 11.7-19 after speaking to the crowds in veiled terms about John and John's relationship to both Jesus and the kingdom of Heaven, Jesus finally announces: 'and if you want to receive it, he [John] is Elijah, the one about to come ['who is to come', RSV].' Jesus reinforces this announcement with the phrase: 'The one having ears, let him hear' (11.15). The same phrase is repeated by Jesus at the conclusion of the enigmatic parable of the sower told to both the disciples and the crowds (13.9) and at the conclusion of his eschatological explanation of the tares to the disciples (13.43). In other words, the righteous will understand the significance of what he has said; outsiders will not (13.10-17, 51). Those having ears—characters in the story and the implied reader—will understand the fact that John is Elijah and all that this implies. Apparently the crowds are not able to receive this truth. The disciples, however, in 17.10-13 clearly can. After seeing Elijah, Moses, and Jesus transfigured on the mount, the disciples are warned not to speak of the vision until the Son of Man is raised from the dead.[1] They ask 'Then why do the scribes say that first Elijah must come?' (17.10). Jesus replies: 'Elijah indeed is come (or is coming) and will restore all things; but I tell you that Elijah already came, and they did not recognize him, but did to him whatever they wanted. Thus also the Son of Man is about to suffer by them' (17.11-12). Then the narrator explicitly tells the reader that 'the disciples understood that he spoke to them concerning John the Baptist' (17.13). Others did not recognize him. But Jesus, the implied reader, and now the disciples do.

b. *John and Jesus: Speech, Actions, and Reactions*

It is apparent that even when discussing repetitions designed to establish John's character, that John's relationship to Jesus is a central

described in 14.1-12? μέλλω plus *present infinitive* occurs in only five places in Matthew: 11.14; 16.27 (the Son of Man is about to come in the glory of his father); 17.12 (the Son of Man is about to be delivered or will be delivered into the hands of men); 17.22 (the Son of Man is about to be delivered or will be delivered into the hands of men); and 20.22 (Can you drink the cup I am about to drink?). Was one 'coming' of John his passion and death?

1. The baptism and the transfiguration, linked by the repetition of the voice (3.17 = 17.5 [15 words in common] = 12.16 [6 words in common]), are also both linked to John. The words of the voice and the identity of John help to anchor firmly Jesus' identity as messiah and Son of God.

concern of the narrative. Indeed, it would not be too much to say that the character of John is introduced in order to *establish the identity and character of Jesus* as well as to foreshadow the fate of Jesus (and secondarily of the disciples). Although important distinctions are made between John and Jesus (3.11, 14; 11.10-11, etc.), the overwhelming impression created is that of a parallel between John and Jesus. Repetition plays no small role in drawing this parallel. Verbal repetitions establish a parallel between John and Jesus through what they say and through what others say about them. In both cases the first occurrence of the phrases is related to John.

Jesus repeats many of John's words which appear in the first episode following the birth story. John 'arrives' (παραγίνεται) in 3.1. Before Jesus 'arrives' (παραγίνεται) in 3.13 to be baptized, John has the opportunity to preach, baptize the crowds, and chastise the Pharisees and Sadducees.[1] John's first act is the proclamation 'Repent, for the kingdom of heaven has come near' (3.2). This is exactly what Jesus' first proclamation is in 4.17 (nine words in common). It is also exactly what Jesus commissions the disciples to proclaim to Israel in 10.7 (seven words in common). The message of John, Jesus, and the disciples is of one piece. Jesus also repeats the rest of John's words in 3.1-12 later in the narrative. Jesus repeats twice the epithet 'Brood of Vipers' with which John greets the Pharisees and Sadducees (3.7). Once it is directed to the Pharisees alone (12.34); once to the Pharisees and Scribes (23.33). John's question 'Brood of vipers, who warned you to flee (φυγεῖν) from the coming wrath?' (3.7) is linked to Jesus' question in 23.33. 'Serpents, brood of vipers, how flee (φύγητε) you from the judgment of Gehenna?'[2] Jesus repeats John's admonition about the need to produce fruit twice (3.8, 10 = 7.16-20 against false prophets[3] in the Sermon on the Mount = 12.33-35

1. The combination of scribes and Pharisees appears five times in Mt. 3.7; 16.1, 6, 11, 12. The only other place the combination appears in the New Testament is in Acts 23.7 where a dispute between the two groups is described. While some have made a historical point arguing that Matthew cannot be Jewish and/or close in time to Jesus and combine the two groups, this is probably a literary device to indicate the Jewish establishment. The group of the Jewish leaders is discussed later in this chapter.

2. The context in ch. 23 is a discussion of the Pharisees as murderers of the prophets.

3. The identity of the false prophets is not made explicit. This problem is discussed below in the section on the Jewish leaders.

directed against the Pharisees; 3.10b = 7.19, eleven words in common). Finally, John's eschatological harvest imagery appears on the lips of Jesus (3.10 = 13.42a, 50, three words in common; 3.12 = 13.30, seven words in common). John warns of the events which will accompany the arrival of the 'coming one' in the same words that Jesus uses about the Son of Man (3.12 = 13.30, seven words in common).[1]

John's words, then, establish in prospect a strong parallel between John and Jesus, and to a lesser degree Jesus' disciples. The phraseological alignment of John and Jesus aligns them ideologically as well. Their message and their enemies are the same. In addition, the repetition of these words on the lips of two reliable characters confirms and reinforces them. The parallels between John and Jesus verbal repetition establishes also encourage the implied reader to look for other parallels. Among other things, the implied reader is prepared for the strong antagonism between the Jewish leaders and Jesus. The comparison between Jesus and John is solidified. The Pharisees and Sadducees are already characterized unfavorably prior to their first confrontation with Jesus.

Such preparation is also accomplished by other verbal parallels. These are found both in the description of John's fate and in the judgment of others about John and Jesus. In 4.12 the reader learns of John's imprisonment and of Jesus' reaction to it: 'Now hearing that John was delivered up, he departed to [the] Galilee.' This verse is separated from the baptism only by the temptation. It also provides the motivation for Jesus' move to Galilee. Jesus begins his proclamation, echoing John in 4.17. In terms of repetition 4.12 is worthy of attention for two reasons. First, the verb παραδίδωμι, refers to the fate of disciples twenty times in Matthew (including 5.25).[2] In many Christian traditions this verb technically refers to the passion of Jesus.[3] Second, Jesus' reaction to John's arrest is the same reaction he

1. John's words concerning the children of Abraham find an echo although not by verbal repetition (except for the key word Abraham) in Jesus' words concerning the faith of the Roman centurion and the fate of the sons of the kingdom in 8.10-12.

2. In Matthew, whenever it is used of persons it refers to John, Jesus or the disciples. Four times it is used of things (11.27; 25.14, 20, 22). See also the discussion of the Johannine subplot in Chapter 4.

3. See N. Perrin, 'The Use of *(para)didonai* in Connection with the Passion of Jesus in the New Testament', in E. Lohse (ed.), *Der Ruf Jesu und die Antwort des Gemeinde* (Gottingen: Vandenhoeck & Ruprecht, 1970), pp. 204-12.

has to John's death: 'Now hearing [of John's death] Jesus departed thence to a wilderness place privately...' (14.13; 4.12 = 14.13, four words plus meaning in common). Jesus withdraws. The time is not yet ripe for Jesus to be delivered up and killed. Perhaps also there is the implication that Jesus, the protagonist, regrets and mourns first the arrest, and then the death of John. The repetition serves to underline the worthiness of John. It also holds the possible future parallel between the fate of Jesus and John before the implied reader. Given the earlier verbal parallels between John and Jesus, after 14.1-13 the reader cannot avoid wondering whether Jesus will meet the same fate as John. This is reinforced when Herod fears that Jesus is John *redivivus* (14.1-2) and others say Jesus is John as well (16.14).[1] The fate of John hangs in the background of the activities of Jesus and the disciples.

This foreboding and the comparison between John and Jesus is only reinforced when the Jewish leaders respond in the same way to the popularity of John and Jesus. In 14.5 the narrator supplies the reader with an inside view of Herod. Herod wanted to kill John, but '...he feared the crowd, because they had him as a prophet.' In 21.26 this is recalled and reiterated in a different context closer to Jesus' passion. Jesus, refusing to explain directly the source of his authority, poses a difficult question to the chief priests and the elders of the people: 'The baptism of John, whence was it? From heaven or from men?' (21.25a). In another inside view the narrator reports to the reader they are afraid to answer from men: 'we fear the crowd: for all have John as a prophet' (21.26). A repetition with variation occurs only a short time later in 21.46. There the reader learns that the priests and the Pharisees share the same fear in relation to Jesus: 'And seeking him, to seize [him] they feared the crowds since they had him for a prophet (21.46).' Indeed the parallels between the reactions to John and Jesus and their fate have already been predicted by Jesus in 17.12: 'But I tell you that Elijah already came, and they did not recognize him, but did by him whatever they wished; this also the Son of Man is about to suffer by them.' The fulfillment of the prediction can be seen in the parallel responses of the leaders and the crowds to John and Jesus in 14.5 = 21.26 and 21.46. First, the views of Herod and the chief priests and elders about John are given. Finally, the same views

1. Herod the elder tries to kill the baby Jesus. Herod the younger kills John.

are expressed about Jesus. The reliable narrator reports these responses to the reader as inside views in all three cases. There can be no mistake about the repeated and parallel responses.

c. *Conclusion*

Verbal repetition helps to establish the character of John the Baptist. Such repetitions include the label, 'the Baptist', scriptural citations, and allusions to Elijah. Perhaps more significant are the verbal repetitions which create and enhance links between John and Jesus. Parallels between their messages, pronouncements about the Jewish leaders, arrests, and executions are brought into focus by verbal repetition. They shape the implied reader's response over the course of the narrative. Verbal repetition also brings into focus parallels between the reaction of the crowds and Jewish leaders to John and Jesus. In addition to developing the characters of John and Jesus, these parallels contribute to the development of the plot. The latter function will be discussed in Chapter 4.

3. *Simon Peter*

Many repetitions help to establish the character of Peter, the most fully developed of all the disciples in Matthew. Some of these repetitions establish Peter's role as spokesman and leading disciple. Others highlight Peter's strengths and weaknesses and create irony. Various types of verbal repetition are involved. These include labeling; repeated actions; double stories; the repetition of the same phrase by Peter and other characters; a reliable character speaking the same words to Peter that he speaks to others, including epithets; and, finally, a reliable character predicting Peter's actions and the repetition of the prediction in the narrator's description of its fulfillment.

a. *Labeling*

The first form of repetition which establishes Simon Peter's role and highlights his strengths is labeling. The label or allegorical name Peter or 'Rock' appears repeatedly even before its significance is revealed in the climactic name change of 16.18. When he is introduced in 4.18: and when he is numbered among the twelve in 10.2, Simon is identified by the narrator as 'Simon, the one called Peter'.[1] Again prior to 16.18 the narrator simply identifies him as Peter in 8.14, 14.28, 29; and 15.15. In 16.16 Jesus addresses him as Simon Peter. After 16.18, he is always called Peter except in 17.24-25 where Simon and Peter again appear together.[2] The allegorical or quasi-allegorical function of the name 'Rock' is similar to that of Allworthy, for example, in Henry Fielding's *Tom Jones*.[3] Edward Hobbs's free translation, 'Rocky Johnson', for (Simon) Peter bar Jonah, may indicate better to the English-speaking reader the striking character of the appellation.[4] For the reader who does not know of the name change, the existence and repeated use of the name prior to 16.18 creates a puzzle. Why is this character called 'Rock'; what is there about him that leads the narrator to label Simon, The One Called 'Rock'? There is a blank or gap in the text which the reader must actively fill or bridge. Peter's role as one of the first disciples called and as spokesman provides guidance. However, Peter's failure at walking on the water and the epithet 'little faith' in 14.28-31 provide contradictory clues. Thus, the significance of the scene in ch. 16 for understanding the character of Peter is heightened. It provides the solution to the puzzle. There is no *clear* indication that the implied reader knows the exact reference of the name prior to 16.18.[5] Actual readers past and present may know the story of the blessing and name change

1. I am not sure that one can make a theoretical argument for salvation-historical primacy and typicality out of the three occurrences of Simon Peter in 4.18, 10.2, and 16.16 as J.D. Kingsbury does in 'The Figure of Peter in Matthew's Gospel as a Theological Problem', *JBL* 98 (1979), p. 74. The name *Simon* is a commonplace name. The Hebrew counterpart is Shimeon. Shimeon was the second son of Jacob and Leah. In Gen. 29.33 the name is derived from *shoma* 'to hear'. Shimeon was also a tribal name and in Ezra 10.31, a post-exilic Jew with a foreign wife. See BAGD and BDB.

2. The narrator identifies him as Peter in 17.24 and Jesus addresses him as Simon in 17.25.

3. See Wellek and Warren, *Theory of Literature*, p. 219, on the use of names and labels. They offer Allworthy and others as examples of allegoric or quasi-allegoric names.

4. Hobbs used this phrase repeatedly in a series of lectures given at the St Olaf Summer Theological Conference, Northfield, Minnesota, during July 1980. BAGD indicate that Peter 'as a name can scarcely be pre-Christian'; although they say one should 'see on the other hand [. . .] A. Dell, esp. 14-17', p. 66.

5. Unless the narrator's phrase, 'Simon, the one called Peter' and the use of the name alone prior to 16.18 are taken to indicate such prior knowledge.

from the beginning, and so possess in advance the solution to the puzzle. They would read earlier portions in the light of 16.18 from the beginning. Uninformed readers would only do so in retrospect. Both would read the narrative from 16.18 on with the key supplied there in mind. In either case the repeated use of the name 'Rock' vividly and economically characterizes Peter. From 16.18 on the use of the name 'Rock' can create irony. The one who is the rock upon which the church is to be built rebukes Jesus, thinking the things of men (16.22-23), and denies him (26.69-75).

b. *Peter as Spokesman: Repeated Speech Actions*

Other types of repetition also subtly characterize Peter. The repeated actions of Peter and the disciples help to establish Peter's role as a spokesman for the group. Although this role has often been noted, the part verbal repetition plays in establishing this has not been fully emphasized.[1] William G. Thompson has noted that the sequence 'disciples...Peter' appears often: 14.26...14.28; 15.12...15.15; 16.13 ...16.16; 16.21...16.22; 18.1...18.21; 19.25...19.27. 'In each case,' he points out, 'Jesus speaks to the disciples, and then Peter makes a request (14.28; 15.15), asks a further question (18.21; 19.27) or responds to the Master's words (16.16; 16.22).'[2] To this list could be added 17.1...17.14 where Peter speaks for James and John and 26.33 and 35a (Peter)...26.35b where Peter speaks and the disciples all reiterate his words. In five of these cases Peter's words are introduced with the phrase: 'And (δὲ) answering him Peter said:...' or 'And (δὲ) answering Peter said:...'[3] In a sixth case the introduction reads: 'Then (τότε) answering Peter said to him:...'(19.27). The repetition of the same introductory phrase, given the same context, is a verbal

1. See R.E. Brown, K.P. Donfried, and J. Reumann (eds.), *Peter in the New Testament* (Minneapolis: Augsburg, 1973), pp. 77-78; and Kingsbury, 'Figure of Peter', pp. 71-72.

2. Thompson, *Matthew's Advice*, p. 205.

3. 14.28; 15.15; 16.16; 17.4; 26.33; in 16.16 the phrase reads 'And answering Simon Peter said:...' See also 16.22: 'And taking him Peter began to rebuke him saying:...'; Mt. 18.21: 'Then approaching Peter said to him:...'; and 26.35a: 'Says to him Peter:...' These patterns are similar to two other patterns Thompson notes: '*kai/tote*—aorist participle *proselthon(ontes)*—subject-verb of saying *auton*(*on*) found in 4.3; 8.19; 13.10; 15.12; 15.23; 16.2; 18.31; 28.18; and *proselthon(-en)* or *proserchontaiauto* -subject-*legon* (*ontes*)' (Thompson, *Matthew's Advice*, p. 204 and pp. 51-52).

reinforcement of the content pattern. With each repetition the predictability of the pattern is increased. In a form of assent, the reader assumes more and more that Peter will speak for the disciples. Since no new or striking information is conveyed and the phrases are predictable (redundant), absorbing them requires little effort. The effect is persuasive. Indeed, through the repeated pattern, for the reader, Peter *is* the spokesman.

c. *Peter as Prototypical Disciple: Linked Episodes and the Epithet 'Little-faith'*

Peter is also seen as a prototypical disciple in two other cases where verbal repetition occurs between similar episodes. The first episode involved is that of Peter walking on the water in 14.22-32. This story is an expanded doublet of the stilling of the storm in 8.23-27.[1] Among other verbal similarities Peter's cry, 'Lord, save me' (14.30b) essentially repeats the disciples' cry in 8.25,[2] and Jesus' response to Peter: 'and says to him: Little-faith, why did you doubt?' (14.31b) echoes his earlier response to all of the disciples: 'And he says to them: why are you fearful little-faiths?' (8.26) The implied reader reads the second episode in the light of the first and, in retrospect, the first in light of the second. The reader can compare and contrast Peter to the disciples. In 14.22-32 Peter stands out and exhibits greater faith than the others by leaving the boat. In his cry, however, he also exhibits the little-faith and faltering typical of the disciples in the earlier episode. Jesus makes the same judgment about him that he made previously about the whole group. The epithet he uses, 'Little-faith', also highlights Peter's role and yet labels him as typical by means of links with other passages. In addition to 8.26 Jesus uses the epithet 'Little-faiths'[3] to characterize the disciples in 6.30 and 16.8 and the closely related 'of little-faith' in 17.20. Yet Peter is the only

1. For further analysis see Chapter 4, 'Double and Triple Stories'. An interesting difference in the second storm episode is that the disciples now 'worship' Jesus and respond, 'Truly you are the Son of God' (14.33) whereas in 6.27 the men marvel, saying, 'What sort of man is this, that even winds and sea obey him?' An advance in understanding has taken place, although there is still 'little-faith'.

2. Note that only the disciples, Jewish outcasts, and Gentiles of faith address Jesus as Lord.

3. According to BAG this word appears in Sextus 6; elsewhere only in Christian writings. In the New Testament only in Matthew and in Lk. 12.28.

individual to be singled out as a 'little-faith'. Peter is the prototypical disciple. At the same time he stands out from the group as special. The occurrence of this expanded doublet builds toward the special and prototypical role Peter assumes in ch. 16 where he confesses Jesus as Christ and Son of God, is blessed, and then rebukes Jesus.

A second set of episodes which link Peter with the disciples by means of verbal repetition is the blessing at Caesarea Philippi and the community discourse. Jesus grants the power to bind and loose to all of the disciples in the community discourse in the same words he used previously to grant it to Peter at Caesarea (16.19b = 18.18, 19, nineteen words in common). These are also the only two contexts in Matthew where the word *ecclesia* appears (16.18 and 18.17, twice). There is a long history of discussion about whether Peter is given additional unique powers in ch. 16.[1]

Why is one episode linked to the other? How is each to be read in the light of the other? The implied reader must make the connections. Why is a power initially granted to Peter alone extended to the group later? Whatever the answer actual readers provide, there can be no doubt, because of the exact verbal repetition that Peter as an individual and the disciples as a group are given the same power to bind and loose. Peter again is characterized as a unique, but prototypical disciple.

d. *Peter's Strengths and Weaknesses and Dramatic Irony: Characters' Repeated Speech*

In addition to repetitions which develop Peter as the prototypical disciple, there are also repetitions which highlight the strength and weakness of Peter's character and create dramatic irony.[2] These repetitions involve both what Peter says and what is said to him. They

1. See Brown, Donfried and Reumann (eds.), *Peter in the New Testament*, pp. 95-101. See also G. Bornkamm, 'The Authority to "Bind" and "Loose" in the Church in Matthew's Gospel: The Problem of Sources in Matthew's Gospel', in D. Miller and D. Hadidian (eds.), *Jesus and Man's Hope* (Pittsburgh: Pittsburgh Theological Seminary, 1970), pp. 46-49.

2. 'Dramatic irony', according to Abrams (*Glossary* [3rd edn], p. 91), 'involves a situation in a play or narrative in which the audience shares with the author knowledge of which a character is ignorant: the character acts in a way grossly inappropriate to the actual circumstances, or expects the opposite of what fate holds in store or says something that anticipates the actual outcome, but not at all in the way he means it.'

occur in two scenes where Peter expands into a round character, the confession and rebuke at Caesarea Philippi (16.13-28) and the trial before the high priest with the intercalated denial by Peter (26.57-75).

In the first scene Jesus speaks to the disciples privately. He asks first, 'Who do men say the Son of Man is (εἶναι)?' Second, 'But you, whom do you say I am (εἶναι)?' (16.15b). Men and disciples are contrasted and Son of Man and I equated. Peter answers Jesus. His answer is introduced by the characteristic phrase repeated when Peter serves as spokesman for the disciples: 'And answering, Simon Peter said...' (16.16a). The answer Peter gives: 'You are the Christ, the Son of the living God', is repeated in the form of a question by the high priest when he seeks to convict Jesus for blasphemy as Peter looks on (26.53-64). Although there are other confessions of Jesus as Son of God in the Gospel,[1] these are the only two passages where Christ and son of the living God appear together (16.16b = 26.63, nine to ten words in common).[2] In both cases the confession or anti-confession is followed by further teaching by Jesus concerning his role as Son of Man. Thus Peter's confession and the trial with Peter's denial intercalated are to be read in the light of one another. Dramatic irony is created when the confession of Jesus' leading disciple is found as an anti-confession on the lips of a chief opponent—when the two are phraseologically aligned in these two crucial scenes. Peter is portrayed as flawed. In retrospect his confession, although correct, is seen to be flawed. This irony is compounded by what occurs immediately following Peter's confession and Jesus' blessing of Peter. Jesus teaches the disciples that he must 'go to Jerusalem and suffer many things from the elders and the chief priests and scribes and be killed and on

1. The disciples confess Jesus as Son of God in 14.34, 'Truly Son of God you are', after the second stilling of the storm. The centurion and guards do also in 27.54b, 'Truly Son of God was this one', after the miraculous portents following the crucifixion. Demonic forces address Jesus as Son of God in 4.3, 6 and 8.29. He is also mocked as Son of God in 27.40, 43.

2. The high priest's question does not directly use 'Son of the living God', but reads as follows: 'I adjure you by the living God that you tell us if you are the Christ, the Son of God.' Kingsbury has noticed the resemblance of 16.16-17 to 26.63-64, but he cites the parallel to argue that the title Son of Man does not supersede the title Son of God in 26.63-64 (*Matthew: Structure*, p. 74). Hawkins lists the expression τοῦ θεοῦ τοῦ ζῶντος XVI, 16; XXVI, 63 as a formula peculiar to Matthew although he notes it also appears in Acts once, Paul six times, and the rest of the NT seven times, *Horae Synopticae* (1909/1968), no. 14, p. 168.

the third day be raised' (16.21). This is what is happening and about to happen in ch. 26. Furthermore, Peter's response to the passion prediction is to rebuke Jesus. Jesus' true identity may have been revealed to Peter, but he refuses to accept or does not understand all that it implies. Already in ch. 16, the seeds of Peter's denial have been planted, a denial made ironic by the fact that the words the high priest uses to condemn Jesus are virtually the same words Peter used to confess him.

That the seeds of Peter's denial are planted and a certain weakness of character revealed in ch. 16 can also be seen in another repetition. Jesus' response to Peter's rebuke is: 'Go behind me Satan: an offence you are to me because you think not the things of God but the things of men' (16.23). Jesus' opening sally, 'Go behind me, Satan', is exactly what Jesus had earlier said to the devil after the third temptation: 'Go, Satan. For it has been written: Lord, the God of you, you shall worship and him only you shall serve' (4.10). That verse is the only verse in the temptation scene where 'Satan' is used. The rest of the verses refer to the 'tempting one' or the 'devil'. Repetition has established a link between Peter's rebuke and the temptation. Reading ch. 16 with the earlier context in mind, the reader sees Peter as tempter. Peter, thinking 'the things of men', is tempting Jesus to worship and serve not God, but Satan. Asked to prove he was the Son of God by means of miracle[1] and offered all of the kingdoms of the world, Jesus had resisted temptation. Now Peter, seeing Jesus as a miraculous Son of God wielding worldly power, tempts Jesus again. He has changed sides in the antithesis men/disciples introduced at the beginning of the episode at Caesarea (16.13-28).

Finally, the dramatic irony of the blessed Peter becoming tempter and denier, the mixture of strength and weakness in Peter's character, is reinforced by repetition in one last context. As is well-known Jesus predicts Peter's denial in 26.34. In 26.33 Peter professes that even if everyone else is offended (σκανδαλισθήσονται) by Jesus, Peter will not be. Indeed, even if he must die with Jesus, Peter says he will never deny him (26.35). Then, Jesus predicts Peter's denial. His prediction is repeated word for word by the narrator when it is fulfilled (26.34 =

1. The phrase, 'If Son you are of God', used in 4.3 and 4.6 is exactly what mockers shout to Jesus on the cross in 27.40, calling for him to prove his Sonship by coming down from the cross.

26.75, eight words in common). The Peter who professes complete loyalty is the very same man who denies Jesus to protect his own life.

e. *Conclusion*

After examining the various verbal repetitions associated with Peter, it can be seen that some function to characterize Peter as leading disciple and spokesman; others serve to highlight his related strength and weakness and create dramatic irony. Many means of characterization are involved: repeated labeling; repeated actions; a double story; epithets; repeated dialogue, linking Peter and other characters and allowing comparison and contrast; and, finally, the prediction of Peter's action by a reliable character and the repetition of that prediction in the narrator's description of its fulfillment. The temporal dimension of reading involving anticipation and retrospection is particularly important to these functions.

4. *The Jewish Leaders*

There are various names given to the sub-groups which form the character group, the Jewish Leaders.[1] However, the way these terms

1. See the terms listed in van Tilborg, *The Jewish Leaders*. With my own additions, the names are:

a. *The Pharisees*: 9.11, 14, 34; 12.2, 14, 24; 15.12; 19.3; 22.15 (and the Herodians), 34, 41.
b. *The Sadducees*: 22.23, 34.
c. *Pharisees and Sadducees*: 3.7; 16.1, 6, 11, 12.
d. *The Scribes*: 7.29; 9.3; 17.10.
e. *The Scribes and Pharisees*: 5.20; 12.38; 15.1; 23.2, 13, 15, 23, 25, 27, 29.
f. *The Chief Priests*: 26.14; 27.6; 28.11.
g. *The presbyters-elders*: not mentioned alone, except in 15.2 which only speaks of the elders in an attributive clause.
h. *The chief priests and elders* (τοῦ λαοῦ): this formulation peculiar to Mt.: 21.23; 26.3, 47; 27.1, 3, 12, 20; 28.11-12. τοῦ λαοῦ in 21.23; 26.3, 47; 27.1 as representatives of the people.
i. *The chief priest and the Pharisees*: 21.45 and 27.62.
j. *The chief priests and scribes*: 2.4; 20.18; 21.15; 2.4 chief priests, scribes.
k. *The chief priests and the whole Sanhedrin*: 26.59.
l. *The scribes and the elders*: 26.57 (and the chief priest also there).
m. *The elders and chief priests and scribes*: 16.21 and 27.41.

are used indicates that there are no sharp distinctions between the sub-groups.[1] All of the sub-groups are portrayed as representatives of the Jewish establishment. It should be noted that 'the Jewish Leaders' is a designation for a Matthean character group, not for any actual Jewish leaders past or present.

Although Jewish leaders appear in many more passages than either John or Peter, there are few nuances in their characterization. As the Gospel's principal antagonists, they are flat characters, types. They are a group of wicked, hypocritical enemies of Jesus. The implied reader is not led to feel sympathy for them.[2] Extended verbal repetition displays and emphasizes their evil nature. It also develops their growing opposition to Jesus. Earlier portions of the narrative prepare the implied reader for the Jewish leaders' eventual role in Jesus' death. Their motivations are revealed and initial portraits of their character are progressively blackened. Their actions stem appropriately from their character.

Since the Jewish leaders appear in so many passages and the narrative order is so important, the reader should consult a chart outlining the passages in order on the following pages. Passages involving repetition which characterizes the Jewish leaders are marked with an asterisk. The characterizing repetitions will then be discussed by type rather than function because they all have essentially the same functions. The reader may wish to refer to the chart from time to time as they are discussed.

n. *Herod, the King*: 2.1, 3, 7 (9, the king), 12, 13, 15, 16, 19, 22.
o. *Herod, the Tetrarch*: 14.1, 3, 6.

1. See van Tilborg's argument in *The Jewish Leaders*: 'Matthew looks upon the representatives of Israel as a homogeneous group. The many names he eventually gives the Jewish leaders are not meant as further historical information. He does not want to introduce a distinction between Pharisees, Sadducees, scribes, high priests, and elders' (p. 1; the data are presented on pp. 1-7).

2. Again I emphasize that I am speaking of Matthew's character group, not of any actual Jewish leaders past or present. The implications of Matthew's portrayal of the Jewish leaders should be a matter of concern for all of us. The issue has been taken up by Lloyd Gaston, Fred W. Burnett, and others. The probable historical situation of opposition between first-century Jew and Christian should not be considered normative for a different context.

Chart of Scenes in Which the Jewish Leaders Appear and References to Them in Discourse Sections

Ch. 2 Conflict with Herod and Jerusalem troubled by the Magi's question about the King of the Jews.

*3.7-12 John condemns the Pharisees and Sadducees. He uses fruit imagery, the epithet, 'brood of vipers', and eschatological imagery.

Chs. 5–7 Jesus warns that righteousness must exceed that of the scribes and Pharisees, 5.20. *Jesus forbids divorce, 5.31-32. *Jesus warns that one should not do acts of piety to be seen by men as the hypocrites do, 6.1-18. *Jesus warns about false prophets, using fruit imagery, 7.15-20. The narrator tells the reader that Jesus teaches 'as one who has authority, and not as their scribes', 7.29.

9.1-8 Jesus forgives a paralytic's sins. The scribes say among themselves, 'This man blasphemes' (9.3). Jesus 'knows their thoughts' and says, 'Why do you think evil things in your hearts? For which is easier to say: "Your sins are forgiven" or "Rise and walk"? But that you may know the Son of Man has authority on earth to forgive sins—' (9.4-6).

*9.10-13 The Pharisees ask the disciples why Jesus eats with tax collectors and sinners (9.11). Jesus overhears, answers with a proverb and enjoins them to 'learn what it is: Mercy I desire and not sacrifice; for I came not to call the righteous but sinners' (9.13).

*9.32-34 Exorcism of a dumb demoniac. The crowd says, 'It never appeared, thus in Israel.' The Pharisees respond: 'By the ruler of demons he expels the demons.'

*10.16-42 Jesus warns the disciples of persecution to come. In 10.25b Jesus tells the disciples, 'If they called the housemaster Beezeboul, how much more the members of his household.'

*12.1-8 The Pharisees question Jesus about his disciples plucking and eating grain on the Sabbath. Jesus cites Scripture and says, 'But if you had known what it is: Mercy, I desire and not sacrifice, you would not have condemned the guiltless. For the Son of Man is lord of the sabbath' (12.7-8).

*12.9-15a Jesus enters 'their synagogue'. The Pharisees seek to 'accuse' Jesus by questioning him about the lawfulness of healing on the Sabbath. Jesus responds with a legal argument and heals a man with a withered hand. 'And when the Pharisees went out, they took counsel against him, in order that they might destroy him. But Jesus, knowing, departed thence.'

*12.22-37 Exorcism of a blind and dumb demoniac. The crowds say, 'Is this not the Son of David?' The Pharisees say, 'This man does not expel the demons except by Beezeboul ruler of the demons.' But knowing their thoughts, Jesus responds with a lengthy condemnation including fruit imagery and the epithet, 'brood of vipers'.

*12.38-42	The scribes and Pharisees request a sign. Jesus refuses offering only the sign of Jonah and condemns 'this evil generation' for sign-seeking.
*14.1-13a	The story of John's death at the hands of Herod the Tetrarch. Initially Herod fears the crowd who have John as a prophet (14.5). When Jesus learns of John's death, he departs to a desert place.
*15.1-11	The scribes and Pharisees ask why Jesus' disciples do not wash whenever they eat bread. Jesus asks why they transgress God's commandment on account of their tradition and calls them hypocrites.
*15.12-14	The disciples ask whether Jesus knows the Pharisees were offended. Jesus says they are blind guides.
*16.1-4	The Pharisees and Sadducees, tempting, seek a sign. Jesus offers only the sign of Jonah to an evil and adulterous generation.
*16.5-12	Jesus warns them to beware the leaven of the Pharisees and Sadducees. They eventually understand.
*16.21	Jesus predicts his passion at the hand of the Jewish leaders and resurrection in indirect discourse.
*17.9-13	Jesus tells Peter, James and John not to tell anyone about the Transfiguration until the Son of Man is raised from the dead, 17.9. The disciples ask why the scribes say Elijah must come first. Jesus says Elijah already came and 'they' did to him whatever they wished; and thus 'also the Son of Man is about to suffer by them', 17.11-12. The disciples understand he speaks about John the Baptist, 17.13.
*17.22-23	Jesus predicts that 'the Son of Man is about to be delivered into the hands of men, and they will kill him, and on the third day he will be raised'.
*19.3-9	The Pharisees tempt Jesus with a question about divorce.
*19.16-22	A rich young man calls Jesus 'Teacher' and asks what he must do to inherit eternal life.
*20.17-19	Jesus predicts the passion at the hands of the Jewish leaders and the resurrection.
21.15-17	The chief priests and scribes are incensed when they see Jesus' marvels and the children crying out, 'Hosanna to the Son of David' in the temple. They ask Jesus if he knows. He responds yes, cites Scripture and departs.
*21.18-22	Jesus curses the unfruitful fig tree.
*21.23-32	While Jesus teaches in the temple the chief priests and elders of the people ask the source of Jesus' authority. They fear the crowd who have John as a prophet. Jesus tells the parable of the two children and condemns them.
*21.33-46	Jesus tells them the parable of the wicked tenants. The 'kingdom of God will be taken from them and given to a nation producing its fruits.' The chief priests and Pharisees, hearing his parables, know he speaks about them. They seek to seize him, but fear the crowds who have Jesus as a prophet.

22.1-14	Jesus answers and speaks again in parables. He tells of the wedding feast and wedding dress.
*22.15-22	The Pharisees, leaving, take counsel to ensnare him in a word. They send their disciples and the Herodians. They call him Teacher and question him about tribute to Caesar. He 'knows their wickedness' and says, 'Why do you tempt me, hypocrites?' He answers, they marvel and leave.
*22.23-33	Sadducees question Jesus about the resurrection. They call him Teacher. The crowds are astounded at his teaching.
*22.34-40	The Pharisees gather and a lawyer, tempting, questions Jesus about the greatest commandment. He calls Jesus Teacher.
22.41-45	Jesus questions the Pharisees about how the Christ can be the son of David. No one is able to answer him a word nor dared to question him anymore from that day.
*Ch. 23	Warnings and woes against the scribes and Pharisees. Jesus calls them hypocrites and blind guides. He predicts they will persecute his messengers and that Jerusalem will be destroyed.
Chs. 24–25	Predicts the destruction of Jerusalem and speaks the apocalyptic discourse.
*26.1-2	Jesus predicts that the Son of Man will be delivered to be crucified after two days.
*26.3-5	The chief priests and the elders of the people counsel in order to seize and kill Jesus, but not at the feast lest there be a riot among the people.
26.14-16	Judas conspires with the chief priests to deliver Jesus.
*26.45b	Jesus tells Peter, James and John 'the hour has drawn near' and 'the Son of Man is delivered into the hands of sinners'.
26.47-56	A crowd from the chief priests and elders come and seize Jesus.
*26.57-75	Jesus is led away to Caiaphas the high priest where the scribes and elders were assembled and is tried while Peter denies him in the court outside.
*27.1-2	The chief priests and elders of the people take counsel to put Jesus to death and deliver him to Pilate.
*27.3-10	Judas repents. The chief priests take counsel and buy the potter's field with his blood money.
27.12-13	Jesus is accused by the chief priests and elders. Pilate asks if Jesus hears their evidence.
27.18	Pilate knows the Jewish leaders delivered Jesus out of envy.
27.20	The chief priests and elders persuade the crowds to ask for Barabbas and destroy Jesus.
27.25	The people (ὁ λαός) take Jesus' blood upon themselves.
27.41-43	The chief priests, scribes, and elders mock Jesus.
*27.62-66	The chief priests and Pharisees ask Pilate to seal the tomb. They seal it with a stone and place a guard.
*28.11-15	The chief priests and elders bribe the guards to say the body was stolen. The narrator says the rumor was spread 'until today'.

The Jewish leaders are characterized in a number of ways which involve repetition. They include: epithets; repeated reactions to, or descriptions of, the leaders by reliable characters; repeated words and actions of the leaders—some depicted, some described; doublets; Jesus offering an authoritative legal interpretation and the leaders challenging it in a later narrative; and the repetition by the leaders of the words of another character. Particularly interesting is the way in which general statements about wicked behavior or attitudes early in the Gospel are specifically applied to the Jewish leaders later in the Gospel. Each type of repetition will be discussed in turn.

a. *Epithets (Used by Reliable Characters): Jesus and John the Baptist*

One device that has always struck readers of the Gospel is the use of vivid epithets by reliable characters to address the Jewish leaders. These epithets characterize the leaders economically, capturing their essence in a word or phrase. Several, 'brood of vipers' and 'blind guides', are striking metaphors. The epithets are repeated in different contexts. The implied reader reads each appearance in the light of the others over the course of the narrative.

Brood of vipers. The first epithet or label to appear is 'Brood of Vipers' (3.7; 12.34; 23.33). When the Pharisees and Sadducees come to the baptism, the first words out of John the Baptist's mouth are: 'Brood of Vipers, who warned you to flee from the coming wrath?' (3.7). This is the first appearance of the Jewish leaders following the birth story.[1] At the first meeting of the leaders and a reliable character, that character labels them a brood of vipers. The second time the leaders are addressed as a brood of vipers occurs in 12.34.

By 12.34 the Pharisees have already taken counsel against Jesus in order to destroy him (12.14). They have claimed that Jesus exorcizes by the power of the ruler of demons rather than by the power of the Holy Spirit. Jesus characterizes them as opponents (12.30). Using the same fruit imagery that John employed in 3.7-10 (see below), he claims that their character is revealed by the evil fruit they bear. He asks: 'Brood of Vipers, how can you speak good things, being evil?'

1. There Herod was portrayed as an enemy of the infant Jesus. All Jerusalem was troubled at the magi's question about the birth of the king of the Jews. The chief priests and scribes of the people appeared briefly, but only to explain that the messiah was to be born in Bethlehem.

Jesus, the most reliable character, labels them with the same epithet introduced by his forerunner, John. The reoccurrence occurs in a context where their antagonism to Jesus is obvious. John's judgement is confirmed and reinforced.

The third instance in which the Jewish leaders are labeled as a brood of vipers occurs in 23.33. Many episodes have intervened and the plot is moving toward its climax. After a series of tests of Jesus by the Jewish leaders that end with the narrator announcing that no one dared to question Jesus any longer, ch. 23 is devoted to the so-called woes against the scribes and Pharisees. Jesus, echoing John's question in 3.7, asks, 'Serpents, Brood of Vipers, how can you flee from the judgement of gehenna?' (3.7 = 23.33). Again the condemnation comes in direct discourse from the most reliable character. According to Jesus the scribes and Pharisees claim they would never have murdered the prophets. They will, however, murder the prophets that Jesus sends. Because they thus participate in the blood guilt from Abel on, they will be destroyed along with Jerusalem. In the first instance they were charged to produce fruit worthy of repentance. In the second they were condemned as bearing evil fruit. In the last their well-deserved judgment is announced.

Hypocrites. Another term used to characterize the Jewish leaders is 'Hypocrites' (6.2, 5, 16; 15.7; 22.18; 23.13, 15, 23, 25, 27, 29; 24.51).[1] This term is introduced in the Sermon on the Mount, ch. 6. There, Jesus warns the audience, disciples, and crowds[2] not to be like the hypocrites who give alms in order to be glorified by men (6.2), who pray before men (6.5), and who, when they fast, ensure that they appear so to men (6.16). The hypocrites are not identified with any particular character group. They are defined in these verses as those who do acts of piety in order to be honored by men. They are contrasted with those who do not do acts of piety for gain and receive a reward from the father who sees in secret. That these references to hypocrites apply to the Jewish leaders becomes apparent to the implied reader only later in the narrative sequence as the plot develops. Jesus, the most reliable character, uses the epithet 'Hypocrites' to address the

1. The term hypocrite is also used as a pejorative, but not specifically in reference to the Jewish leaders in 7.5.

2. The audience is difficult to determine. It probably includes two tiers: the disciples in the inner circle and the crowds beyond.

scribes and Pharisees in 15.7, the disciples of the Pharisees and the Herodians in 22.18, and the scribes and Pharisees in 23.13, 15, 23, 25, 27 and 29. In 15.7 the contrast between outward and inward piety is again emphasized. The Pharisees and scribes have questioned the disciple's failure to observe laws of cleanliness. Jesus responds by condemning their interpretation of the law as annulling the word of God. He calls them hypocrites who fulfill Isaiah's prophecy of the people who honor God with their lips, but not their hearts (15.7). In 22.15-22 the plot, leading to the passion, has progressed to the point that the Pharisees have taken counsel in order to ensnare Jesus (22.15). Their disciples and the Herodians pose the question of tribute to Caesar, pretending to honor Jesus' opinion as a teacher of truth who does not look to the face of men (22.16-17). The narrator indicates that Jesus knows their duplicity ('But knowing Jesus, the wickedness of them...' 22.18a). Jesus asks, 'Why do you [test or] tempt me, hypocrites?' Again, the outward-inward contrast is reiterated. The use of πειράζω here and in 16.1 and 19.3 indicates that the leaders are tempters like Satan (cf. 4.1, 3, where the devil is described as tempting Jesus). Finally, in a litany of concentrated repetition, Jesus addresses the scribes and Pharisees as hypocrites in 23.13, 15, 23, 25, 27 and 29. The connections between chs. 23 and 6 are made explicit through the use of repetition (6.1-2 = 23.5-7, six words in common). The scribes and Pharisees do works 'in order to be seen by men' and like the chief place in the suppers, synagogues, and greetings in the marketplaces. If there was any doubt in the reader's mind that they are the hypocrites of 6.2, 5, 16, Jesus' condemnation: 'Woe to you, scribes and Pharisees, hypocrites...' would allay it. The final use of the term hypocrites occurs in 24.51. There Jesus warns parabolically that the slave who behaves wickedly because his master is delayed will be cut off and find his place with the hypocrites, where there will be weeping and gnashing of teeth (24.48-51). Although the category hypocrites may include more than the Jewish leaders (see 7.5), it certainly includes them (15.7; 22.18; 23.13, 15, 23, 25, 27, 29). They are prime candidates for judgment (see 3.7-12; 23.13-36) and belong with those who weep and gnash their teeth (see 8.12; 22.13; perhaps also 13.42, 50).

Through the use of the epithet 'Hypocrites', the Jewish leaders are characterized as those who are outwardly righteous, but inwardly lawless and wicked. Early non-specific references to hypocrites prepare the implied reader for this characterization. When Jesus, the most reliable character, addresses them in this fashion the implied reader connects them and their behavior with other references to the hypocrites in the Gospel. This is especially true of ch. 6 where hypocrites and imitation of their behavior are condemned. When the Jewish leaders exhibit that behavior later, the reader is ready to perceive them as wicked; a verdict confirmed by Jesus' form of address, 'Hypocrites'.

Blind guides. The last epithet which characterizes the Jewish leaders is 'blind guides'. In 15.14 Jesus warns his disciples that the Pharisees are blind guides of the blind. In this context the disciples wonder if he knew he had offended the Pharisees when he called them hypocrites and denounced their tradition concerning hand-washing as violating God's law (15.1-11).

Jesus reiterates the epithet 'Blind Guides' in ch. 23. In one of the woes against the scribes and Pharisees, Jesus replaces the epithet, 'Hypocrites' with the epithet, 'Blind Guides' (23.16). Again at issue is their interpretation of the law. They are also addressed as blind guides in 23.34. They have valued the weightier aspects of the law less than the lighter: 'Blind Guides, the ones straining the gnat, but swallowing the camel' (23.24). Through the use of this epithet the Pharisees are characterized as blind leaders who mishandle the law and who will lead all who follow into trouble.

b. *Repeated Description by Reliable Characters*

A second form of characterization of the Jewish leaders is the repeated description of the Jewish leaders by reliable characters. This includes speeches reliable characters make to the leaders and comments on the leaders made to other characters.

Fruit imagery. One example of this form of characterization is the repeated use of fruit imagery to portray the Jewish leaders as evil trees who produce evil fruit or no fruit at all. They are contrasted to those who do the will of the father in heaven, the bearers of good fruit. The nature of the Jewish leaders can be determined by the fruit they produce.

As with the epithet 'Brood of Vipers', John the Baptist is the first to use fruit imagery. In the first appearance of the Jewish leaders following the birth story[1] John sees the Pharisees and Sadducees coming to the baptism and speaks to them: 'Brood of Vipers, who warned you to flee from the coming wrath? Produce therefore fruit worthy of repentance...And already the axe is laid at the root of the trees; therefore every tree not producing good fruit is cut down and is cast into the fire' (3.7-8, 10). John, a reliable character, the forerunner of the messiah, is the first to cast aspersions on the Jewish leaders as a group. The reader learns early in the narrative that the Jewish leaders are a brood of vipers who will be judged if they do not produce good fruit, fruit worthy of repentance. When this group appears again in the narrative the reader will look for evidence that confirms or denies John's evaluation. As the narrative progresses the reader will look to see what kind of fruit the Jewish leaders produce.

The next instance of fruit imagery is in the Sermon on the Mount. There Jesus warns the disciples and the crowds about false prophets in sheep's clothing. They are to be known by their fruits (7.16a = 7.20, which forms an inclusio around the teaching on fruit). Good trees cannot produce evil fruits and vice versa (7.17-18). 'Therefore every tree not producing good fruit is cut down and is cast into the fire' (7.19). These are the exact words John had spoken to the Pharisees and Sadducees in 3.10b (3.10b = 7.19, eleven words in common). This suggests to the reader that 7.15-20 is an indirect reference to the Jewish leaders similar to the condemnations of the hypocrites in ch. 6.[2] Since Jesus does not specify the identity of the false prophets beyond the fact that they are to be recognized by their fruits, the implied reader must fill in the gap or indeterminate opening in the narrative. Repetition leads the implied reader to suspect, at least provisionally, that the false prophets in sheep's clothing are the Jewish leaders. The implied reader might change his or her mind in retrospect after the text supplies more data. However, the fact that

1. Herod, of course, seeks to kill the infant Jesus. The chief priests and scribes of the people are assembled to find out where the messiah is to be born (2.4). This is an ironic reference. Through their interpretation of Scripture Jesus' messiahship is confirmed.

2. W.D. Davies suggest other connections between the Sermon on the Mount and ch. 23 in *The Setting of the Sermon on the Mount* (Cambridge: Cambridge University Press, 1966), pp. 291-92. He notes 'that the characteristics condemned in the Pharisees in xxiii are almost precisely those described in the SM' (*Setting*, p. 291).

Jesus specifically applies similar words to them in 12.33-34 confirms the initial identification.[1] Even if the implied reader does not identify the false prophets directly with the Jewish leaders, he or she may link them indirectly. Both are antagonists who must be judged by their fruits.

The next reference to producing fruit is directly connected with the Jewish leaders by Jesus. In 12.33-34 Jesus openly condemns the Pharisees as a brood of vipers, producing bad fruit, being evil. He does this after they have attributed his healing of a blind and dumb demoniac to the power of Beezeboul rather than the Holy Spirit. They have blasphemed against the Holy Spirit, a sin that cannot be forgiven. Jesus' open condemnation echoes his own words in the Sermon on the Mount concerning the false prophets (7.16 or 20 and 7.17 = 12.33, eleven words in common) and confirms the words of John in 3.7-10 (3.10 = 12.33, four words in common, 3.7 = 12.34, brood of vipers). The Jewish leaders are increasingly revealed as evil and incapable of the repentance for which John called. The repetition of fruit imagery reinforces this characterization for the implied reader. This characterization is also seen in their behavior in the first twelve chapters. This episode and the following request for a sign form a climax to the initial series of confrontations between Jesus and the Jewish leaders.

1. Some scholars using other methods object to the identification of the false prophets in 7.15-20 with the Jewish leaders. For primarily historical and/or redactional reasons the false prophets have been identified variously as Zealots (A. Schlatter according to G. Barth, 'Matthew's Understanding of the Law', *Tradition and Interpretation in Matthew* [Philadelphia: The Westminster Press, 1963], p. 74); Hellenistic Christian anti-nomians (Barth, *Tradition*, pp. 73-75, 159-64); Christian enthusiasts (Kingsbury, *Matthew: Structure*, p. 151 in a position similar to Barth's); or gnostics (B.W. Bacon and J. Weiss as reported by Barth, *Tradition*, p. 164 and Davies, *Setting*, p. 199, and of A. Schlatter according to Davies, p. 199). Those who argue that the false prophets are Christian insiders often treat 7.15-23 as one unit. Thus 7.15-20 and 7.21-22 which refers to those who call Jesus 'Lord' and prophecy and exorcize in his name are seen as descriptive of the same group. The reference to sheep's clothing is also seen as indicative of insiders. But see 10.6 and 15.24 where the sheep are Israelites and note the contrast between 'inner' and 'outer' typical of Jesus' descriptions of the Jewish leaders. Another argument treats the false prophets of 7.15-20 and 24.11 and 24.24 as 'Christians'. Barth argues that 7.15 and 24.11 refer to anti-nomian Christians because the terms 'false-prophets' and 'lawlessness' appear in both contexts (*Tradition*, p. 75). However, the scribes and Pharisees are accused of lawlessness in 23.28 (see Davies on ἀνομία, p. 205). They can also lead the faithful astray (23.3).

The leaders have reacted negatively to Jesus during his ministry.[1] The narrator has already told the implied reader that the Pharisees are plotting against Jesus in 12.14. The portrait of the Jewish leaders as the evil antagonists of Jesus is well-established. The reader knows them by their fruits and through the words of John and Jesus against them.

The final references to the Jewish leaders as those who produce evil fruit or no fruit at all come in ch. 21. In ch. 21 Jesus triumphantly enters Jerusalem, cleanses the temple, and heals the blind and lame there. The chief priests and scribes are incensed at the marvels he has done and the cries of the children, 'Hosanna to the Son of David' (21.15). After they confront him, he leaves the city for Bethany. On his return the fruit imagery becomes concrete. He curses a barren fig tree which withers instantly. Re-entering the Temple he again confronts the Jewish leaders. The chief priests and elders of the people question the source of his authority. He responds with a question concerning the authority of John. They dare not answer because they fear the crowd who 'have John as a prophet' (21.26). Jesus proceeds to tell them two parables, the parable of the two sons (21.28-32) and the parable of the wicked tenants (21.33-41). He concludes by saying, 'Therefore, I tell you, that the kingdom of God will be taken from you and will be given to a nation producing the fruits of it' (21.43). Although the phrase is very short, the implied reader hears the echoes of 3.7-10; 7.15-20; and 12.33-34 where the Jewish leaders and the production (ποιέω) of fruit are linked. Like the fig tree, the Jewish leaders are barren. They do not do the will of the father (21.31 = 12.50, five words in common). They have not responded properly to Jesus. They do not render the fruits of God's vineyard to God. They will be judged and wither as the cursed fig tree. The chief priests and Pharisees know that Jesus tells the two parables concerning them and seek to seize him. However, they fear the crowds who have Jesus, like John, as a prophet (21.46 = 21.26, five words in common). The Jewish leaders are portrayed as the enemies of John and Jesus, who

1. In 9.3 scribes think Jesus has blasphemed by forgiving sins. In 9.11 the Pharisees question Jesus' disciples about why he eats with tax collectors and sinners. In 9.34 the Pharisees say Jesus exorcized a dumb demoniac by the ruler of the demons. In 12.2 the Pharisees challenge him for allowing the disciples to pluck grain on the Sabbath in order to accuse him; and, finally, in 12.14 after he heals on the Sabbath they take counsel against him in order to destroy him.

both warn the reader that the character of the leaders can be known by their fruits.

Jesus' use of Hosea 6.6. A second example of the characterization of the Jewish leaders by means of the repeated words of a reliable character is the use of Hos. 6.6 by Jesus in 9.13 and 12.7 (seven words in common). In ch. 9, following the exorcism of the Gadarene demoniacs (8.28-34), Jesus enters his own city. There the scribes believe Jesus blasphemes by forgiving the sins of a paralytic. Jesus calls Matthew, a tax collector, and eats with tax collectors and other sinners. The Pharisees question Jesus' disciples: 'Why does your teacher eat with tax collectors and sinners?' (9.11b). Jesus responds with the proverb that the sick are those who need a doctor and says, 'But learn what it is: Mercy I desire and not sacrifice, for I came not to call righteous ones but sinners' (9.13).

In ch. 12, following Jesus' saying about his light yoke (11.28-30), the Pharisees question the lawfulness of the disciples' plucking grain on the Sabbath. Jesus points to the actions of David and the temple priests. He continues:

> And I tell you that a greater thing than the Temple is here. But if you had known what it is: Mercy I desire and not sacrifice, you would not have condemned the guiltless. For Lord of the Sabbath is the Son of Man (12.6-8).

The episode that follows is another in which the Pharisees charge Jesus with Sabbath breaking (12.9-13). It concludes with the Pharisees going out and taking counsel against Jesus in order to destroy him (12.14).

In both contexts, 9.10-13 and 12.1-8, the Pharisees challenge Jesus' behavior according to their understanding of the law. In both cases Jesus responds with a quote from Hosea: 'Mercy I desire and not sacrifice'. The Pharisees are characterized as unmerciful sticklers who do not understand the heart of the law. The repetition not only emphasizes their repeated behavior which calls forth this repeated response, it also shows the reader that the Pharisees have not changed in the course of the narrative. There is repetition with variation. In 9.13 Jesus had charged them to *learn* (μάθετε)[1] the meaning of Hos. 6.6. They have not learned this lesson by 12.1-8. If they 'had known'

1. The same root as disciple (ὁ μαθητής).

its meaning, they 'would not have condemned the guiltless' (12.7). The repeated quotation is introduced differently in each case. Repetition with variation in different contexts influences the reader as the narrative progresses.

Passion predictions. A third way the Jewish leaders are characterized by means of the repeated words of a reliable character is through Jesus' predictions of the passion.[1] The narrator reports Jesus' words in the first prediction (16.21). The rest are in direct discourse (17.12d; 17.22-23a; 20.18-19; 26.2 and 26.45b; see also 17.9b and 20.28, related Son of Man sayings). All occur in private and are directed to the disciples. Therefore, these predictions are privileged communications which the implied reader shares only with the narrator and the disciples. Further the narrator tells only the implied reader explicitly in 16.21 that the predictions concern Jesus Christ. Since it is in indirect discourse, the narrator adds his or her authority to that of Jesus. This first prediction occurs at a turning point of the narrative, the movement of Jesus toward Jerusalem and the passion.[2] The next four predictions which speak of the Son of Man very strongly reiterate the first prediction in direct discourse at points along the way. The ties between 16.21 and the lengthier predictions of 17.22-23a and 20.17-19 are particularly strong (16.21 = 17.22-23a, six words in common; 16.21 = 20.18-19, ten words in common; 17.22-23a = 20.18-19, ten words in common). These three predict both the passion and the resurrection, 'and on the third day he will be [or is to be] raised'.[3]

1. 16.21 = 17.22-23a, (six words in common); 16.21 = 20.18-19 (ten words in common); 17.12d = 17.22-23a (five words in common); 17.12d = 20.17-19 (five words in common; 17.12d = 26.2 (four words—the Son of Man only); 17.12d = 26.45b (four words, the Son of Man only). Mt. 17.22-23a = 20.18-19 (ten words in common); 17.22-23a = 20.28 (four words: the Son of Man only); 17.22-23a = 26.2, (six words in common); 17.22-23a = 26.45b (seven words in common); 20.17-19 = 20.28 (four words: the Son of Man only); 20.17-19 = 26.2 (five words in common); 20.17-19 = 26.45b, (five words in common); 20.28 = 26.2 (four words: the Son of Man); 20.28 = 26.45b (four words: the Son of Man); 26.2 = 26.45b (six words in common).

2. See Kingsbury, *Matthew: Structure*, pp. 7-25 who makes 16.21, parallel to 4.17 a major division of the Gospel. See also Chapter 4 on plot.

3. Chapter 17.9b also refers to the resurrection of the Son of Man. Another related saying is 12.40 which speaks of the Son of Man being in the heart of the earth

One function of these predictions is to characterize the Jewish leaders.[1] The protagonist and most reliable character predicts that the Jewish leaders will kill him. Although their antagonism is implied from the very beginning of the Gospel with Herod's search and slaughter of the innocents and the mention of plot to destroy Jesus in 12.14,[2] 16.21 is the first detailed prediction of the passion.[3] With each succeeding prediction new details are revealed. The evil actions of the leaders are depicted not only as they occur, but many times prior to their occurrence in the predictions. The implied reader perceives the leaders in the light of the events which are ultimately revelatory of their character *even before those events occur.* The implied reader is repeatedly directed to see the leaders' true nature and prepared for the deeds they will do. Their actions do not come as a surprise, but as recognized fulfillments of predictions. There is an economy of characterization here. With these repeated predictions, there is less need to describe the leaders' opposition and motivations when the events occur. The repetitions also emphasize the Jewish leaders' responsibility for Jesus' death and downplay the responsibility of the Romans.[4]

Variations in the terms used for those responsible for the passion emphasize the sinful nature of the Jewish leaders. This can be seen in the progression of predictions. The first prediction, 16.21, specifies that it is the elders, chief priests, and scribes who will cause Jesus to

three days and three nights. The chief priests and Pharisees report the following words of Jesus to Pilate: 'After three days I am raised', and request that he seal the tomb 'until the third day' lest the disciples steal the body and say 'He was raised from the dead' (27.63-64). References to 'three days' or the 'third day' are found in 12.40; 16.21; 17.22-23a; 20.17-19; 27.63; 27.64. See also 26.61 and 27.40.

1. Plot development is perhaps the primary function. See Chapter 4.

2. Destroy (ἀπόλλυμι) in the active tense of persons can mean ruin, kill, or put to death.

3. The sign of Jonah doublet (12.38-42 = 16.1-4) refers to the Son of Man being in the heart of the earth three days and three nights.

4. 20.17-19, for example, predicts that the chief priests and scribes will deliver Jesus to the Gentiles to be mocked, scourged, and crucified. The mocking, scourging, and crucifixion (27.26, 29, 31, 35) by the Romans is seen in prospect as the responsibility of the Jewish leaders. This, of course, is supported by such verses as 27.18, 20, 25.

suffer (παθεῖν)[1] and to be killed. The second, 17.12, emphasizes the nearness of the suffering of the Son of Man and associates it with the death of John the Baptist at 'their' hands.[2] The third prediction, 17.22-23a, says that the Son of Man is about to be delivered (παραδίδοσθαι, a technical term for the passion) into *the hands of men* and killed. This emphasizes that Jesus' opponents are human and his death the result of human actions.[3] The identity of the men is made explicit by repetition in 20.17-19 where Jesus predicts that the Son of Man will be delivered to the chief priests and scribes who will condemn him to death. The final prediction, 26.45b, following the watch in Gethsemene, announces the imminent deliverance of the Son of Man 'into *the hands of sinners*'. This echoes 17.22-23a. The hands here are described not merely as the hands of men, but as 'the hands of sinners'. Variation in the repeated predictions plays a role in portraying the Jewish leaders in an even more negative light as the narrative proceeds.

General descriptions made specific by repetition. A fourth way the repeated words of a reliable character characterize the Jewish leaders occurs when general descriptions are made specific later in the narrative. Jesus speaks about evil persons in general and repeats the words later in the narrative, applying them specifically to the Jewish leaders. These later repetitions all occur in ch. 23, the climactic condemnation discourse against the scribes and Pharisees. Passages involved are 6.1-2 = 23.5-7 (ten words in common); 10.17, 23 = 23.34, 36 (seven words in common), similar also to 5.10-12[4] and the use of the epithet hypocrites discussed above.

The first pair of passages concerns the 'hypocrites' who do their piety 'in order to be seen by men' (6.1 = 23.5) especially 'in the synagogues' (6.2 = 23.6). In ch. 6 of the Sermon on the Mount Jesus

1. The verb in another form also appears in 19.12d with reference to Jesus.

2. The only antecedent of 'they' and 'them' in 17.12 that is possibly specified in the context is the scribes mentioned by the disciples in 17.10. It is not clear whether the scribes are specifically intended.

3. See the contrast between 'the things of God' and 'the things of men' in 16.23.

4. Another example may be 5.34-35 = 23.22 (six words in common). The problem is that Jesus forbids swearing in 5.34-37, while in 23.16-22 he questions the scribes' and Pharisees' decisions on which oaths are binding, not swearing in general.

warns in the second person not to do as the hypocrites do. In ch. 23 Jesus is warning the crowds and the disciples, again in direct discourse, about the scribes and Pharisees in the third person.

The second pair of passages concerns persecution of God's messengers. They will be persecuted from city to city and scourged (10.17 = 23.34). Then the judgment will occur (10.23 = 23.36). In ch. 10, the missionary discourse, Jesus warns the disciples who will be persecuted in the second person. In ch. 23 he addresses the scribes and Pharisees, the persecutors, in the second person.[1]

Both pairs of passages are connected not by the exact repetition of whole sentences, but by the repetition of words, phrases, and content. In both cases the initial occurrence is a warning Jesus presents without specifically identifying the culprits. Hypocritical behavior and persecution are condemned as evil. The implied reader is left to search for the persons to whom the descriptions apply. Throughout the central section of the narrative many clues are provided, such as the application of the epithet 'hypocrites' to the Jewish leaders. By the time Jesus launches into a thoroughgoing diatribe the implied reader is not surprised and can easily accept Jesus' characterization of the scribes and Pharisees as hypocrites and persecutors of the righteous. The initial passages prepare the implied reader for Jesus' characterization of the scribes and Pharisees in ch. 23.

c. *Repeated Actions or Words of the Jewish Leaders*

Taking counsel. Repeated actions and words of the Jewish leaders are another form of characterization. Some are described; others are depicted. One example is the narrator's repeated description of the leaders 'taking counsel (συμβούλιον λαμβάνειν)', primarily against Jesus.[2] Important in plot development, the narrator's use of this

1. 23.1 indicates Jesus is addressing the crowds and disciples. He speaks about the scribes and Pharisees. In 23.13, however, he shifts to speaking to the latter. A discussion of persecution recurs shortly after 23.34-36 in 24.9-13 when Jesus again warns the disciples of persecution preceding the end (10.17-19 = 24.9a, παραδώσουσιν ὑμᾶς; 10.22a = 24.9b, seven words in common; 10.22b = 24.13, seven words in common).

2. 12.14 = 22.15, six words in common; 12.14 = 27.1, five words in common; 12.14 = 27.7, three words in common; 12.14 = 28.12, two words in common; 22.15 = 27.1, three words in common; 22.15 = 27.7, three words in common; 22.15 = 28.12, two words in common; 27.1 = 27.7, three words in common ; 27.1 = 28.12, two words in common ; 27.1 = 27.7, three words in common; 27.1 =

phrase repeatedly and authoritatively characterizes the leaders as antagonists. They are crafty, deliberate, and intentional in their opposition to Jesus. They *plot* against Jesus. The first two instances are probably the most significant in this regard. In 12.14-15 the first clear indication of a plot against Jesus during his ministry occurs: 'And going out the Pharisees *took counsel* against him, so as him they might destroy. But Jesus knowing departed thence.'

The narrator reveals the Pharisees' plans initially only to the implied reader. Jesus, aligned with the narrator in important respects, shares this knowledge. The Pharisees *taking counsel* follows two episodes (12.1-8 and 12.9-13) in which they have been in conflict with Jesus over the Sabbath laws. Their defeat in the first with the injunction to learn the meaning of Hosea 6.6 and Jesus' veiled reference to the Son of Man as Lord of the Sabbath (12.8) leads them to pose the question of healing on the Sabbath in the second 'in order that they might accuse him' (12.10). Jesus bests them in legal interpretations for the second time. This is the context for their plotting in 12.14. The antagonism between Jesus and the Jewish leaders, especially the Pharisees, continues throughout ch. 12. It climaxes in a lengthy and vivid condemnation of the Pharisees as evil opponents who will be judged (12.25-37).

The next instance in which the Jewish leaders *take counsel* against Jesus has a similar context and echoes the first: 'Then going, the Pharisees took counsel so as him they might ensnare in a word' (22.15; 12.14 = 22.15, six words in common). Again the Pharisees are characterized as crafty opponents. Again their plotting occurs after Jesus has offended them—this time with three parables concerning their unworthiness and replacement by others.[1] Again they try to trap him with a legal question. They send their disciples and the Herodians

28.12, four words in common; 27.7 = 28.12, two words in common. The noun συμβούλιον is found elsewhere in the New Testament, according to Moulton-Geden, only in Mk 3.6, TWHmgR; 15.1, TWHmg; and in Acts 25.12.

1. 22.15 follows the parables of the two sons, the wicked tenants, and the wedding feast. The narrator indicates that the Pharisees and chief priests know that Jesus told the first two parables against them and sought to seize him, but feared the crowds (21.45-46). It is easy to see why, given the pointed applications of 21.31b 'Amen, I tell you, that the tax collectors and the harlots are going before you into the Kingdom of God' and 22.43 'Therefore I tell you that the Kingdom of God will be taken from you and given to a nation producing the fruits of it.'

to ask about the lawfulness of tribute to Caesar (22.16-17). Again the narrator indicates that Jesus (along with the implied reader) knows their motives, 'But Jesus, knowing their wickedness, said, "Why do you tempt me, hypocrites?"' (22.18). This episode is followed by episodes in which the Jewish leaders question Jesus about the resurrection of the dead and the greatest commandment. In the latter episode one of the Pharisees is again described as tempting (πειράζων, 22.35) Jesus. The plotting of the Jewish leaders and these conflicts lead to an extended condemnation, in this case the woes of ch. 23.

These repeated descriptions of the Jewish leaders *taking counsel* emphasize the continuing conflict between Jesus and the leaders. Repetition fixes the leaders as those who react to Jesus' superior knowledge of the law and condemnations, not with repentance and faith, but by consorting against him. Jesus' superiority is emphasized in both cases, since Jesus knows that they seek to trap him. The variations in the second case show a deepening opposition and widening gap between Jesus and the leaders. This prepares the implied reader for the leaders' final 'counsels' and deliverance of Jesus out of 'envy' (27.18).

The continued craftiness of the Jewish leaders in their plots against Jesus is also emphasized in the other occurrences of the phrase *taking counsel*. In 27.1 the chief priests and elders of the people (τοῦ λαοῦ)[1] take counsel 'against Jesus so as to put him to death', and deliver Jesus to Pilate so that an execution may occur. In 27.7 the chief priests and elders 'take counsel' in order to determine what to do with the blood money of Jesus' betrayer and buy the potter's field. In 28.12 the chief priests and elders again 'take counsel'. After hearing the story of those guarding the tomb, they bribe the soldiers to say that the disciples stole the body. This repetition shows that the Jewish leaders remain crafty, plotting enemies of Jesus even after his death.

One final instance portraying the Jewish leaders as counseling against Jesus must be mentioned. Although not an exact repetition of the phrase *take counsel*, the chief priests and the elders are described as counseling against Jesus in order to seize him by means of guile and kill him in 26.3-4. The verb συνεβουλεύσαντο, a counterpart to the phrase συμβούλιον λαμβάνειν, is used. This is the only time the

1. One should remember the distinction between 'the crowds (οἱ ὄχλοι)' and 'the people (ὁ λαὸς)'. The elders here officially represent the 'people' Israel.

verb appears in Matthew.[1] This *counseling* is the first action of the Jewish leaders following their abandonment of all attempts to question Jesus in 22.46. They decide not to seize Jesus during the Passover, lest a riot break out. However, they find the means to seize him when Judas offers his services as a betrayer in 26.14-16. Thus this instance of counseling precedes the final steps in the plotting of the 'wicked' leaders. Through repetition, the implied reader sees the final actions of the leaders which lead to the cross as characteristic of the actions they have taken from the beginning. Their character and motivation, emphasized by the repeated *taking counsel*, are consistent.

Tempting. A second example of the narrator's repeated description of the Jewish leaders' actions is the use of the word 'tempt or test' (πειράζω):

16.1 And approaching the Pharisees and Sadducees *tempting* asked him for a sign from the heaven to show to them.

19.3 And approached Pharisees to him *tempting* him and saying: '[If] Is it lawful to dismiss his wife for every cause?'

22.35 And questioned one of them [the Pharisees] a lawyer *tempting* him: 'Teacher, what commandment [is] great in the law?'

Even though these passages are linked verbally by at most only four words (16.1 = 19.3), the pattern is similar and the word *tempting*[2] is striking. It appears elsewhere in Matthew only in 22.18, where Jesus accuses the Pharisees and Herodians of tempting him, and in the temptation scene. There the narrator says that Jesus was led into the wilderness to be tempted by the devil (4.1) and the devil is labeled 'the tempting one' (4.3).

In each case where the Jewish leaders are involved, including 22.18, they have come to question Jesus. The use of the word 'tempting' by the narrator, or the closely aligned Jesus, indicates that the leaders

1. Moulton-Geden: found only here and in Jn 18.14; Acts 9.23; and Rev. 3.18 in the New Testament.

2. The translation of πειράζω as 'tempting' each time it appears highlights the links created by the repetition of the word. It also preserves the negative connotations associated with attempts to entrap Jesus. For a detailed discussion of πειράζω see *TDNT*, VI, pp. 23-36. There it is argued that πειράζω ought to be translated 'to tempt' in the temptation scene and 'to test' in the scenes involving the Jewish leaders because 'There can be no question of an attack by Satan in and with the words of the questioners' (p. 36). My point is that the use of the word does align them with Satan.

seek not an answer, but to entrap Jesus. In so doing they place themselves on the side of the devil or 'tempting one' (4.3) rather than on the side of God. The first case, 16.1, is part of the second sign of Jonah episode. In 12.38-42 the scribes and Pharisees make the first request for a sign. There Jesus says that only an evil and adulterous generation seeks signs. He adds that this evil generation will be like a man exorcized of one demon who ends up possessed by eight. They have been answered and warned once. Their second request is clearly identified as ill-motivated. They are *tempting* him.

In the last three cases, including 22.18, the leaders question Jesus concerning the law. This is appropriate since one of the main issues between them is the correct interpretation of the law (see e.g. 15.1-11). However, with the use of *tempting* it is clear that the leaders' questions are not properly motivated. The second case, 19.3, is particularly interesting in this regard. The Pharisees question Jesus concerning grounds for divorce. Jesus, however, had already stated his position on divorce in the Sermon on the Mount (5.32). This is an example of a frequent phenomenon discussed below, the Jewish leaders questioning or disputing with Jesus a legal teaching that he has already authoritatively decided. The same is true to a certain degree of 22.35. In answer to the question about the greatest commandment, Jesus speaks of love of God and love of neighbor. He had already emphasized love of neighbor in 5.43-47 and 19.19. The last two instances of *tempting*, 22.18 and 35, occur near the end of a section in which Jesus and the leaders engage in controversy with one another. This section precedes the stinging condemnations of the scribes and Pharisees in ch. 23. The repeated labels of ch. 23 and the repetitions of *tempting* lead the implied reader to recall earlier passages. They also reinforce one another. The Jewish leaders deserve these condemnations because they are hypocrites (23.13, 15, 23, 25, 27, 29) and blind guides (23.16, 24) who do not seek to learn the correct understanding of the law from Jesus, but rather repeatedly 'tempt' him as the devil earlier had done (4.1, 3). They test, as the *tempting one* did, his interpretation of the law (4.4, 6-7, 10).

Fear of the crowds. A third example of the repeated actions and words of the Jewish leaders involves both the narrator's repeated descriptions of the Jewish leaders' thoughts and motives (14.5 and 21.46) and their private verbal expression (21.26). The narrator provides the implied reader with a repeated unflattering inside view. The Jewish leaders repeatedly fear to take action because the crowds have John or Jesus as a prophet. The passages involved, 14.5, 21.26, and 21.46, are discussed above in the section on John the Baptist. It should be reiterated here that the Jewish leaders' reactions to John and the crowd in 14.5 and 21.26 foreshadow their reaction to Jesus (21.46). They are afraid to express their true opinion about John (21.26) and their desire to kill John and Jesus (14.5 and 21.46) for fear of the crowd. This repeated fear emphasizes not only their hypocrisy, but sets them over and against the crowds. The crowds are shown more positively because they at least see Jesus as a prophet; this even though the Jewish leaders sway them against Jesus in the end.

Teacher. A fourth example of the repeated speech of the Jewish leaders is their use of the title or label 'teacher'. This characterizes the Jewish leaders as Jesus' opponents. The only characters who address Jesus as teacher (διδάσκαλε) are members of the Jewish establishment.[1] These include a scribe in 8.19; scribes and Pharisees in 12.38; the rich young man in 19.16; the disciples of the Pharisees and the Herodians in 22.16; the Sadducees in 22.24; and the Pharisaic lawyer in 22.36 (see also 'your teacher' in 9.11 and 16.24b). The narrator, the disciples, those seeking healing, and some Gentiles call him Lord, Son of David, Son of God, or Christ.[2] The repeated use of solely the title teacher emphasizes the attitude of the Jewish leaders toward Jesus in contrast to the attitudes of other groups. In the first three instances, especially the first, their use of the label seems to indicate respect—although not faith or understanding. In the last three, they use the title as an outward form of respect while inwardly they seek to trap Jesus. In 22.15-16 the narrator warns that they seek to ensnare Jesus in a word. Jesus 'knows their wickedness', asks why they tempt him, and calls them hypocrites (22.18). In 22.23-28 the Sadducees pose an absurd hypothetical test case. In 22.34 the lawyer is described as 'tempting' Jesus as he poses his question. As the plot progresses and the antagonism between the Jewish leaders and Jesus increases, the

1. This is an example of the use of an epithet by unreliable characters. The implied reader would question it as a characterization of Jesus.

2. The Jewish leaders do call Jesus Son of God when questioning or mocking him in the passion, 26.63, 65; 27.40, 43. For a discussion of various character groups' use of the titles, see Kingsbury, *Matthew: Structure*, pp. 53-54 and 92-93.

implied reader sees the use of the label *teacher* as an indication of the Jewish leaders' hypocrisy and failure to understand Jesus' true identity.

Stealing the body. The final characterization of the Jewish leaders involving repeated words and actions occurs after Jesus' death. It involves their fear that the disciples will steal Jesus' body and their creation of such a rumor (27.64 = 27.66, three words in common; 27.64 = 28.13, five words in common). The progression appears as follows:

27.64 'Command therefore to be made fast the grave until the third day lest coming the disciples may steal him and may say to the people: "He was raised from the dead, and will be the last deceit worse [than] the first."'

27.66 And they going made fast the grave sealing the stone with the guard.

28.13 Saying: 'Say that the disciples of him by night coming stole him while we slept.'

28.15b And was spread about this saying by Jews until today.

The repetition shows that their character remains unchanged even by the resurrection. The last calumny of the Jewish leaders in the narrative is the rumor they inspire. The first passage depicts their fear. Naming Jesus 'the deceiver', they recall his prediction: 'After three days I am raised' (27.63). They request that Pilate post a guard and seal the tomb 'lest coming the disciples may steal him and may say to the people: "He was raised from the dead, and will be the last deceit words [than] the first'" (27.64). When the guards report to them following the resurrection, the leaders bribe the guards. They provide the guards with a story: 'Saying, Say that the disciples of him coming by night stole him while we slept' (28.13). This story echoes the fears they expressed to Pilate (27.64 = 28.13, five words in common). Even though their own devices, the guards and stone, would have prevented what they feared, they do not believe the truth. Not only are they unconvinced, they cause this lie to be spread among the Jews 'until today', the time of the implied author and implied reader.[1] The last words and actions of the Jewish leaders in the story connect them with evil in the day of the reader.

d. *Double Stories*

The double stories which characterize the Jewish leaders are the expanded doublet and phrase concerning Jesus exorcising by

1. See Chapter 2, page 63.

Beelzeboul, ruler of demons (9.32-34 = 12.22-27, sixteen words in common, related to 10.25) and the sign of Jonah (12.38-42 = 16.1-4, twenty-four words in common). Each doublet involves the repeated words and actions of both Jesus and the leaders. In each case there is not only repetition, but also variation in the second episode. From the point of view of the implied reader, each half of a doublet must be read in light of the other half, in prospect and retrospect. Variations between the stories and the changing contexts in which each story is found are also important. Both double stories will be discussed further in the next chapter.

Exorcising by Beelzeboul, the ruler of demons. The first double story involves two exorcisms of demoniacs (9.32-34 = 12.22-27). These episodes develop Jesus' conflict with the Pharisees and their struggle for the hearts of the crowd. The different reactions of the crowds and Pharisees to Jesus' exorcisms force the implied reader to compare and distinguish the two character groups. In the first episode Jesus exorcizes a dumb demoniac. The crowd marvels, 'Never was anything like this seen in Israel.' The Pharisees responded, 'He casts out demons by the ruler of demons.' This is the first time the Pharisees openly oppose Jesus.[1] With this open opposition a section of miracles and questions concerning Jesus' identity and activities is brought to a close. The Pharisees are characterized as not only misunderstanding, but also as opposing Jesus. If one assumes that the implied reader knows that Beelzeboul is the ruler of demons, the reader is reminded of the Pharisees' opposition in 10.25 when the disciples are warned using *qal wachomer* that if 'they' call the teacher Beelzeboul, how much more the disciples.[2] If the reader does not know that Beelzeboul is the ruler of demons, the meaning of the term becomes a puzzle. The puzzle will only be solved when the second half of the doublet (12.22-27) is read. There 'Beelzeboul' and 'the ruler of demons' are in apposition. This would draw even more attention to the doublet and the Pharisees'

1. Although in 9.3 the scribes claim he blasphemes and in 9.11 the Pharisees ask the disciples why he eats with tax collectors.

2. The exact historical meaning of the term is uncertain. See W.C. Allen, *A Critical and Exegetical Commentary on the Gospel According to St Matthew* (Edinburgh: T. & T. Clark, 3rd edn, 1977), pp. 107-108 and A.H. McNeile, *The Gospel According to St Matthew* (New York: Macmillan, 1915; reprint edn, Grand Rapids: Baker Book, 1980), pp. 143-44.

opposition. Although Jesus does not directly identify the 'they' who call the teacher Beelzeboul in 10.25, the allusion is clear; if not with reference to the first half of the doublet, then certainly in the light of the second. Other generalized descriptions of opponents in the missionary discourse of ch. 10 are specifically applied to the scribes and Pharisees elsewhere as well.

The characterization of the Jewish leaders as Jesus' opponents is developed further in the second demoniac exorcism found in 12.22-37. In ch. 12 the controversy between Jesus and the Pharisees again comes to a head. After two incidents of Sabbath breaking, the Pharisees plot Jesus' destruction (12.14). Jesus withdraws. The narrator indicates that this withdrawal fulfills Isa. 42.1-4. This prophecy echoes God's words in the baptism and foreshadows the transfiguration. The Pharisees plot against God's own son. They are contrasted to the Gentiles who have hope in the servant. Against this backdrop the demoniac incident recurs with several significant variations. This exorcism is even more miraculous than the first. The demoniac is blind as well as dumb. The crowd is not only amazed, but wonders if Jesus is the Son of David. They have grown in their openness and are willing to entertain the possibility.[1] The Pharisees, however, persist in their misunderstanding and opposition. The narrator reveals their private reaction. Uniting the phraseology of 9.34 and 10.25 they say, 'It is only by Beelzeboul, ruler of demons, that this man casts out demons.' This time, however, the episode is expanded. Instead of withdrawing Jesus explodes in a condemnation which gathers force by using many phrases from previous passages. The Pharisees have recognized neither the power of the Holy Spirit nor the dawn of the Kingdom of God. They are enemies who will not be forgiven (12.30-32).

The characterization of the Pharisees is carried forward by means of the second episode. This is the second time they have misread Jesus' authority as demonic. On the one hand, they are consistent in their opposition. On the other, considering the intervening opportunities to change, they are developing characters. Their opposition has increased (note also 12.14). The expansion of the second episode also moves

1. Even if J.D. Kingsbury is right in asserting that the *meti* anticipates a negative answer, 'The Verb *Akolouthein* ("To Follow") as an Index to Matthew's View of his Community', *JBL* 97 (1978), p. 61.

forward their characterization. Jesus, the most reliable character, charged twice with using demonic power, characterizes them with his condemnation. The implied reader is prepared for this, since it is the second such episode. In retrospect, the characterization of the Jewish leaders in the first episode is seen as apt since it foreshadowed their behavior in the second.

The sign of Jonah: Two requests for a sign. The second doublet which characterizes the Jewish leaders is their request for a sign (12.38-42 = 16.1-4, twenty-four words in common). The first request follows the second Beelzeboul episode and precedes Jesus' rejection of his mother and brothers. These three episodes form a climax to the rejection of Jesus' words and deeds prior to the parable discourse. In the first pericope some of the Pharisees and scribes answer Jesus' charges by saying: 'Teacher,[1] we wish to see a sign from you.' Jesus answers: 'An evil and adulterous generation seeks a sign; but no sign shall be given to it except the sign of Jonah the prophet.' He interprets the sign as the Son of Man being in the heart of the earth three days and three nights. He then says 'this generation' will be condemned in the judgment because they do not listen to a 'greater thing' than either Jonah or Solomon. He drives home his point with the story of the unclean spirit, illustrating what will happen to 'this evil generation' (12.39 and 12.45b form a sort of inclusio around Jesus' condemnation). Jesus' tirade is only brought to an end by the appearance of his family. Although this anger is specifically directed at the Pharisees, 12.46 indicates that the crowd has been present the whole time. In the second sign of Jonah pericope, the only audience present is the Pharisees and this time the Sadducees (see 15.36 and 16.5). Their request for a sign is specifically identified as an effort to *tempt* Jesus.[2] The Pharisees are becoming more perverse in the course of the narrative. Jesus' answer includes a reference to the ability of the Pharisees to read the signs of the sky, but not the signs of the times (16.3). There is no interpretation of the sign of Jonah. None is necessary. The implied reader already knows its meaning from the first pericope. The Pharisees have not learned a thing. They are portrayed as characters with no faith or understanding. They still seek a sign. The second episode also allows the implied reader to contrast their behavior with that of the

1. See the discussion of the Jewish leaders' use of this label on pp. 118-19.
2. See the discussion of *peirazo* on pp. 116-17.

Canaanite woman (15.21-28) and the crowds who marvel at Jesus' healing power and glorify Israel's god (15.29-32). These two episodes and the second feeding (15.32-39) precede it. It forms a bridge between the feeding of the four thousand and Jesus' warning to the disciples concerning the leaven of the Pharisees and Sadducees.

e. *Legal Interpretation and Challenge*

Another form of repetition which characterizes the Jewish leaders occurs when Jesus gives an authoritative interpretation of the law and the Jewish leaders question him about it later in the narrative. Jesus' authoritative interpretation occurs in direct discourse addressed to the implied reader as well as to characters in the narrative. The rhetorical effect is to portray Jesus as the true interpreter of the law and the Jewish leaders as false interpreters.

Divorce. The first example is Jesus' prohibition of divorce except for unchastity. In the Sermon on the Mount Jesus offers a series of antitheses contrasting what was said by the men of old with Jesus' stricter interpretation.[1] In 5.31-32 he cites requirement of a bill of divorce[2] and authoritatively forbids divorce except for unchastity (πορνείας). In 19.3-9, following the community discourse and Jesus' entrance into Judea, the Pharisees tempt him with a question concerning the grounds for divorce. They refer to the passage he had mentioned in 5.31 asking, 'Why then did Moses command [us] to give a bill of divorce and to dismiss?' (5.31 = 19.7, three words in common). Jesus replies that Moses allowed this because of their hardness of heart. He then repeats the authoritative interpretation (or command) of 5.32 with very slight variation (19.9 = 5.32, twelve words in common).[3] This provides the occasion for the disciples' question concerning marriage and Jesus' teaching on celibacy.

Through the repetitions of the requirement of a bill of divorce and Jesus' authoritative teaching on the grounds for divorce the Jewish leaders are characterized as representing the old order and false

1. Here Barth's interpretation is followed, 'Matthew's Understanding of the Law', *Tradition*, pp. 93-95.

2. The phrase is reminiscent of Deut. 24.1-3. See McNeile, *St Matthew*, p. 66 and Allen, *St Matthew*, pp. 51-52.

3. The exact parallel is nine words, but there are three additional words shared in the final clauses with different senses.

interpretation of God's will. In the first passage Jesus speaks to the disciples and crowds. In the second he is in dialogue with the Pharisees. Having read the first, the implied reader already knows the answer to the legal question the Pharisees pose in order to 'tempt' Jesus in 19.3. After Jesus cites Genesis, the implied reader can even anticipate the Pharisees' parry since he or she already read that 'it was said' there should be a bill of divorce. When they do cite Deut. 24.1-3, they fulfill the implied reader's expectation that they represent the old order and a false interpretation of the law opposed to that of Jesus. Because they question Jesus only to tempt him, the implied reader knows they do not really seek Jesus' authoritative interpretation, an interpretation he or she already possesses. This places the implied reader in a superior position aligned with Jesus over against the Pharisees. In addition, in the second passage Jesus offers a reason for Moses' permission for divorce: 'Moses in view of your hardness of heart allowed you to dismiss your wives; but it has not been so from the beginning' (19.8). What the Pharisees have viewed as a commandment was only a concession to hard-heartedness.[1]

The greatest commandment. The Pharisees also 'tempt' Jesus with a legal question in 22.34-40. There a Pharisaic lawyer addressing Jesus as 'Teacher', asks which is the greatest commandment (22.35). Jesus responds that love of God (Deut. 6.5) is the greatest commandment and love of neighbor (Lev. 19.18) the second (22.37-39). Jesus has already directly referred to the second in answer to the rich young man in 19.19 (and indirectly in 5.43; 19.19 = 22.39, six words in common, 'You shall love your neighbor as yourself' and 5.34b = 19.19 = 22.39, four words in common, 'You shall love your neighbor').[2]

1. It is difficult to tell whether the 'your' and 'you' is meant to apply to the Jewish leaders alone or as representatives of the hardhearted among Israel, or to the people (ὁ λαὸς) as a whole.

2. In the Sermon on the Mount Jesus tells the crowds and disciples, 'You have heard it was said: You shall love your neighbor and hate your enemy. But I tell you: Love your enemies and pray for those who persecute you' (5.43-44). 5.43b is found no where in the Tanach or the rabbinic materials. W.D. Davies suggests a possible Essene origin (*Setting*, pp. 245-48). 5.43 suggests an interpretation of Lev. 19.18 which extends the commandment to love the members of the community to hatred of enemies. Jesus insists that the interpretation be radicalized in the opposite direction, love of enemies and the perfection of the heavenly Father (5.44-48). It is not clear

In 19.16 the rich young man, also addressing Jesus as Teacher, asks what he must do to inherit eternal life. Jesus tells him to keep the commandments. The young man asks, which ones? Jesus answers with four of the ten words plus Lev. 19.18, giving it a high level of importance. The young man says he has kept all these commandments and asks what he still lacks. Jesus replies, 'If you wish to be perfect, go sell your belongings and give to the poor, and you shall have treasure in heaven, and come follow me.' The young man fails to accept this invitation to discipleship because he has many possessions. This episode (19.16-22) occurs after Jesus has entered Judea (19.1-2). It is separated from the controversy with the Pharisees about divorce and the teaching about celibacy (19.3-12) only by Jesus' blessing the children in 19.13-15. It is followed by a section in which Jesus teaches the disciples about the difficulty of the rich entering heaven and the rewards of sacrificial discipleship (19.23-30). The disciples will judge the twelve tribes of Israel and inherit eternal life as the rich young man will not.

The Pharisee's question concerning the greatest commandment (22.34-40) occurs after Jesus has entered Jerusalem (21.1-11). It is the third and final episode in a series of confrontations between the Jewish leaders and Jesus in which they attempt to entrap him.[1] It immediately precedes Jesus' question concerning the Christ and the Son of David which leaves them speechless and unable to question him any more and the condemnation of the scribes and Pharisees in ch. 23.

The repetition of Lev. 19.18, the command to love the neighbor, probably reflects more about the thematic concerns of Jesus' teaching than the characterization of the Jewish leaders. However, in both episodes members of the Jewish establishment ask about the heart of the law. In both cases they call Jesus, 'Teacher'. In the first case the rich young man says he has obeyed the commandments including love of neighbor, but refuses to give his wealth to the poor and follow Jesus. In the second case the Pharisees have no response to Jesus' summary of the law. They are silenced by the question Jesus asks them. In neither case are they ready to accept Jesus' authoritative interpretation of the law.

how 5.43 is related to 19.19 or 22.39 in terms of characterization of the Jewish leaders.

1. The first two are the tribute to Caesar (22.16-22) and the Sadducees' question about resurrection (22.23-33).

f. *Repetition of the Words of Another Character*
Ironic repetition of Peter's confession. The last form of characterization of the Jewish leaders is their repetition of the words of another character.[1] The passages in question, Peter's confession (16.17) and the high priest's question (26.64), have already been discussed in an earlier section of this chapter. The important thing to remember here is the dramatic irony created by the repetition. The high priest's question used to condemn Jesus for blasphemy is ironically the closest the Jewish leaders ever come to the truth about Jesus' identity. It contains the same words for which Peter earlier was blessed. The repetition characterizes the Jewish leaders as blind, mortal enemies of the Christ, the Son of the Living God.

5. *Conclusion*

This chapter has explored characterization and the ways in which repetition contributes to the characterization of John the Baptist, Peter and the Jewish leaders. This exploration has revealed several recurring types of characterizing repetition. For the most part these categories are drawn from the typical means of characterization outlined in the introduction. They include labels or epithets; actions of a character, depicted or described by the narrator or a reliable character; dialogue of a single character (independent of labels or double stories); dialogue of one character repeated by another; and double stories. The actions and dialogue treated in separate categories are those which are independent of double stories. Of necessity, double stories contain repeated dialogue and actions. They constitute a unique category, however, because they are repetitions of a whole episode or scene. A review of the recurring types listed above and some of their functions will conclude this chapter.

a. *Labels or Epithets*
Labels or epithets characterize John the Baptist, Simon Peter, and the Jewish leaders. John is called 'the Baptist' by the narrator. Simon Peter is called Peter or 'Rock' by the narrator and Jesus. The Jewish

1. Other repetitions involving the Jewish leaders which do not seem to have primary significance for their characterization include 9.14-15 = 15.1-3, ten words in common and 15.4 = 19.19, six words in common.

leaders are called 'Brood of Vipers' by John and Jesus and 'Hypocrites' and 'Blind Guides' by Jesus. Labels also characterize other actors in the Gospel. Jesus calls the disciples 'Little-faiths' in 6.30, 8.26, 14.31 and 16.8 (cf. also the related 'of little faith' in 17.20). The narrator identifies Judas as the Iscariot in 10.4 and 26.14 and as 'the betraying one' in 10.4, 26.25, 26.46, 26.48 and 27.3. The narrator and various characters use christological titles.

When the narrator or a reliable character repeatedly uses a label or epithet an important aspect of a character or character group is economically identified, highlighted, and fixed in the mind of the implied reader.[1] Paradoxically, repeated labels make the work of the reader easier and more difficult. On the one hand, a repeated label performs a limiting function. It helps to distinguish characters, especially two with the same name, such as John the Baptist and John the son of Zebedee. It may also capture in a word or phrase the essence of a character and his or her role in the narrative. Judas is 'the betraying one'. The Jewish leaders are a 'brood of vipers'. The more times a label is associated with a character the more predictable it becomes. The characterization is not only reinforced, the implied reader also expects and accepts the identification.[2] On the other hand, repeated labels appear in different contexts as the narrative proceeds. The implied reader must react to the resonances and echoes the use of the label creates in different contexts, sometimes on the lips of different characters or the narrator and a character. This is especially true of highly metaphoric labels. The reader not only must decide, for example, what it means for Simon to be called 'Rock' or the Jewish leaders 'Blind Guides', but also react to the labels as they appear in different contexts in the course of the narrative.

Thus the scene in which Jesus gives Simon the name Peter in ch. 16 sheds light on earlier and later repetitions of the name. So, too, Jesus' non-specific use of the label 'Hypocrites' early in the narrative

1. As Wellek and Warren note in *Theory of Literature*, p. 219. 'The simplest form of characterization is naming. Each "appellation" is a blend of verifying, animizing, individuating.' They also suggest that labeling—whether with an introductory label or a mannerism, gesture or saying such as Dickens' Mrs Gummidge 'always thinking of the old un'; or with a symbol such as Zenobia's red flower—is an economical means of characterization.

2. For a discussion of predictability and persuasion see the section on the communication model in Chapter 1.

prepares the reader for its application to the Jewish leaders. It also prepares the reader for the characterization it embodies. When it is applied to the Jewish leaders earlier uses are also seen from a new perspective. The three contexts in which Jesus uses the epithet 'Blind Guides' (15.14; 23.16; 23.24) illumine the epithet and vice versa. In each context the Jewish leaders' treatment of the law is at issue. 'Blind Guides' captures Jesus' characterization of the Jewish leaders as false interpreters of the law. The repetition reinforces the characterization, but also creates links between the various situations causing the reader to associate one with the other.

Finally, the repeated use of a label or title by unreliable characters should be noted. When only members of the Jewish establishment call Jesus 'Teacher'—and they do so repeatedly—the implied reader learns more about their failure to truly understand Jesus' identity than about Jesus. As the narrative progresses the label, originally a respectful title, becomes an indication of their hypocrisy.

b. *Repeated Actions of a Character, Depicted or Described by the Narrator or a Reliable Character*

In many cases the repeated actions of a character underscored by verbal repetition serve the same functions as those of a repeated label employed by the narrator or a reliable character. The repeated action establishes and highlights something that is typical of a character. Peter is the spokesman for the disciples. This is underlined by the repeated phrase, 'And (then) answering (him) Peter said...' The Jewish leaders are repeatedly described as 'taking counsel'. The behavior of Peter and the leaders becomes predictable. The contexts and the temporal dimension of narrative are also important. For example, the continuing and deepening opposition of the Jewish leaders is emphasized by the repeated descriptions of them as 'taking counsel' and 'tempting' in various contexts as the narrative progresses.

c. *Repeated Dialogue of a Character Independent of Labels or Double Stories*

Most of the repeated dialogue of a single character in Matthew occurs on the lips of Jesus. Other characters rarely repeat their own speeches except in double stories. This is not surprising since Jesus has by far the greatest percentage of dialogue. Some of this dialogue consists of favorite expressions such as, 'The one having ears, let him hear'

(11.15 = 13.9 = 13.43) or 'There will be the weeping and the gnashing of teeth' (8.12 = 13.42, 50 = 22.13 = 24.51 = 25.30). Some takes the form of inclusio, setting off a unit of teaching, such as, 'You shall know them by their fruits' (7.16 = 7.20) or 'The first shall be last and the last shall be first' (19.30 = 20.16). Other examples are repeated predictions like the passion–resurrection predictions and repeated sections of teaching. Examples of the latter are the teaching on divorce (5.31-32 = 19.3-9, fifteen words in common) and that concerning parts of the body which cause one to sin (5.29-30 = 18.8-9, thirty words in common). Jesus' repeated words characterize him in the sense that they establish consistent speech patterns and values. However, given the role Jesus plays in the Gospel's rhetoric described in Chapter 2—a reliable protagonist whose point of view is aligned closely with the narrator's in important ways—the repetition of Jesus' words often has other functions as well. It may characterize other actors, further the plot, or develop themes. This is true of words addressed repeatedly to the same audience or first to one, and then another audience.

In this chapter there are a number of examples of repeated words of Jesus which characterize another character. Peter is characterized as a prototypical disciple when Jesus grants the power to bind and loose that he first granted to Peter to the other disciples (16.19b = 18.18-19, nineteen words in common). In ch. 16 Peter's misunderstanding is revealed when Jesus rebukes him with the same phrase he had earlier used in addressing the tempter, 'Go [behind me] Satan' (4.10 = 16.23). The earlier context in which the phrase appeared colors the implied reader's view of Peter and Peter's refusal to accept Jesus' passion prediction in 16.21-22. Another example is Jesus' use of the quotation from Hos. 6.6, 'Mercy I desire and not sacrifice' (9.13 = 12.7). In both contexts in which it appears the Jewish leaders question Jesus' behavior based on their interpretation of the law. The repetition of the quote establishes the failure of the Jewish leaders truly to understand the law or Jesus' authority. A slight variation in Jesus' introduction of the quote, 'But going learn what it is:...' (9.13) versus 'But if you had known what it is:...' (12.7), indicates their failure to change in the course of the narrative. The last two examples show how context, slight variations, and the temporal dimension of narrative come into play in this type of character repetition. These factors can also be seen in those cases where Jesus describes evil persons in general and repeats the words when applying them to the Jewish leaders later in the narrative. The passages involved include those where the epithet hypocrites appears, and the descriptions of those who do their piety 'in order to be seen by men' (6.1-2 = 23.5-7, ten words in common), and those who persecute God's messenger (10.17, 23 = 23.34, 36, seven words in common). Repetition of a phrase which characterizes a single character or group has a persuasive power since it establishes something as typical. Here the initial instances lead the implied reader to seek the identity of those described as he or she reads. They prepare the implied reader for the negative characterization of the Jewish leaders when Jesus repeats the phrase.

d. *Dialogue of One Character Repeated by Another*

In this chapter the overwhelming majority of repetitions of the words of one character by another are repetitions of John's words by Jesus. In fact a high proportion of the words spoken by John in 3.1-12 are repeated by Jesus later in the narrative. Jesus proclaims 'Repent for the Kingdom of Heaven has come near' and tells his disciples to do the same (3.2 = 4.17, nine words in common = 10.7, seven words in common). He calls the Jewish leaders a 'Brood of Vipers' (3.7 = 12.34 = 23.33); speaks of the need to produce good fruit (3.8, 10 = 7.16-20 = 12.33-35; 3.10b = 7.19, eleven words in common), and uses eschatological harvest imagery (3.10 = 13.42a, 50, three words in common; 3.12 = 13.30, seven words in common). Other repeated words include the echoes of Peter's confession, 'You are the Christ, the Son of the living God' in the high priest's command, 'I adjure you by the living God, that you tell us if you are the Christ, the Son of God' (16.17 = 26.63, ten words in common); those of the tempter and the mocking passersby at the cross, 'If you are the Son of God' (4.3 = 4.6 = 27.40, five words in common); and the angel's repetition of Jesus' prediction that he would be raised and go before the disciples into Galilee (26.32 = 28.7, six words in common).

In terms of characterization these repetitions create a link between the characters involved. Some characterize one character by revealing similarities to another, such as Jesus' similarities to John or the mocking passersby to the tempter. Some reinforce characters' reliability. This is the case with the repetitions linking the words of John and Jesus and those of the angel and Jesus. In terms of point of view, when one character's words are repeated as another character's own words and not as a quotation, the characters' points of view are partially aligned on the phraseological plane. In Matthew, this often indicates that two characters share, at least partially, an ideological point of view as well. Thus Jesus and John share very similar ideological perspectives on the Jewish leaders, for example. As with the repeated dialogue of a single character, dialogue repeated by a different character can increase predictability. However, the variation of a different speaker and other variations in context are very important. Thus when Jesus preaches the same message as John, it is not surprising to find him telling the disciples to do the same. The same is true of the three passages concerning fruits. When first John and then Jesus speak of producing fruit, the third appearance on the lips of Jesus is not surprising. In the first case *John* warns the *Jewish leaders* of the need to produce good fruits. In the second Jesus speaks of knowing true from false prophets by means of their fruits (7.15-20) without a specific application. In the third case the imagery is again applied to *the Jewish leaders*; this time by *Jesus*. The first two instances prepare the implied reader for the climactic application by Jesus to the Jewish leaders. These two examples illustrate how this type of repetition can create expectations. In some cases, however, the repetition of dialogue by a different character can create surprise or dramatic irony. The variation of speaker and context are extremely important. When the words of Peter's confession of Jesus as 'the Christ, the Son of the Living God' are echoed in the high priest's question at Jesus' trial dramatic irony is created. The words of confession for which Jesus blessed Peter become an anti-confession on the lips of the high priest. The high priest is characterized as one who rejects Jesus, not realizing that the true answer to his question is yes. Peter also is characterized as flawed. The anti-confession echoing Peter's original confession occurs as part of the trial, an episode intercalated into the story of Peter's denial of Jesus. The high priest's words help the implied reader to recall Peter's earlier bold confession and contrast it with his present behavior.

e. *Double Stories*

Double and triple stories are an important form of verbal repetition in Matthew. These episodes contain both repeated words and actions. Some are almost exact duplicates. Others are repeated with a greater degree of variation. Several involve a doublet which is an expanded version of an earlier story. All contribute greatly to characterization and the development of plot. They are treated as a group in greater detail in the next chapter. In this chapter three double stories were discussed: Peter walking on the water, an expanded doublet of the stilling of the storm (8.23-27 = 14.22-33, seventeen words in common); the expanded doublet and phrase concerning exorcism by the power of Beezeboul, ruler of demons (9.32-34 = 12.22-27, twenty-two words in common, related to 10.25); and the sign of Jonah (12.38-42 = 16.1-4, twenty-four words in common). These double stories characterize both Jesus and the other characters who appear. As with the other types of characterizing repetition, double stories can establish, emphasize, and highlight character traits. They can also create expectations. If a character or group behaves the same way in the same situation twice, the implied reader expects that this behavior is typical. As with the other types of repetition as well, the differences or variations between similar stories and the point at which repetitions appear in the narrative are important. The sign of Jonah episodes, for example, characterize the Jewish leaders as lacking faith and understanding. But the repetition of the episode does more than underscore this characterization. The Jewish leaders' second request shows they learned nothing from Jesus' reply to their first request or from the episodes which occur in the interlude between the two. Variations between the episodes are also important. In the second episode Jesus does not spell out again for the Jewish leaders the meaning of the sign which they failed to understand. Further, they are described as *tempting* Jesus when they ask for a sign. The location of this slight variation shortly before the first prediction of Jesus' passion at the hands of the Jewish leaders (16.21) gives it added significance. The characterization developed by the repetition with variation of the request for a sign helps the reader to understand the nature and motivation of the leaders and their actions.

Although double stories have many of the same functions as other types of characterizing repetition, they are lengthier than most. They are unique in that they are repeated *episodes* containing dialogue and action. They may contain several of the types of characterizing repetition already discussed. The fact that whole episodes are involved may account for the significant contributions they make to the development of both character and plot.

Chapter 4

Plot

1. *Introduction*

This chapter will focus on the role of verbal repetition in shaping the plot of the Gospel.[1] Before discussing various devices involving repetition, several previous structural proposals will be examined. Literary terms associated with plot will be defined and a general overview of the Matthean plot offered. The devices to be examined include (1) summary passages, (2) anticipation and retrospection, (3) the Johannine sub-plot and (4) double and triple stories. Since there are so many, not all repetitions involved in the plot will be discussed. A representative sample will be offered.

1. For subsequent discussions of plot in Matthew see Kingsbury, *Story*, pp. 2-9 and 'The Plot of Matthew's Story', *Int* 46 (1992), pp. 347-56; M.A. Powell, 'The Plot and Subplots of Matthew's Gospel', *NTS* 38 (1992), pp. 187-204; F.J Matera, 'The Plot of Matthew's Gospel', *CBQ* 49 (1987), pp. 233-53; and Howell, *Matthew's Inclusive Story*, pp. 93-160. Powell offers an analysis of Kingsbury's and Matera's views on plot as well as the concept of plot implied by Edwards's reader-response analysis of Matthew in *Matthew's Story of Jesus*. He makes a very helpful distinction between a concentration on narrative flow, causality, and conflict which he ascribes to Edwards, Matera, and Kingsbury respectively. While appreciating their contributions, Powell also argues against the overall descriptions of the Matthean plot by Matera and Kingsbury. Against Matera, Powell argues that Matthew is not essentially a story about God fulfilling God's promises to Israel, Israel rejecting the Messiah, and the promises passing to the Gentiles. He also disagrees with Kingsbury who emphasizes Jesus' conflicts with the religious leaders and the disciples, and describes Matthew as the intertwining of three story lines: the story of Jesus, the story of the religious leaders, and the story of the disciples. Instead, Powell argues that Matthew has a main plot and several subplots. The main plot centers on God's plan to save to save God's people from their sins and Satan's challenge to this plan. Two subplots concern (a) the conflict between Jesus and the religious leaders and (b) the conflict between Jesus and the disciples.

2. *Previous Outlines*

Many scholars have sought to describe the design of the Gospel of Matthew.[1] Most of the proposed outlines have focused on structure rather than plot. Plot involves the temporal arrangement of the episodes of a story, the motivation for events, and the pragmatic effects of arrangement and motivation upon the reader. Structure emphasizes other ordering principles. Structural outlines of Matthew have been based on criteria such as geography, the distinction between narrative and sermon (discourse, speech), formulas, topic or theme, view of salvation history, and analogy to other works (the Torah, Tanach, Mark, etc.). Topical outlines which divide the Gospel into sections according to perceived changes in subject matter have come the closest to a concentration on plot. The most influential structural outline of the Gospel is that of B.W. Bacon.

a. *B.W. Bacon*

B.W. Bacon proposed the following outline of the Gospel of Matthew:

Preamble or Prologue		1–2. The birth narrative
Book I:	(a) 3.1–4.25	Narrative material
	(b) 5.1–7.27	The Sermon on the Mount
	Formula: 7.28-39	'And when Jesus finished these words...'
Book II:	(a) 8.1–9.35	Narrative material
	(b) 9.36–10.42	Discourse on mission and martyrdom
	Formula: 11.1	'And when Jesus had finished instructing his twelve disciples...'
Book III:	(a) 11.2–12.50	Narrative and debate material
	(b) 13.1-52	Teaching on the Kingdom of Heaven
	Formula: 13.53	'And when Jesus had finished these parables...'

1. Kingsbury, *Matthew: Structure*, p. 107, has a good discussion of various structural proposals. He divides them into two categories (*apropos* of his own proposal), topical and salvation historical outlines. He then offers his own proposal, pp. 7-25. See also B.M. Nolan, *The Royal Son of God* (Gottingen: Vandenhoeck & Ruprecht, 1979), p. 98 and n. 1; The most recent and comprehensive study of Matthean structure is D.R. Bauer, *The Structure of Matthew's Gospel: A Study in Literary Design* (BLS, 15; JSOTSup, 31; Sheffield: Almond Press, 1988). Luz (*Matthew 1–7*, pp. 33-46) also has a recent, helpful consideration of structure and genre. Although he considers sources, he also speaks of Matthew as a narrative 'intended to be read from beginning to end' (p. 43). He argues that Matthew was based on the Markan narrative model.

Book IV:	(a) 13.54–17.21	Narrative and debate material
	(b) 17.22–18.35	Discourse on church administration
	Formula: 19.1	'And when Jesus finished these words...'
Book V:	(a) 19.2–22.46	Narrative and debate material
	(b) 23.1–25.46	Discourse on eschatology: farewell address
	Formula: 26.1	'And when Jesus had finished all these words...'
Epilogue:	26.3–28.20	From the Last Supper to the Resurrection[1]

Three primary factors determine Bacon's outline. The first factor is the transitional formulas which end each of the five major discourses—7.38; 11.1; 13.53; 19.1 and 26.1. The second is an analogy with the Torah and other five-book works. The third is division into narrative and discourse, a section of each per 'book'. Various historical and theological inferences have been drawn from this outline.[2]

Scholars have offered major criticisms of Bacon's proposal.[3] One critique questions the weight placed on the formulas as a structural criterion.[4] Perhaps they are merely transitional or liturgical formulas. Another faults the analogy to the Torah because each book of the Torah does not begin with narrative and end with discourse. Related critiques are that there are more than five major discourses in Matthew (if one includes chs. 11 or 23, 3.8-12 and/or 28.16-20); the New Moses typology does not seem as prominent in Matthew as Bacon's outline suggests; and content parallels between Matthew's and the Torah's books are lacking. For example, the birth story would correspond better with Genesis and the Sermon on the Mount with Exodus. A fifth critique questions the division within each of Bacon's 'books' into narrative and discourse. There is more discourse in Bacon's narrative sections than his outline suggests. These criticisms attack either Bacon's criteria or his application of them. A final critique brings in different criteria. It questions the designation of the birth story and passion–resurrection narratives as prologue and epilogue because of the importance of their contents to the plot of the

1. Bacon's outline as presented in Thompson, *Matthew's Advice*, pp. 14-15.

2. Thompson, *Matthew's Advice*, pp. 2-4.

3. In this section I follow Kingsbury, *Matthew: Structure*, pp. 4-5 and Davies, *Setting*, who offers a good discussion of the Bacon hypothesis and alternatives, pp. 14-25.

4. Davies, *Setting*, pp. 17-18 and Kingsbury, *Matthew: Structure*, p. 5.

Gospel and early Christian preaching.[1] It seems especially strange to place the climax of the Gospel outside its main structure.

b. *J.D. Kingsbury*

A second structural outline given prominence in recent years is that of Jack Dean Kingsbury in *Matthew: Structure, Christology, Kingdom.* He divides the Gospel into three principal sections: (1) The Person of Jesus Messiah (1.1–4.16); (2) The Proclamation of Jesus Messiah (4.17–16.20); and (3) The Suffering, Death, and Resurrection of Jesus Messiah (16.21–28.20).[2] Kingsbury bases his argument in broad terms on topical and salvation-historical criteria.

He relies on 1.1, 4.17, and 16.21 as literary and thematic dividing points. They are superscriptions for and describe the contents of each section of the Gospel. In terms of salvation history, Kingsbury sees Matthew's vision as including two epochs, 'the Time of Israel (Old Testament)' and 'the Time of Jesus (Messiah)'.[3] He bases this on his interpretation of 3.1's, 'In those days...', as an eschatological phrase initiating the public manifestation of the time of messianic fulfillment begun with Jesus' birth; Matthew's 'theological affinity' for the categories of prophecy and fulfillment evidenced by the fulfillment quotations;[4] and the fact that the time of the church is a part of the time of Jesus. The latter, he argues, is evidenced by a lack of distinction between the earthly and exalted Jesus, the portrait of the disciples as representative church members, and a lack of textual indications of a separate epoch.[5] The Christology of Matthew (the time of Jesus) is the 'controlling element' in Matthew's concept of salvation history. Kingsbury argues that this view of salvation history as christologically centered, combined with the christologically centered topical outline, shows that it is primarily Matthew's Christology that has shaped the Gospel.

Kingsbury's arguments generally have been well-received.[6]

1. Davies finds the importance of the death and resurrection in early Christian preaching most telling (*Setting*, p. 25).

2. Kingsbury, *Matthew: Structure*, pp. 7-25.

3. Kingsbury, *Matthew: Structure*, p. 31.

4. Kingsbury, *Matthew: Structure*, p. 31.

5. Kingsbury, *Matthew: Structure*, pp. 32-34.

6. Favorable review articles include F.W. Danker, 'Review of *Matthew: Structure, Christology, Kingdom* by Jack D. Kingsbury', *Dialog* 16 (1977), pp. 64-

However, as with Bacon, Kingsbury can be criticized for his choice and application of criteria. Why should the phrase, 'From then Jesus began...' in 4.17 and 16.21 receive a greater weight than the transitional formulas at the end of the discourses? Are there not greater connections between the three major sections, 1.1-4.16, 4.17-16.20, and 16.21-28.20 than this division allows? M.D. Goulder has raised these points rather caustically:

> the formulas at 4.17 and 16.21 do not operate like 'Chapter Two' [as is obvious from the ease with which he is able to override Bacon's formulas]. Matthew is much less of a compartmentalizer than a modern author. There is something fantastic about a division of his Gospel into three which puts 'You are Peter, and upon this rock...' in Part II, and 'You are a stumbling-stone to me' five verses later, in Part III. There are several miracles and a lot of public teaching (e.g., Chapter 23) in Part III.[1]

Another criticism arises from Kingsbury's creation of conflicting structural and salvation-historical outlines. Why should 3.1 serve as a major division in one and not the other? What criteria are primary for what purposes? In the salvation-historical outline Kingsbury argues that 3.1 marks a dividing point from what has gone before. Yet he links 3.1-4.16 with what has gone before in the structural outline by means of the 'structural sign' of the particle δε.[2] δε, of course, can indicate stronger or weaker transitions depending on the context. J.P. Meier argues against Kingsbury's interpretation saying that the 'nature of the transition intended must be judged from the context and not the context from a very pliable *de*'.[3] He feels that the shift in time and the introduction of a totally new figure along with the formula beginning of 3.1 'forbid a close connection with chapters 1–2 as a part of one uniform section called a prologue'.[4]

It should be said in Kingsbury's defense that the divisions at 4.17 and 16.21 do mark turning points in the plot, if not major structural

75; F.H. Borsck, 'Matthew's Intricate Fabric', *Int* 31 (1977), pp. 73-76; D.R.A. Hare, 'Review of *Matthew*... Kingsbury', *JBL* 96 (1977), pp. 307-308; and R.E. Brown, 'Review of *Matthew*... Kingsbury', *USQR* 31 (1976), pp. 299-300.

1. 'Review of *Matthew: Structure, Christology, Kingdom* by J.D. Kingsbury', *JTS* 28 (1977), p. 145.

2. Kingsbury, *Matthew: Structure*, p. 13.

3. 'Review of *Matthew: Structure, Christology, Kingdom* by J.D. Kingsbury', for the CBA Task Force on Matthew, unpublished paper, pp. 11-12.

4. Meier, 'Review', p. 12.

divisions. One might consider all prior to 4.17 as the exposition.[1] It is also true that 16.21 is the first detailed anticipation of the passion and resurrection, which together form the climax and dénouement of the plot. Yet this defense raises the issue of plot and other structural devices. Kingsbury's divisions are based on *one* repeated formula and a topical-theological outline that only hints at plot. Are there other structural markers that should also be considered? Are there things about the Gospel's structure which might be revealed by a literary analysis in terms of plot?

c. *C.H. Lohr*

A third structural proposal is that of C.H. Lohr:[2]

Chapters	Section
1–4	Narrative: Birth and Beginnings
5–7	Sermon: BLESSINGS, ENTERING KINGDOM
8–9	Narrative: Authority and Invitation
10	Sermon: MISSION DISCOURSE
11–12	Narrative: Rejection of this generation
13	Sermon: PARABLES OF THE KINGDOM
14–17	Narrative: Acknowledgement of disciples
18	Sermon: COMMUNITY DISCOURSE
19–22	Narrative: Authority and invitation
23–25	Sermon: WOES, COMING OF KINGDOM
26–28	Narrative: Death and rebirth

This proposal views Matthew as a giant chiasm. It relies on concentric repetition, theme, and division into narrative and sermon as structural criteria. Lohr argues that the Sermon on the Mount focusing on blessings and entering the kingdom corresponds to the woes against the scribes and Pharisees and apocalyptic discourse, considered as one sermon focusing on the woes and the coming of the kingdom. The mission discourse and the community discourse, both directed to the disciples, correspond. Chapter 13, the parable discourse, concerning the nature of the kingdom, is the center and high point of the Gospel.

1. Although the entrance of the adult Jesus in 3.13 marks the end of the opening narrative frame as described above on pp. 67-68.

2. 'Oral Techniques in the Gospel of Matthew', *CBQ* 23 (1974), pp. 424-34. A modified form of Lohr's outline appears in P.F. Ellis, *Matthew: His Mind and Message* (Collegeville, MN: Liturgical Press, 1974), pp. 10-13. J.D. Fenton, *The Gospel of Matthew* (Pelican Gospel Commentaries; Harmondsworth: Penguin Books, 1963), pp. 16-17 also suggests a chiastic arrangement.

The birth corresponds to the resurrection (rebirth), the baptism to the crucifixion, the triple temptation to the 'triple agony' in the garden, etc. Lohr also provides charts to show the 'interlocking echoes' between (a) chs. 8–9 and 19–22, and (b) chs. 11–12 and 14–17. For example:

7.28	22.33	'The crowds were astounded at his teaching.' This formula is a modification of Mk 11.18b, but Matthew has changed the context in the latter place, and simply inserted it in the former.
11.5	15.31	'The blind see and the lame walk.' The former is parallel to Lk. 7.22; the latter to Mk 7.37, except that Matthew has adapted his source so that it resembles the former passage more closely.[1]

Lohr indicates the advantages of his outline as (a) it shows the attempts to find five books, each containing one sermon and one narrative, false because there are always six narratives; (b) 'it provides a solution to the problem of the motive of Matthew's rearrangements of Markan and other materials in 4.23 to 13.58'; and (c) 'an understanding of this structure supplies us with a key to the meaning of the Gospel as the Evangelist himself saw it.'[2] Lohr's arrangement does avoid the most frequently cited criticism of Bacon—the reduction of the birth and passion-resurrection narratives to dispensable prologue and epilogue. This is why he ends up with six rather than five narratives.[3] Although Lohr's claim to have found a key to the meaning of the Gospel 'as the Evangelist himself saw it' is naive, his approach has an important virtue. He uses the recurrence of phrase and topoi as criteria for developing his concentric arrangements. This is a virtue because the criteria are not limited to a few verses nor are they external to the text. There is no doubt that they exist in the text as well as in the reader.

However, like Bacon and Kingsbury, Lohr can be criticized either on the basis of his choice of criteria or his application of them. In terms of application, one of the same criticisms applied to Bacon's proposal applies to Lohr's. Can the Gospel be so neatly divided into narrative and discourses? Lohr combines ch. 23 with 24 and 25,

1. Lohr, 'Oral Techniques', pp. 428-29.
2. Lohr, 'Oral Techniques', p. 428.
3. Bacon treated chs. 1–2 as prologue and 3.1–4.25 as the Book One narrative. Lohr treats chs. 1–4 as his first narrative. This is why Lohr ends up with six rather than seven narratives.

eliminating one major portion of discourse Bacon included in a narrative section. But, what about ch. 11 or other large chunks of discourse in 'narrative' sections? A second related critique is that often just as many repetitions or echoes can be found between certain sermons and narratives, and/or other theoretically non-corresponding sections as between sermons or between narratives. For example, Lohr links chs. 10 and 18, the missionary and community discourses, with phrases containing thirty repeated words. However, there are more links between chs. 10 and 23–25 (thirty-seven words in common) or ch. 10 and a single narrative, ch. 16 (thirty-six words in common). Third, the decision concerning the major thematic content of each section is inevitably subjective. Why should chs. 8–9 and 19–22 both be labeled 'Authority and Invitation' and the Sermon on the Mount, 'Entering Kingdom?'

d. *Conclusion*

Examination of three major structural proposals for the Gospel of Matthew shows that different sets of criteria lead to different outlines of the Gospel. Criticism of a structural proposal usually focuses on choice or application of criteria. All of this is but another way of stating the old saw that the questions one poses determine the answers one finds.

From the point of view of the narrative critic, two things stand out. First, attention has been given to internal structural devices such as formula and repetition. But scholars seem to focus on a limited number rather than developing a catalog.[1] Second, the plot of the Gospel and the role various devices play in it have received little attention.

This chapter will focus on plot as a key to the design of the Gospel and the role verbal repetition plays in it. The focus on plot will

1. With the exceptions of the recent contributions of David Bauer and Ulrich Luz. Bauer draws up a list of rhetorical features or compositional relationships which structure the relationships between the various literary units and sub-units of the Gospel (Bauer, *Structure*, pp. 13-20). One of these features is repetition. Luz speaks of the seamless character of Matthew and its use of formulaic language. He develops a catalog of means of structuring shorter sections which includes grouping similar materials, correspondence of length, number schemes, repetition of key words, central verses or generalizations at the beginning and ending of sections, doublets, inclusions, chiastic ring compositions, and signals or anticipations (*Matthew: 1–7*, pp. 37-41).

provide a new way of looking at the Gospel's design. The focus on repetition will reveal a number of important plot devices. Some of these devices have already been recognized. Some have not. The examination of both types in terms of plot provides new insights. A comprehensive plot outline will not be offered since repetition is only one factor involved in the development of the plot.

3. *General Description of Plot*

a. *Definitions*

Literary critics have defined plot in various ways since Aristotle spoke of 'the action', the 'arrangement of incidents'.[1] Most emphasize one or more of the following: the temporal or sequential element, motivation, or the effects of the arrangement of events on the reader. Various distinctions have been made between (a) story and plot, and (b) the fable or story and the *sujet*. E.M. Forster emphasizes the importance of motivation when he defines a story as 'a narrative of events arranged in their time-sequence' and a plot as 'a narrative of events, the emphasis falling on causality'.[2] '"The king died and then the queen died," is a story', he writes. While, '"The king died, and then the queen died of grief" is a plot.'[3]

The distinction between fable and *sujet* emphasizes the effects of the

1. Loeb edition, *Poetics* 6.8. Typical modern definitions are those of Scholes and Kellogg: 'Plot can be defined as the dynamic, sequential element in narrative literature. Insofar as character, or any other element in narrative becomes dynamic, it is part of the plot' (*Nature*, p. 207); and Abrams: 'The plot in a dramatic or narrative work is the structure of its actions, as these are ordered and rendered toward achieving particular emotional and artistic effects' (*Glossary*, 3rd edn, p. 127); and R.S. Crane, 'the particular temporal synthesis effected by the writer of the elements of action, character, and thought that constitute the matter of his invention... with a power to affect our opinions and emotions in a certain way' ('The Concept of Plot and the Plot of *Tom Jones*', in *idem* [ed.], *Critics and Criticism* [Chicago: University of Chicago Press, abridged edn, 1957 (1952)], pp. 66-67). I have deliberately avoided the semantic jungle of most recent structuralist examinations of plot since they are not as familiar to the average reader as the traditional definitions learned by most American high school and college students. I am also not yet convinced that any of the proposed systems would enhance greatly the description of repetition I am undertaking.

2. Forster, *Aspects*, p. 130.

3. Forster, *Aspects*, p. 130.

arrangement of actions. Wellek and Warren define fable as 'the temporal-cause sequence which, however it may be told, is the "story" or story-stuff'. This includes all the events described or referred to in chronological order. This definition is the same as Forster's. *Sujet*, on the other hand, is 'narrative structure'—'The artistically ordered presentation of the motifs'—'the plot as mediated through point of view'.[1] This is the arrangement of events in narrated order. The reader perceives the events differently depending on their arrangement. The distinction between story and plot (*sujet*) also allows Wellek and Warren to speak of fable or story time, 'the total period spanned by the story', and narrative or plotted time (corresponding to *sujet*), 'reading time, or "experienced time"...controlled by the novelist, who passes over years in a few sentences, but gives two long chapters to a dance or tea party'.[2] Others make a further distinction between narrative or plotted time, the events as arranged and depicted in the narrative, and reading time, time as it relates to the reader's experience of reading the narrative.[3] G. Genette notes that the order of the events, the duration or length of events, and the frequency of events can be varied to achieve rhetorical effects.[4]

Given the emphasis on arrangement and motivation, other important terms have been developed in plot analysis. Aristotle noted that a plot is a whole with a beginning, middle, and end.[5] He spoke of the complication (tying) and dénouement (loosing).[6] These terms have been expanded in speaking of typical plots to include the *exposition* or introduction (setting the stage), the *rising action* or complication often involving *conflict* between the protagonist and antagonist,[7] the *climax*, the point to which the rising action has been leading,[8] and the *dénoue-*

1. Wellek and Warren, *Theory*, p. 218. Another way to speak of this is that of Chatman who speaks of plot as the 'story-as-discoursed'. He says, 'The events in a story are turned into a plot by its discourse, the modus of presentation', *Story and Discourse*, p. 43.

2. Wellek and Warren, *Theory*, pp. 218-219.

3. Petersen, *Literary Criticism*, pp. 50-80.

4. See *Narrative Discourse: An Essay in Method* (Ithaca, NY: Cornell University Press, 1975) and Chatman, *Story and Discourse*, pp. 63-79.

5. Loeb edition, *Poetics* 7.2-3.

6. Aristotle, *Poetics* 18.1-3.

7. There may also be a conflict with nature, fate, circumstances, or within the protagonist.

8. Sometimes distinguished from the *crisis* or turning point, Abrams, *Glossary*,

ment or conclusion. This rising and falling plot outline is sometimes called Freytag's pyramid.[1] The exposition and the rising action create questions in the mind of the implied reader and the climax and dénouement provide the answers. The questions range from, 'What will happen?' to 'how?' and 'why?' The arrangement of episodes creates *suspense* and sometimes surprise when the unexpected occurs. Surprise may be most effective when it 'turns out in retrospect, to have been well-grounded in what has gone before...'[2]

Two further terms also refer to the response of the implied reader and indicate the importance of the plotted, temporal arrangement of the story. They are anticipation and retrospection.[3] Anticipation or foreshadowing prepares the implied reader for events to come. Retrospection reviews what has already occurred. Both allow the implied author to guide the memory and perceptions of the implied reader. There are various types of anticipation ranging from a vague hint to a detailed prediction of a future event. There are also shorter or longer intervals between anticipation and fulfillment. In some cases anticipations foreshadow events which occur after the narrative has come to a close, that is, in story, but not in plotted time. An anticipation can be provided directly by a third person omniscient narrator or indirectly through characters with a greater or lesser degree of reliability. It can be provided to the implied reader alone or it may be integrated into the plot and therefore available to certain characters as well. When there are a number of detailed anticipations provided by reliable sources, the implied reader 'will ask "how" instead of "what"'.[4] The effect of detailed anticipation by an omniscient narrator in the ancient Greek romances is described as follows by Hägg:

3rd edn, p. 130.

1. See Abrams, *Glossary*, 5th edn, pp. 140-41 for a brief discussion of these terms using 'Hamlet' as an illustration.

2. Abrams, *Glossary*, 5th edn, p. 140.

3. The discussion of these categories is informed by G.E. Duckworth, 'Foreshadowing and Suspense in the Epics of Homer, Apollonius, and Vergil' (PhD dissertation, Princeton University, 1933) and T. Hägg, *Narrative Techniques in Ancient Greek Romances* (Skrifter Utgivna Av Svenska Institutet I Athen. 8, VIII; Acta Institutet Atheniensis Regni Sueciae 8, VIII; Stockholm, 1971), chs. 6 and 7 and pp. 323-32.

4. Hägg, *Narrative Techniques*, p. 215.

> Consequently, the author is able to influence directly the reading technique both by pointing out where the important issues in the romances are to be looked for and by shifting the emphasis from suspense about the outcome to interest in the various stages of development of the plot or vice versa.[1]

Such a use of foreshadowing creates 'suspense of anticipation' rather than 'suspense of uncertainty'.[2] The implied reader 'remains in a state of emotional tension and is on the lookout for something which he either wishes or dreads to see happen'.[3]

Retrospection is another way of creatively focusing the memory and response of the implied reader. As with anticipation, it may occur at shorter or longer intervals and be more or less specific. It may either be integrated into the plot in the speech or thoughts of characters, or appear in omniscient narration. Since an event has already occurred, retrospection is often a compressed, shorthand recollection or recapitulation. Retrospection may refer to events which occurred before a narrative begins, that is, events within story, but not plotted time.

b. *Overview of the Matthean Plot*

The plot of the Gospel of Matthew combines two common Western plot types, the biography and the journey.[4] As a biography, the story begins with Jesus' birth and ends with his death (and resurrection).

1. Hägg, *Narrative Techniques*, p. 215.

2. Duckworth, *Foreshadowing*, p. 37, also cited in Hägg, *Narrative Techniques*, p. 325.

3. Duckworth, *Foreshadowing*, p. 37; also cited in Hägg, *Narrative Techniques*, p. 325.

4. By plot type, I do not mean a historically specific genre such as Hellenistic biography. Rather I speak in the very general sense that over the centuries two common plots are one that tells of the life of a person from birth to death and one which recounts a journey. In 'Biblical Hermeneutics and the Ancient Art of Communication', *Semeia* 39 (1987), pp. 100-101 Werner Kelber has noted that neither Albert Lord nor John Miles Foley has ever encountered an oral story that covers a hero's life from birth to death. Thus, he argues that it is unlikely that Mark is a transcription of an oral performance. Rather it stands in tension between orality and literacy, between elaborately plotted nineteenth- and twentieth-century novels and the episodic arrangement of totally oral narrative. I think the case is similar with Matthew. I will argue that the plotting in Matthew is fairly significant, if not of the same nature as that in *War and Peace*. Thus, I think that some elements of Freytag's pyramid are relevant to Matthew despite W.J. Ong's comments about the absence of a rising and falling plot in oral narratives in *Orality and Literacy: The Technologizing of the Word* (London: Methuen, 1982), pp. 142-47.

The typical biographical form is altered, however. Instead of closing with the protagonist's death, the Gospel opens outward with the resurrection and Great Commission.[1] The movement from birth to resurrection corresponds with a journey from Judea (birth) to Galilee (ministry) to Judea, specifically Jerusalem (death and resurrection) to Galilee (resurrection commission to the disciples). The specific geographic movements associated with plotted events occur as follows: Jesus is born in Judea and his life is threatened by Herod the King who lives in Jerusalem. Jesus' family flees to Egypt, returning not to Judea but to Nazareth in Galilee. Jesus emerges from Galilee to be baptized in Judea by John and to be tempted in the wilderness. When John is delivered up, Jesus returns to Galilee, but dwells in Capernaum, not Nazareth. From 4.17 on he ministers in Galilee, emerging only twice into Gentile territory (Gadara, 8.28-34 and Tyre and Sidon, 15.21-28, counting Caesarea Phillipi as part of Galilee). He reaches his goal in 21.10 and dies there. He appears after his resurrection once outside of Jerusalem to the women. After this he returns to Galilee for the Great Commission. Symbolically Judea, particularly Jerusalem, is the stronghold of his adversaries, the Jewish leaders, and represents threat of death and death itself. Galilee is its opposite, Galilee of past and future ministry, Galilee of the Gentiles (4.15 and 28.19).

One can also view the plot in terms of exposition, rising action or complication involving conflict, climax, and dénouement. Jesus, the plot's protagonist, is introduced in the birth story. His identity, purpose, and location in space and time are established. The conflict with the Jewish leaders and the extension of his mission to the Gentiles are foreshadowed there as well.[2] Whether John's conflict with the Pharisees and Sadducees (3.1-12), the baptism of Jesus (3.12-17), the temptation (4.10-11), and/or Jesus' move to Capernaum (4.12-16)

1. In this it fulfills Forster's desire in *Aspects*, p. 145 and his practice in *A Passage to India*—although the Gospel is not cyclical. It also resembles certain Greek epics described by F.M. Stanwell in Duckworth, *Foreshadowing*, p. 28: 'the typical epic, though it must have a close does not have an end... and instinctively the supreme epic poets close their work in such a way as to leave us with this vivid sense of *going-on*.' See the comments on the frame of the Gospel in Chapter 2, pp. 67-68 for the effect on the reader.

2. The shock of Jerusalem and Herod's attempt to kill him foreshadow the conflict with the Jewish leaders. The attitudes of the magi and perhaps the inclusion of the women in the genealogy foreshadow positive interaction with the Gentiles.

should be considered part of the exposition or the beginning of complication is a matter that can be debated. In terms of the point of view discussed in Chapter 2 the first portion of the 'frame' ends with Jesus' entrance in 3.13. From 3.13 until Jesus' death, the temporal and spatial points of view of Jesus and the narrator are closely aligned. Certainly, with the beginning of Jesus' ministry and the call of the first four disciples (4.17-22) the complication has begun. The success and failure of Jesus' proclamation and his relationship with the disciples are developed throughout the rest of the Gospel. As the plot proceeds Jesus also becomes involved with the crowds, supplicants, individual Gentiles, and the Jewish leaders. Conflict arises over which groups will recognize, understand, and accept Jesus' identity and mission. Suspense is created as the implied reader asks who will help or hinder Jesus, when, why, and how? As the plot progresses the groups take various stances vis-à-vis Jesus and he toward them. The plot plays the groups off against one another as foils, revealing motivation at appropriate points in the temporal sequence. The Jewish leaders are perhaps the most obvious in their position as antagonists who plot against Jesus. They eventually achieve an ironic victory, one which really marks their defeat. The crowds initially lean toward Jesus, attracted by the authority with which he speaks, his healings and exorcisms. Eventually, they side with the Jewish leaders in calling for his crucifixion. The disciples waiver between faith and understanding on the one hand and 'little-faith' and misunderstanding on the other. They receive a commission in ch. 10, but abandon Jesus in his final hour of trial. They confess Jesus as Son of God, but do not accept the necessity of suffering and death. Finally, however, after the resurrection they are reunited with him and given the Great Commission. The supplicants have great faith in Jesus and are healed by him. They provide a strong contrast with the Jewish establishment who would view them as outcasts. The same is true of most of the Gentiles. An important part of the developing plot is how the Gentiles receive Jesus and how he begins to extend his mission beyond Israel.[1] This

1. The one group of Gentiles who do not respond favorably to Jesus are the Gadarenes. The reason, perhaps, is that Jesus came to exorçize demons in Gadara 'before the time' (8.29). A notable advance in the movement towards the Gentiles is the healing of the Canaanite woman's daughter in the region of Tyre and Sidon in 15.22-28. This will be discussed below in the section on double and triple stories.

culminates in the Great Commission to go to all the nations or Gentiles.[1] As noted in the above description, many of the threads of the plot are brought together in the climactic passion, and most are untied.[2] Given the frequent anticipations of the passion, the implied reader has been filled primarily with the suspense of anticipation. Both suspense of uncertainty and suspense of anticipation are released at the Gospel's close except for several unresolved questions. These center on eschatological anticipations—especially the parousia predictions—and the Great Commission. They leave the implied reader with the expectation of events yet to occur in story time. Given earlier patterns of fulfillment in the narrative, the suspense which remains is primarily that of anticipation.[3]

4. *Summary Passages*

Summary passages provide an example of the relation of story time and plotted time. In this section passages which summarize in a few sentences several actions over an extended period rather than presenting a single event will be discussed. Summary passages allow the narrator to indicate the passage of story time in a very short reading time. They have an effect on the pace, allowing the narrator to telescope time as a number of events are touched on without being illustrated at length. They give body to the narrative economically. The designation of summary passages involves a certain degree of subjectivity. A list of Matthean summary passages would include at least the following:

4.23-25 And he went about in all Galilee, teaching in their synagogues and proclaiming the Gospel of the kingdom and healing disease and every illness among the people (τῷ λαῷ). And the report of him went into all Syria; and they brought to him all the ones ill having suffered from various diseases and tortures, demon-possessed and lunatics and paralyzed and he healed them. And followed him many crowds from Galilee and Decapolis and Jerusalem and Judea and beyond the Jordan.

1. For the translation of πάντα τὰ ἔθνή as 'all the Gentiles' see D.R.A. Hare and D.J. Harrington, 'Make Disciples of All the Gentiles', *CBQ* 37 (1975), p. 363.

2. Whether the passion or the resurrection appearance scene is the precise climax of the narrative is a matter that can be debated.

3. At least as far as the parousia is concerned. Given their earlier defects, the implied reader might suspect that the disciples' path toward fulfilling their commission may not be entirely straight.

8.16 (plus scriptural comment of v. 17): And evening coming they brought to him many being demon-possessed; and he cast out the spirits with a word, and all the ones ill having he healed (so that was fulfilled the thing spoken through Isaiah the prophet saying: He took our weaknesses and bore the diseases).

9.35 And Jesus went about all the cities and villages teaching in their synagogues and proclaiming the Gospel of the kingdom and healing every disease and every illness.

11.1 And it came to pass when Jesus ended giving charge to his twelve disciples, he removed thence to teach and proclaim in their cities.

12.15-16 (plus fulfillment quotation vv. 17-21): But Jesus knowing departed thence. And many followed him, and he healed them all, and warned them that they should not make him manifest; (in order that might be fulfilled the thing spoken through Isaiah the prophet saying: Behold, my servant whom I chose, my beloved...).

14.13-14 And hearing Jesus departed thence in a ship to a desert place privately; and hearing the crowds followed him afoot from the cities. And going forth he saw a great crowd, and was filled with tenderness over them and he healed their sick.

14.34-36 And crossing over they came onto the land to Gennesaret. And recognizing him the men of that place sent into all that neighborhood, and brought to him all the ones ill having, and besought him that only they might touch the fringe of his garment; and as many touched were completely healed.

15.20-31 And removing thence Jesus came by the sea of Galilee, and going up into the mountain he sat there. And approached to him many crowds having with themselves lame, maimed, blind, dumb and many others, and cast them at this feet; and he healed them; so that the crowd marvelled seeing dumb men speaking, maimed whole and lame walking and blind seeing; and they glorified the God of Israel.

19.1-2 And it came to pass when Jesus ended these words, he removed from Galilee and came into the borders of Judea across the Jordan. And many crowds followed him and he healed them there.

A number of these summary passages coincide with suggested structural markers including geographical references (4.23-25, 14.34-36, 15.29-31, 19.1-2, and perhaps 9.35 and 11.1), fulfillment quotations (8.16-17; 12.15-21), and discourse-ending transitional formulas (11.1 and 19.1-2). All are associated with Jesus' movements except 8.16 which refers to people being brought to him. They are analogous to 'stage directions'. All except 11.1 include references to Jesus' healing activities. Most refer to crowds following him.[1]

1. Only 8.16, 9.35, 11.1, and 14.34-36 have no direct reference to 'crowds'. 8.16 and 14.34-36 imply the presence of a crowd.

Various summaries are connected to one another by fairly long repetitions:

4.23 = 9.35, twenty words in common = 11.1, three words—teach, proclaim, cities
4.24 = 8.16, eight words—(they) brought (to) him... all the (ones) ill having... demon possessed... healed, = 14.35-36, five words—and all the (ones) ill having
4.24-25 = 12.15b = 19.2, six words—And followed him many (and he) healed them, = 14.13b-14, five words—And followed him and (he) healed
4.25 = 19.1b, eight words—from the Galilee... and Judea... beyond the Jordan
11.1 = 19.1, seven words in common—transitional ending formula plus μετέβη
12.15 = 14.13-14, ten words—And [δὲ] ὁ Jesus [knowing-hearing] departed thence. And followed him and [he] healed.

Some are also connected by repeated key words and phrases to other passages. This is natural since the summary passages summarize many of Jesus' actions of which individual incidents are examples. Passages with such connections include:

14.14 = 9.36, four words—And seeing (he saw) crowd (crowds) ἐσπλαγχνίσθαι [he was filled with tenderness] over [ἐπ' περὶ] them
14.14 = 15.32b, three words—σπλαγχνίζομαι [I am filled with tenderness] over crowd and 14.14 = 18.27 = 20.34, one word—σπλαγχνισθεὶς
14.36 = 9.20-21, nine words—touched (touch) the fringe of [the] garment [of] him; only touch (touched) [shall be] healed (were completely healed)
14.36 = 8.34, one word—παρεκάλεσαν
4.23 = 9.35 = 10.1, seven words—and healing (to heal) every disease and every illness; 15.30 = 21.14, eight words—And approached [to] him blind [and] lame... and [he] healed them.

The chief function of most of the repetitions which link the summary passages to one another is to emphasize repeatedly that crowds follow Jesus wherever he goes, seeking healing which he provides. The summaries indicate typical behavior and build toward future events. Every so often the narrator offers one of these summaries to indicate that the crowds and healings which spread Jesus' fame (4.23-25) continue to follow in his wake. The summaries give through repetition a background and unifying texture to Jesus' movements. They lead up to the triumphal entry in 21.2-11 where the crowds shout, 'Hosanna to the Son of David'; announcing Jesus as 'the prophet, the one from Nazareth of Galilee'. Jesus does not disappoint them. Once again in the temple he heals the blind and lame (21.14 = 15.30, eight words—And approached [to] him blind [and] lame... and [he] healed them; 21.14 =

4.24 = 12.15 = 19.2, three words—and [he] healed them; and 21.14 = 4.23 = 8.16 = 9.35 = 14.14, some form of θεραπεύω). The crowd's response to Jesus all along the way is a source of irritation to the Jewish leaders (9.33-34; 12.23-24; 21.15-16; and 21.46). It is only at the trial before Pilate that the crowds are won over to the side of the Jewish leaders (27.20) and become one with the leaders as 'the people' (ὁ λαὸς) (27.25).

Another repetition which links two summaries has more specific functions. This is the most striking repetition involving summary passages, 4.23 = 9.35 (twenty words in common). A number of scholars have argued that this repetition has a structural significance.[1] These verses form an inclusio around Jesus' teaching (chs. 5–7) and healing (chs. 8–9) activities. The Sermon on the Mount and the miracles of chs. 8–9 are concrete examples—individual scenes—illustrating two of the activities summarized in 4.23 and 9.35. Thus they are appropriately included in the ring, just as the parable of the workers in the vineyard is appropriately encircled by the phrase, 'The first will be last and the last first' (19.30 = 20.16), or the warning about good and evil trees is encircled by the phrase, 'By their fruits you will know them' (7.16 = 7.20).[2] As in each of these cases the first half of the inclusio relates to what has gone before. Thus 4.23 also recalls 4.17, Jesus' beginning of the proclamation of the kingdom, emphasizing that it continues. Both also serve as bridges to what immediately follows: 'And seeing the crowds…' (5.1 = 9.36). The sight of the crowds gathered from Galilee, the Decapolis, Jerusalem and Judea and beyond the Jordan by his teaching, proclaiming and healing (4.23-25) causes Jesus to ascend the mountain, the disciples to approach, and Jesus to begin the Sermon on the Mount. The sight of the crowds

1. See H.J. Held, 'Matthew as Interpreter of the Miracle Stories', in G. Bornkamm, G. Barth and H.J. Held (eds.), *Tradition Interpretation in Matthew* (trans. P. Scott; Philadelphia: Westminster Press, 1963), pp. 249-50; J.D. Kingsbury, 'The "Miracle Chapters" of Matthew 8–9', *CBQ* 40 (1978), pp. 566-67; W.G. Thompson, 'Reflections on the Composition of Mt. 8:1–9:34', *CBQ* 33 (1971), pp. 366 n. 5, 366-68.

2. There are a number of other examples of inclusio appearing at close range. J.C. Fenton cites Lagrange's list: 6:19/20; 7:16/20; 9:14/15; 12:2/8; 12:39/45; 15:2/20; 16:6/12; 18:1/4; 18:10/14; 19:3/9; 19:13/15; 19:30/20:16; 21:23/27; 21:33/41; 22:43/45 to which he would add 1:1/17; 5:3/10; 13:54/56 ('Inclusio and Chiasmus in Matthew', *SE* 1 [TU 73; Berlin: Akademie-Verlag, 1959], pp. 174-75).

gathered by his activities summarized in 9.35 evokes Jesus' compassion and the commissioning of the disciples as workers in the harvest in the missionary discourse (9.36–10.42). The summary passages are also linked to the missionary discourse by repetition (4.23 = 9.35 = 10.1, seven words in common). As Jesus heals every disease and every illness, so he gives the disciples the authority to do the same. The disciples are also commissioned to proclaim that the kingdom has drawn near as Jesus and John the Baptist have (3.1-2 = 4.17 = 10.7, seven words in common) and as the summaries emphasize Jesus continues to do (4.23 = 9.35 = 10.7, three words in common). They are also to go into the cities and villages of Israel (10.11, 23) as Jesus does. The only activity summarized that they are not given to do is teaching. This is reserved until the Great Commission (28.20). After the missionary discourse the transition to the next episodes recalls through repetition the earlier summaries emphasizing, however, only the teaching and preaching in 'their cities' (4.23 = 9.35 = 11.1, three words—teach, proclaim, cities). The summaries 4.23 and 9.35 are both anticipatory and retrospective summaries. They are linked together as an inclusio and with what precedes and follows each. They both conclude a section of narrative and anticipate what is to come. In addition to creating temporal plot connections, they also provide motivational/causal linkages for the implied reader.

Two other repetitions, linking a summary passage to a scene, merit mention. 14.36 is related to 9.20-21 by nine words: touched (touch) the fringe of [the] garment [of] him; only touch (touched) [shall be] healed (were healed). By repetition the implied reader imputes to people of Gennesaret the same faith as the woman suffering a hemorrhage. 14.34-36 also provides a comparison to the scene in Gadara (8.28-34). Both the Gadarenes and the Gennesarites beseech (παρεκάλεσαν[λουν]) Jesus following stilling of the storm scenes. However, the Gadarenes beseech him to depart and the Gennesarites beseech Jesus in order to touch the fringe of his garment. Again, repetition emphasizes typical actions of characters, but also through variation indicates contrasts.

5. *Anticipation and Retrospection*

There is a great deal of anticipation and retrospection in Matthew.[1] Anticipation and retrospection are central ordering devices of the Matthean plot. Anticipation ranges from vague foreshadowing such as Herod's attempt to kill the infant Jesus to detailed predictions such as the passion prediction in 20.18-29. Similarly retrospection ranges from the echo of the birth story's 'God With Us' in the Great Commission, 'Lo, I will be with you always…' to the angel's specific reminder that Jesus had predicted his own resurrection in 28.5-7. Many of the anticipations and retrospections involve repetition. Judas' betrayal (26.47-50), for example, is anticipated in 10.4; 26.14-16; and 26.20-25. These passages are linked with each other and 26.47-50 by various degrees of repetition. Judas's death is anticipated and linked by repetition to 26.14-15 (= 27.3-10, five words in common) and 26.20-25. The death scene is also retrospective calling Judas 'the one who betrayed Jesus' and explaining what happened to 'the thirty pieces of silver' paid Judas in 26.15. Other examples are Peter's denial and charges the disciples have stolen Jesus' body. Jesus' prediction of Peter's denial (26.34) anticipates it and the denial (26.69-75) recalls the prediction. They are linked closely by repetition (26.34 = 26.75, seven words in common).[2] The fear that the Jewish leaders express to Pilate that the disciples will steal Jesus' body and the placing of the guard (27.62-66) anticipate and are linked by repetition to the bribe and charge that the disciples have stolen the body in 28.11-15 (27.62-66 = 28.11, eight words in common).[3]

There are also anticipations and retrospections involving repetition which deal with story time prior to or after narrated events. For example, all of the fulfillment quotations linked to one another by the

1. For a brief discussion see Lohr, 'Oral Techniques', pp. 412-16. There, however, Lohr treats only the formula fulfillment quotations and recapitulative summaries as retrospective. I have treated the summaries separately.

2. Peter's denial and the predictions are discussed on pp. 94-96 above.

3. See above p. 119 and C.H. Giblin, 'Structural and Thematic Correlations in the Matthean Burial–Resurrection Narrative (Matt. 27:57–28:20)', *NTS* 21 (1975), pp. 408, 412-13. Note that 27.62-66 might itself be considered retrospective of 26.60-62 and possibly 12.38-40 and 16.1-4.

repetition of the characteristic formula are retrospective.[1] They recall scriptural anticipations uttered in story time at a point prior to the beginning of the narrated action.[2] The repeated formula forces the implied reader to see the narrated events as part of a pattern relating them to the earlier sacred utterances. Jesus' life is a series of fulfillments of sacred prediction, sacred foreshadowing. Jesus' eschatological predictions move in the other direction. They occur within the narrative frame, but anticipate events which will occur later. Since Jesus is a reliable character who makes other predictions fulfilled in plotted incidents, the implied reader is left to believe that these will be fulfilled in story time as well.[3] Examples of eschatological predictions involving repetition are the Son of Man parousia predictions (10.23; 13.41; 16.27; 16.23; 19.28; 20.18; 24.27, 30, 36-37, 39, 44; 25.31, and 25.64) and the predictions that those who are found wanting will be 'thrown into a fiery furnace' (13.42, 50) or 'cast into the outer darkness' (8.12; 22.13; 23.50) or 'placed with the hypocrites' (24.51) where in all three cases 'there will be the weeping and the gnashing of teeth' (8.12; 13.42, 50; 22.13; 24.51; 25.30).[4]

There are other examples of anticipation and retrospection involving repetition in Matthew. The above enumeration has indicated some of the most important. Three others have been chosen for detailed discussion in this section. They are (1) dreams, (2) passion and resurrection predictions, and (3) the prediction that Jesus will be raised and go before the disciples to Galilee.

a. *Dreams*

The first example of anticipation involving repetition is the use of supernatural revelation of the future by means of dreams. The Gospel contains six such anticipations, each containing the phrase κατ' ὄναρ: 1.20-21; 2.12; 2.13; 2.19-20; 2.22b; and 27.19.[5] The word ὄναρ is

1. See Petersen's discussion of scriptural citations in Mark in *Literary Criticism*, pp. 50-54.

2. Some of the predictors, Isaiah and Jeremiah, for example, fall within the scope of the genealogical frontispiece of the Gospel.

3. See Petersen, *Literary Criticism*, pp. 64-79, for the same principle in Mark.

4. Verses 8.12, 13.42, 50, 24.51 are direct predictions of Jesus; 22.13 and 25.30 are the words of characters who speak indirectly for Jesus in stories he tells.

5. For a discussion of the first five from a redactional point of view see Brown, *Birth of the Messiah*, pp. 105-19. For a brief discussion of the force of this repetition

unique to Matthew in the New Testament. It is found only in these passages. Three passages involve appearances of an angel of the Lord by means of a dream: 1.20-21; 2.13; and 2.19-20, seven words in common. All of the dream anticipations are integrated in the narrative. The information given is available both to the character who has the dream and to the implied reader. However, only one of the characters is portrayed as sharing the contents of the dream with another (27.19). The rest are privileged inside views. These anticipations foreshadow future plot developments for the reader and provide plot motivation. They also contribute to characterization as they reveal characters' responses to the dreams.

Five of the dream anticipations are concentrated in the birth story. Four are revelations to Joseph. The fifth, 2.12, is to the magi. The first, 1.20-21, provides the motivation for Joseph not to divorce Mary and to legitimize Jesus by naming him. It also anticipates an important future role for Jesus in the derivation of his name:

> But while he thought on these things, behold an angel of the Lord by a dream appeared to him saying: Joseph, son of David, fear not to take Mary your wife: for the thing begotten in her is of the Holy Spirit. And she will bear a son, and you shall call his name Jesus; for he will save his people from their sins.

Since the birth story is part of the exposition of the plot and introduces Jesus to the implied reader, this foretelling of Jesus' role is important. The source of the anticipation is significant. The implied reader 'overhears' the angel's words directly so there can be no mistake about their reliability or content. The angel's words are also immediately reinforced and elaborated by a direct authorial comment in 1.22-23. Part of the realization of the anticipation occurs after this comment. In 1.24-25, upon awakening, Joseph obeys the angel's command in words which echo it (1.20-21 = 1.24-25, fifteen words in common). The repetition emphasizes that the commandment was obeyed exactly. This suggests that the rest of the angel's words will come to pass as well. Suspense of anticipation is created. When and how will Jesus save his people from their sins?

The second dream passage occurs in 2.12: 'And having been warned by a dream not to return to Herod, they [the magi] departed by another way to their country.' The narrator explains in this passage

see Lohr, 'Oral Techniques', p. 413.

how the magi know Herod was not sincere in his desire to worship Jesus (1.8) and how Jesus is saved by supernatural intervention. The anticipation and realization occur in the same verse. In a sense the passage also provides stage directions, ushering the magi offstage. Finally, it portrays the magi positively as recipients of divine revelation. This passage is very similar to 2.22b which will be discussed below (2.12 = 2.22, five words in common). The repetition of supernatural intervention by a dream emphasizes the divine oversight of the child. It unifies the events associated with his birth as part of one divine plan. Behind the plot events is the order of God.

The third dream passage immediately follows the second in 2.13: 'When they had departed, behold an angel of the Lord appears by a dream to Joseph saying: Rising, take the child and his mother, and flee into Egypt, and be there until I tell you; for Herod is about to seek the child and destroy him.' The narrator's introduction is almost exactly the same as the introductions to Joseph's first and third dreams (1.20 = 2.13, seven words in common in the introduction; 2.12 = 2.19-20, nine words in common in the introduction). As in those cases the implied reader 'overhears' the angel's words. This time, however, contemporaneity of the implied reader with Joseph and the angel is achieved with the use of the historical present in 2.13 (φαίνεται). This dream anticipates two future plot events, the flight to Egypt and Herod's slaughter of the innocents. Like the magi's dream, it represents divine intervention to save Jesus' life. Through repetition it unites the events of the birth story. It also provides the motivation for the next major action, the flight into Egypt. The divine authority for the flight is also reinforced by the fulfillment quotation of 2.15b. As in 1.24-25, the angel's command is repeated almost word for word in Joseph's fulfillment of it (2.13 = 2.14-15, fifteen words in common). When Herod seeks to kill the baby in 2.16 all of the angel's words except the promise to tell Joseph when to return have been realized. Herod's slaughter of the innocents is narrated after the dream and flight and prior to the foretold dream which brings about the return from Egypt. It is set off by an inclusio mentioning his death (2.15a and 2.19a). It is plotted slightly out of chronological order. Herod cannot kill babies after he is dead (2.15a). It provides retardation; sandwiched between the dream which causes Joseph to flee and that which brings him home.

The introduction and dream which bring Joseph home, 2.19-20, are almost exact duplicates of those which caused him to flee (2.13 = 2.19-20, eighteen words in common). Again the historical present is used. This repetition represents the fulfillment of the angel's promise to tell Joseph when to return (2.13). It also provides the motivation for the next plot event, the journey home: 'But Herod having died, behold an angel of the Lord appears by a dream to Joseph in Egypt saying: Rising take the child and his mother and go into the land of Israel; for the ones seeking the life of the child have died.' This anticipation is immediately realized; again emphasizing by repetition Joseph's obedience and the fulfillment of the anticipation (2.20 = 2.21, twelve words in common).

The final dream in the birth narrative (2.22b-23), like that of the magi, is simply described in the voice of the reliable narrator, rather than displayed. It, too, is a warning to depart in such a way as to escape the ruler (2.12b = 2.22b, five words in common), providing stage directions: 'And being warned by a dream he departed into the part of Galilee and coming dwelt in a city called Nazareth.' It provides the anticipation, motivation, and realization in one sentence. The divine authorization of the move to Nazareth is reiterated by the fulfillment quotation which follows in 2.23b.

What are the effects of the repetitions involved in these dream anticipations? Why are they concentrated in the birth narrative? First, like the fulfillment quotations, which are in their own way retrospective,[1] they authoritatively give divine sanction to Jesus and events of his life. The repetition unifies the episodes and establishes a pattern. That they are divine revelations and not merely supernatural is vouchsafed because an angel of the Lord appears in three major dreams. All of the dreams represent divine intervention to preserve the life and safety of Jesus.[2] Second, the events anticipated almost all occur soon in almost precisely the same words as predicted. This emphasizes not only the obedience of Joseph and the magi, but also the reliability of anticipations as indicators of future events in this narrative—at least those anticipations with divine sanction. A third

1. The anticipation, the original utterance, occurs in story time long before the plotted narrative begins. The narrator draws attention to the fact that certain events have been foretold and now are occurring. The fulfillment quotations recall that earlier point of foretelling.

2. Even the first dream prevents Jesus from being born as an illegitimate child unprotected by a human father.

function of all but the first dream is to provide motivation (*divine* motivation) for the chain of events, for the geographical movements—the arrivals and departures—of characters. They move the action along. In addition, repetitions highlight the symbolic significance of several of these movements in the plot as a whole.

Since the birth story is an important part of the plot's exposition, the clustering of these dreams and of fulfillment quotations there is not surprising. The narrator needs to establish Jesus' identity as well as the context for his life and mission, to set the scene for future plot developments. Thus the first and third functions mentioned above are important. The narrator also is laying the ground rules for the telling of his or her tale and so the second function is important. The same pattern of fulfillment will be seen later in the passion–resurrection predictions made by the divinely authorized Jesus. The implied reader knows from the birth story that authoritative (in the voice of divinely authorized characters or direct narrational) anticipations almost invariably come to pass.

The last instance of the unique phrase κατ' ὄναρ occurs in 27.19. There Pilate's wife tells him of a dream as he sits on the judgment seat: 'Now as he sat on the judgment seat his wife sent to him saying: Have nothing to do with that righteous man; for I suffered many things today *by a dream* because of him.' This dream serves as a plot interlude between Pilate's question, 'Whom do you wish I may release to you. Barabbas or Jesus the one called Christ?' (27.17b) and the chief priests' and elders' persuasion of the crowds to ask for Barabbas and destroy Jesus (27.20). It also provides the motivation for several future plot actions. The first is Pilate's hand-washing and declaration of innocence. The second is the people's acceptance of responsibility for Jesus' death (27.24-25). It is not as clear and detailed an anticipation as the dreams of the birth narrative. It creates a vague foreboding. Neither is it presented directly. Instead Pilate's wife has her dream reported to Pilate along with her interpretation: Pilate should have nothing to do with Jesus. Since the implied reader hears only her report, he or she does not have access to the details of the dream itself. This partially explains the vague hint of doom. The repetition of the phrase κατ' ὄναρ in a new context recalls its use in its earlier context, the birth story. Supernatural portents accompany the key plot events of Jesus' birth and death. This time, however, the dream does not protect Jesus. It does, however, emphasize his innocence.

b. *Passion–Resurrection Predictions*

This section discusses anticipations of the passion and resurrection and highlights their role in the plot.[1] These anticipations are treated as a group first, and then individually. There are three passion and resurrection predictions (16.21; 17.22-23a; and 20.18-19; see also 10.38; 12.40; and 20.28) which are clear anticipations. They are closely related by repetition (16.21 = 17.22-23a, six words in common; 16.21 = 20.18-19, ten words in common; 17.22-23a = 20.18-19, 10 words in common). There are also three related predictions of the passion (17.12d; 26.2; and 26.45b) and one additional anticipation of the resurrection (17.9b, not a prediction).[2] These anticipations are all integrated into the plot. They are delivered to the disciples in private. Thus, the implied reader possesses a foreknowledge shared only by these characters and the narrator. The first prediction is in indirect discourse; the narrator lending his or her authority to that of Jesus. The first prediction also speaks somewhat formally of Jesus Christ.[3] In the rest of the anticipations, the reliable character Jesus speaks of the Son of Man, a title only he uses. The implied reader already knows that Jesus is the Son of Man from earlier passages, especially 16.13. However, the close resemblance of the first prediction to the others doubly ensures that the reference to Jesus is clear.

In terms of development of the Gospel's plot, the predictions are very significant. *Repetition with variation and placement are crucial.* The predictions create a 'suspense of anticipation'—enhanced by repetition—as the implied reader awaits their fulfillment. Each repetition keeps the coming events and their significance before the reader. He or she reads the rest of the text in the light of this foreknowledge.

1. See Chapter 3 for their role in the characterization of the Jewish leaders.

2. 17.9b = 16.21, six words in common; 17.9b = 17.12d, four words in common (the Son of Man); 17.9b = 17.22-23a, five words in common; 17:9b = 20.18-19, five words in common; 17.9b = 26.2, four words in common (the Son of Man); 17.9b = 26.45 b, four words in common (the Son of Man); 17.12d = 17.22-23a, five words in common; 17.12d = 20.17-19, five words in common; 17.12 d = 26.2, 4, four words in common (the Son of Man); 17.12d = 26.45 b, four words in common (the Son of Man); 26.2 = 17.22-23a, six words in common; 26.2 = 20.17, five words in common; 26.2 = 26.45b, six words in common; 26.45b = 17.22-23a, seven words in common; 26.45b = 20.17-19, five words in common.

3. The *UBSGNT*, 3rd edn, adopts the reading 'Jesus', but rates the choice 'C', a considerable degree of doubt whether the text or the apparatus ('Jesus Christ') contains the superior reading.

The 'what' comes as no surprise. The 'when' and 'how' gradually become clearer as the anticipations build to the climax and dénouement of the plot. With each prediction old information is echoed and new information is presented. The closer the passion, the more details are revealed. In 16.21 the implied reader and the disciples learn that Jesus *must* go to Jerusalem and suffer many things before the Jewish leaders, be killed, and on the third day be raised; in 17.22-23a that Jesus as the Son of Man is about to be *delivered* (παραδίδοσθαι);[1] and in 20.17-19 that he will be condemned to death and delivered to the Gentiles to be mocked, scourged, and crucified. As the passion draws near, two predictions of the passion alone echo earlier passion and resurrection predictions and indicate when they will be fulfilled. In 26.2 the implied reader learns that the betrayal will occur after two days; in 26.45b that it is imminent. Both use the prophetic present. Earlier anticipations, including 17.9b and 17.12d, which relate the death and resurrection to the Transfiguration and the death of John, give no indication of when the passion will occur. The first, 16.21, merely says that Jesus must suffer. The second, 17.9b, refers to 'when' he is raised. The rest use the word μέλλει and/or the future tense.

In addition to gradually revealing more details of the how and when of the passion, the three major passion–resurrection predictions enhance the sense of plot movement by highlighting Jesus' geographical progress on his journey toward Jerusalem and the passion. The initial prediction is the first clear indication of the necessity and reason for the journey to *Jerusalem*. The second indicates that Jesus and the disciples are still in *Galilee*, συστρεφομένων, 'gathering'. The group, having entered *Judea* in 19.1, the third prediction notes that they are about to go up to *Jerusalem*. At each of these points along the way the implied reader is reminded of the events that will take place at the end of the road.

As the repeated anticipations with variations build toward the passion, they also echo in each context in which they occur. These anticipations are found in and help to link similar contexts by means of repetition. Although they anticipate the resolution of Jesus' conflict with Jewish leaders, the contexts in which they are found relate the passion to the disciples and discipleship as well. This is not surprising

1. This may or may not be related to Judas, the betrayer (ὁ παραδίδους). παραδίδωμι is a technical term for the passion.

since the disciples are the only characters who hear Jesus' predictions. The repeated anticipations lead the implied reader to view the disciples in the light of their repeated failure to understand and accept the passion–resurrection predictions and the true nature of discipleship. The disciples repeatedly model the wrong response to the predicted passion and resurrection. Jesus repeatedly indicates the way of true discipleship. The similar contexts linked by the repeated passion–resurrection predictions emphasize the disciples' weakness and misunderstanding. They prepare the implied reader for the disciples' eventual flight and Peter's betrayal as well as the reunion in Galilee.

Matthew 16.21

> From then began Jesus Christ to show his disciples that it is necessary for him to go to Jerusalem and to suffer many things from the elders and chief priests and scribes and to be killed and on the third day to be raised.

The first passion–resurrection prediction occurs after Peter's confession of Jesus as Christ and Son of the Living God and the subsequent blessing. Although this confession ironically anticipates the high priest's question in 26.63, it is the only positive confession of Jesus as Christ by a character.[1] It is one of three human confessions of Jesus as Son of God.[2] The reader may feel that now that the disciples realize that Jesus is Christ, Son of God, and Son of Man (16.13-20), they are making progress. Perhaps the disciples are ready to learn along with the implied reader of the coming death and resurrection. Jesus' identity is only to be understood in that light. However, immediately following the prediction, Peter rebukes Jesus and Jesus rebukes Peter (16.22-23). Jesus then offers a teaching on true discipleship, echoing teachings from the missionary discourse (10.38-39 = 16.24-25, twenty words in common; 16.28 = 10.23, nine words in common.) He also predicts the parousia (16.24-28). The exalted status of Jesus as Christ and Son of God is seen in the light of the passion and resurrection. The blessing of Peter for the insight granted him is contrasted with his failure to accept Jesus' necessary suffering. Although Peter, and by implication the other disciples, have not entirely understood Jesus' mission; they, along with the implied

1. Pilate does speak of Jesus as 'the one called Christ' in 27.17, 22.
2. The others are disciples' confession in 14.33 and the centurion's in 27.54.

reader, know clearly for the first time that it is necessary for Jesus to journey to Jerusalem to suffer (παθεῖν) at the hands of the Jewish leaders, die and be raised on the third day.[1] The conflict with the Jewish leaders is not new, but from this point on the implied reader looks toward Jerusalem, the passion, and the resurrection for its resolution. The introduction to the prediction and the use of indirect discourse may alert the implied reader to the significance of the prediction for the plot. The phrase, 'From then Jesus began' ('Aπὸ τοτε ἤρξατο 'Iησοῦς) occurs only here and in 4.17. Although one should not necessarily attribute the determinative structural significance to these verses that Kingsbury does, they to seem to mark turning points.[2] From 16.21 on the narrator, the implied reader, Jesus, and the disciples move toward Jerusalem and the passion. It is always in the background. From time to time it is brought to the foreground by predictions which repeat with variations.

Matthew 17.9b and 17.12d

> Tell no one the vision until the Son of Man be raised from the dead (17.9b) ... thus also the Son of Man is about to suffer by them (17.12d).

The second and third anticipations of the passion (17.12d) and the resurrection (17.9b) occur shortly after the first. They follow the Transfiguration (17.1-8) and are part of Jesus' ensuing discussion with Peter, James and John. Verse 9b is not a prediction, but a command from Jesus, in direct discourse not to reveal the vision of the transformed Jesus until after the resurrection. Verse 12 is Jesus' prediction that the Son of Man will suffer the same fate as John the Baptist. This links the main plot to the Johannine subplot which will be discussed below. It is both retrospective and prospective. Jesus' enemies are the same as John's, and they will put him to death also. Each of these anticipations is tied by the repetition of a key word to 16.21; 12d by the word 'to suffer' (παθεῖν and πάσχειν) and 9b by the word 'be

1. 10.38 and 12.40 offer clues, but very vague ones. Those clues require knowledge of the story on the part of the reader if they are to be deciphered when first read.

2. McNeile also saw them as important. He says they divide the teaching of Jesus into two main parts: 'public preaching about the imminence of the Kingdom'; and 'private instructions to the disciples about His own sufferings, the necessary prelude to His advent to inaugurate the Kingdom' (*St Matthew*, p. 45).

raised' (ἐγερθῆναι and ἐγερθῇ). As does 16.21, they follow a revelation of Jesus as the Son of God—this time by God (17.5)—and precede an example of discipleship weakness—the inability to exorcise due to 'little faith' (17.14-20). The disciples do, however, understand that John the Baptist was Elijah (17.13). Repetition occurs in a similar context and underscores the similarity. Similar event patterns contribute to both plot and character development. Again, the future glory and the suffering of Jesus are kept in tension. Again the understanding and weakness of the disciples are held in tension and displayed. However, the repetition occurs at a later point in the narrative, thus continuing the building of the plot inexorably towards the passion and resurrection.

Matthew 17.22-23a

> As they were gathering[1] in Galilee Jesus said to them: 'The Son of Man is about to be delivered into the hands of men, and they will kill him, and on the third day he will be raised'.

Following the disciples' failure to exorcise due to 'little-faith', Jesus reiterates his prediction of the passion and resurrection. This prediction is closely tied by repetition to the first by six words:

> καὶ ἀποκτενοῦσαν (ἀποκτανθῆναι, 16.21) καὶ τῇ τρίτῃ ἡμέρα ἐγερθήσεται (ἐγερθῆναι, 16.21).

It is less strongly linked by five words, four being the title Son of Man, to 17.9: ὁ υἱὸς τοῦ ἀνθρώπου ἐγερθήσεται (ἐγερθῇ, 17.9); and by five words including the title Son of Man to 17.12d: ὁ υἱὸς τοῦ ἀνθρώπου μέλλει.

The variations from 16.21 consist largely in the use of direct discourse, the title Son of Man, and the reference to Jesus being delivered (a technical term for the passion) into the hands of men, and the reference to being in Galilee rather than the journey to Jerusalem. The main points of 16.21, that Jesus would suffer from and be delivered to his enemies, be killed, and be raised on the third day are repeated. The reference to the hands of men emphasizes the opposition between the side of God and the side of men, as did 16.23.[2] Jesus

1. This translation follows Thompson, *Matthew's Advice*, pp. 17-18.

2. Note that none of the predictions specify the Jewish leaders doing the actual killing of Jesus. In 16.21 Jesus suffers from them and is to be killed. In 17.22-23a

being 'delivered' has echoes in the 'delivery' of John and of the disciples (4.12; 10.17, 19; 17.22; 20.18, 19; 24.9, 10; 26.2, 15, 16, 21, 23, 25, 45, 46, 48; 27.2, 3, 4, 18, 26). It also foreshadows the actions of Judas, ὁ παραδίδους. The introductory reference to Galilee indicates that the events still lie in the future; the journey to Jerusalem has not yet begun. μέλλει, likewise, keeps the anticipated events on the horizon. Jesus does not leave Galilee until 19.1, after the community discourse.

The immediate context is also important. Preceded by the failure to exorcise due to little-faith, 17.22-23a is followed by a sign that the disciples are beginning to grasp the seriousness of Jesus' end: after this prediction, 'they were grieved exceedingly' (17.23b). The prediction is followed by the didrachmae tax incident (including a reference to Capharnaum) and the community discourse. So, although the prediction occurs in close proximity to an incident of 'little-faith', there is no episode showing weak faith following the prediction, unless the question concerning greatness in the kingdom (18.1) is so construed.[1] However, 17.24–18.35 contains teachings on discipleship. The paradox of greatness through humility is again emphasized. The developing responses of Jesus' enemies and the disciples are intertwined. Jesus' own suffering and authority are kept in tension as the passion approaches as well. The power of Jesus is emphasized in the story of the didrachmae tax—not so much in the miracle of the fish, but even more in the freedom from the tax. The repeated prediction keeps the passion and resurrection in the foreground so the implied reader will keep those events in mind as he or she interprets what is occurring.

Matthew 20.17-19

> And being about to go up to Jerusalem Jesus took the twelve privately, and in the way said to them: Behold, we are going up to Jerusalem, and the Son of Man will be delivered to the chief priests and scribes and they will deliver him to the Gentiles to mock and to scourge and to crucify, and on the third day he will be raised.

he is delivered into the hands of *men* and *they* will kill him. In 20.17-19 he is delivered to the Jewish leaders who condemn him to death and deliver him to the Gentiles to be crucified.

1. Some have argued that the disciples are questioning a privilege granted to Peter in the tax incident. See below, p. 166.

The next prediction occurs just prior to Jesus' arrival in Jerusalem. A number of passages intervene between it and the previous prediction: the temple-tax (17.24-27), the community discourse (18.1-35), the entrance into Judea (19.1-2), the Pharisees' question concerning divorce (19.3-9), Jesus' teaching on celibacy (19.10-12), blessing the children (19.13-15), the rich young man's question about eternal life (19.16-22), Jesus' teaching concerning wealth and entrance into the kingdom (19.23-26), his promise the disciples would judge the twelve tribes of Israel (19.27-29), and the parable of the workers in the vineyard surrounded by the inclusio: 'first will be last, the last first' (19.30–20.16). The prediction precedes the request of the mother of the sons of Zebedee (20.20-23), more teaching on true discipleship ['And whoever among you wished to be the first, he shall be your slave'] (20.24-27), the Son of Man saying concerning a ransom for many (20.28), the healing of two blind men at Jericho (20.29-34) and the entry into Jerusalem (21.1-17). The geographical position is emphasized by the repetition of the words 'go up (ἀναβαίνεν, ἀναβαίνομεν) to Jerusalem' in the introduction and the actual prediction. The content of the prediction strongly echoes both 16.21 (ten words in common) and 17.22-23a (ten words in common). It is linked by the title Son of Man and the verb ἐγερθήσεται (ἐγερθῇ, 17.9) to 17.9 and by the same title and similarity of content (the suffering of 17.12d being spelled out in detail in 20.18-19) to 17.12d. Thus repetition recalls and confirms the intimations of the previous anticipations shortly before the point in the plot where Jesus actually enters Jerusalem.

However, there are variations. This prediction foreshadows the events of the passion in more detail. A two-step deliverance, first to the Jewish leaders and second to the Gentiles is predicted. Those who will put Jesus to death are now clearly identified. The condemnation to death foreshadows the trial before the high priest. The mocking, scourging and crucifixion foreshadow the actual indignities and manner of death.[1] The details of the passion are being revealed only to the disciples (and the implied reader) is stressed in the introduction, 'he took the twelve privately'.[2] That the events remain in the future is

1. There is a mention of the cross in 10.38 but at that point it may be taken as metaphorical, not necessarily indicating the precise manner of death. This case is similar to 16.24, a parallel passage (10.36 = 16.24, six words in common; 10.39 = 16.25, fourteen words in common). In retrospect the allusions are clear.

2. The essential equivalence of the disciples and the Twelve in Matthew is a

emphasized by the use of the future tense in vv. 18-19. In addition to confirming earlier hints, as the plot is moving toward its climax more details are revealed. There is less and less suspense about the outcome, even about the 'who' and 'how' of the outcome.

That this prediction occurs shortly before the entrance into Jerusalem, preparing the implied reader for the events of the passion week, is not the only significant aspect of its context. As with earlier predictions there is a dialogue uncovering the weaknesses of the disciples (the request of the mother of the sons of Zebedee, 20.20-24), and teaching on discipleship (20.25-27). As with 16.21 there is also a new Son of Man saying (20.28). This time, however, it entails the suffering, not the parousia, of the Son of Man. The prediction of Jesus' passion and resurrection is again associated with the disciples' weakness and misunderstanding. Again this provides the occasion for teaching that disciples must follow Jesus in humility and suffering to achieve greatness. The repeated predictions of Jesus—ideologically aligned with the narrator—lead the implied reader to see some of the import of the death and resurrection before they occur. The disciples model the wrong responses and Jesus authoritatively indicates the proper ones. The similarity of contexts between the three major passion–resurrection predictions has been noted by William G. Thompson, who perceives a formal pattern:[1]

Passion-prediction:	16.21	17.22-23	20.17-19
Instructions:			
Dialogue	16.22-23	17.24-27	20.20-23
Sayings to the disciples	16.24-28	18.1-20	20.24-28
Dialogue		18.21-35	

Certainly the parallels between the first and third are clear. They can even be expressed in more detail:

Passion–resurrection Prediction	16.21	20.17-19
Dialogue and misunderstanding of Christ's role	16.22-23	20.20-24

matter of dispute. See U. Luz, 'Die Jünger im Mattäusevengelium', *ZNW* 62 (1971), pp. 142-43; Minear, 'The Disciples', p. 27; Sheridan, 'Disciples', pp. 235-40; Thompson, *Matthew's Advice*, pp. 71-72. Confusion exists in these discussions between the disciples as a character group and the way in which a reader or hearer responds to the Gospel.

1. Thompson, *Matthew's Advice*, pp. 94-95.

Teaching on true discipleship: the paradox of greatness and sacrifice	16.24-26	20.25-27
Son of Man saying related to the teaching on discipleship	16.27-28	20.28

The chief difficulties with fitting 17.22-23 into the same pattern are the lack of a concluding Son of Man saying and the interpretation of the didrachmae tax episode. Can the didrachmae tax incident be seen as a parallel to Peter's rebuke and the request of the mother of the sons of Zebedee? Is there a coherent flow of thought from passion-resurrection prediction, to dialogue, to teaching on discipleship? Thompson establishes such a flow based on (A) narrative introductions (17.22a, 24a, 25b; 18.1a), including a parallel to 8.1-17; and (b) his interpretation of the symbolic meaning of the didrachmae as the temple tax. He argues that paying the temple tax was a means of atonement. Jesus argues that the sons of the kingdom will be free because of the death and resurrection (17.22-23, the prediction). They are thus to strive for greatness through childlikeness and humility, forgiveness, etc. (18.1-14). This interpretation of the tax incident fails to make a parallel with Peter's rebuke and the mother's request clear, however. Another interpretation suggests that the fact Jesus has Peter pay the tax for 'me and you' gives a primacy to Peter. This elicits the disciples' question in 18.1.[1] A similar interpretation suggests the question, 'Who *then* is the greater?', that is, 'Why is Peter assumed to be the chief among us?' is raised because the tax collectors single Peter out as representative of the other followers.[2]

However the tax incident is interpreted, it is too much to force the three major predictions and subsequent incidents into a rigid pattern. What can be said is that each repeated prediction is associated with authoritative teaching which views discipleship in the light of the passion and resurrection. The arrangement of episodes explores the role of the disciples as well as that of the Jewish leaders as the plot develops. Their understanding of and responses to Jesus are linked to the passion and resurrection through the repeated predictions.

1. Ellis, *Matthew*, p. 64.
2. Allen, *St Matthew*, p. 191.

Matthew 26.2 and 26.45b

> You know that after two days the Passover occurs and the Son of Man is delivered in order to be crucified (26.2).
> Behold, the hour has drawn hear and the Son of Man is delivered into the hands of sinners (26.45b).

The final two predictions, 26.2 and 26.45b, are shorter than the three major passion–resurrection predictions. They focus on the passion alone. Since they follow the earlier predictions and more immediately precede the events anticipated, they serve as brief reminders before the fact. They recall the earlier major predictions through repetition (26.2 = 17.22-23a, six words in common; 26.2 = 20.17-19, five words in common; 26.45b = 17.22-23a, seven words in common; and 26.45b = 20.17-19, five words in common). The first emphasizes the manner of death; the second the antagonists who cause it. Particularly striking is the parallel between the deliverance into the hands of men in 17.22 and the deliverance into the hands of sinners in 26.45b.

These predictions, however, lack geographical references since Jesus is already in Jerusalem. Instead they focus on *time*. The first indicates that the passion will begin in two days; the second that the deliverance will occur immediately. Both shift into the prophetic present instead of μέλλει (17.12d; 17.22; 20.17) or the future (17.23; 20.18, 19).[1] This use of the present is a counterpart to the historical present used in confident assertions about the future.[2] Here it emphasizes the immediacy of the events foretold as well as the certainty that they are about to occur. Thus this variation from earlier predictions is significant.

The placement of each of these reminders is helpful to the implied reader. The first, 26.2, follows the apocalyptic discourse. It serves as a transition into the final plot events preceding Jesus' arrest. The first verse of ch. 26 contains the transitional formula ending the discourse and the narrator's introduction to the prediction. Verse 2 is the actual prediction addressed to the disciples (and the implied reader). It is immediately followed by the plotting of the Jewish leaders in Caiaphas's court to seize and kill Jesus by guile. The passion and the

1. See the comments of McNeile, *St Matthew*, pp. 373, 392-92 and *BDF*, N. 323 (2).

2. *BDF*, N. 323 (2). Ordinarily, as here, a temporal indication of the future is included in the sentence.

plot which leads to it are highlighted as the climactic events begin to unfold. By this time, through repeated anticipations, the actions of Jesus' antagonists are no surprise to the disciples or the implied reader. This is emphasized by the words 'You know' with which the first prediction begins. The plotting of the Jewish leaders is followed by the woman who anoints Jesus to the dismay of the disciples (26.6-13) and Judas providing the Jewish leaders with the means to seize Jesus without causing a riot (26.14-16). Both incidents again associate the passion with disciple failure. The first represents a failure of perception; the second, unforgivable betrayal. Again the reactions of the Jewish leaders and the disciples are intertwined in the plot. Plot and character development are interrelated.

The second prediction, 26.45b, follows the last supper (26.17-29); Jesus' prediction of Peter's denial and the disciples' flight (26.30-35); and the garden of Gethsemene (26.36-47). It is part of the conclusion of the scene in Gethsemene marking the transition to the arrest in 26.47-56. After the disciples have failed Jesus by falling asleep for the third time, Jesus says, 'Sleep now and rest; behold the hour has drawn hear and the Son of Man is delivered into the hands of sinners. Rise, let us be going; behold the one betraying me has drawn near' (26.45-46). The prediction begins to come true in the next verse. In fact, 26.45b is less of a prediction than an indication *through repetition* that earlier anticipations are being fulfilled. Jesus is being delivered into hands of sinners as repeatedly predicted:

16.21	Jesus Christ... to suffer many things from the elders and chief priests and scribes and be killed...
17.12d	*The Son of Man* is about to suffer by them.
17.22	*The Son of Man* is about *to be delivered into the hands of* men, and they will kill him...
20.18	...*the Son of Man will be delivered* to the chief priests and scribes, and they will condemn him to death...
26.2	...*the Son of Man is delivered* in order to be crucified. (The Jewish leaders appear, plotting, in the next verse.)
26.45b	...*the Son of Man is delivered into the hands of* sinners...

Repeated anticipations have prepared the implied reader for this 'deliverance'. He or she awaits the rest of the predicted events, the climax and denouement of the plot.

c. *After I Am Raised, I Will Go before You to Galilee*

26.31-32	Then says to them Jesus: All you will be offended in me tonight. For it has been written I will strike the Shepherd, and the sheep of the flock will be scattered. But after I am raised I will go before you to the Galilee.
28.5-7	And answering, the angel said to the women: Fear not, for I know you seek Jesus. The one having been crucified: he is not here: for he was raised as he said: Come, see the place where he lay. And quickly going tell his disciples and that he was raised from the dead, and behold he goes before you to the Galilee, there you will see him. Behold I told you.
28.10	Then Jesus says to them: Fear not; go announce to my brothers that they may go away into the Galilee and there they will see me.

In these passages there is both anticipation of future plot events and retrospection. All three passages anticipate 28.16 where Jesus appears on a mountain in Galilee to the eleven. One passage, 28.5-7, is also retrospective because it refers back to the earlier prediction of 26.31-32. The passages are linked not only by content, but also by repetition (26.32 = 28.7, six words in common; 26.31-32 = 28.10, eight words in common including the introduction: Then Jesus says to them; 28.5-7 = 28.10, eight words in common). All are integrated in the plot. All are spoken by very reliable characters, Jesus and an angel. The implied reader shares the knowledge imparted with the disciples in 26.31-32 and with the women in 28.5-7 and 28.10. The main function of the anticipations is to prepare the implied reader (and the disciples in 26.31-32) for the resurrection and reunion in Galilee. The repeated anticipation causes the implied reader to look forward to the events which conclude the narrative. Repetition keeps his or her eye focused upon them and highlights their importance. That the latter two repetitions occur close to their fulfillment and echo the first is also significant. It reminds the implied reader that Jesus had predicted the events which are about to occur. The plot is controlled by a divine order known by Jesus and the angel, and through them recognized by the implied reader.

Matthew 26.31-32. This passage is part of an interlude just after the last supper (26.20-29) and prior to the watch in Gethsemene (26.36-46); the arrest of Jesus (26.47-56a); and the flight of the disciples

(26.56b). In this interlude Jesus predicts the flight of the disciples (26.31, 35b); his resurrection and reunion with the disciples in Galilee (26.32); and Peter's denial (26.34). The interlude also includes the vehement protestations of loyalty by Peter (26.33, 35a); and to a lesser extent, the other disciples (26.35b). The disciples and the implied reader are prepared for events to come by the narrative's most reliable character. The anticipation of the resurrection and reunion in Galilee on the eve of Jesus' arrest and the disciples' flight is especially important for the implied reader. He or she is reminded that Jesus will ultimately be victorious. The implied reader is also prevented from totally rejecting the disciples. They fail Jesus, but will be restored. The fact the Jesus predicts their failure, supporting his prediction with a scriptural citation (26.31c), makes their abandonment seem an inevitable part of the plot. His prediction that he will be raised and go before them to Galilee makes these events seem foreordained as well. There is suspense of anticipation with little suspense of uncertainty.

Matthew 28.5-7. The women followers who remained with Jesus—loyal surrogates for the disloyal male disciples—come to his tomb in 28.1. The angel of the Lord who appears to them announces the resurrection, reminding them that Jesus had predicted it (26.5-7). This forces the implied reader to remember the earlier anticipations of the resurrection: 16.21, 17.9b, 17.23, 20.19, and 26.32 discussed above. He or she experiences the shock of recognition. All had occurred as Jesus predicted—the flight of the disciples, Peter's denial, the passion, and now the resurrection. The angel also instructs the women to tell the disciples that Jesus 'was raised from the dead'—a phrase reminiscent of 17.9b and 27.64—'and behold he goes before you to Galilee: there you will see him. Behold I told you.' The implied reader again experiences the shock of recognition through repetition. Jesus had earlier used almost the same words to anticipate the reunion in Galilee (26.32 = 28.7, six words in common). The last phrase is enigmatic. Is the angel emphasizing that he is making a prediction they should remember when it is fulfilled? Are the women to tell the disciples that an angel told them? Or is the angel, speaking with Jesus' voice, reminding the women and/or the disciples and the implied reader of his earlier prediction? The angel's repetition of Jesus' earlier prediction is not only retrospective, it remains prospective as well. The implied reader is again reminded by repetition that there is an appearance of Jesus in Galilee and a reunion with the disciples yet to come. The repetition keeps the implied reader anticipating this goal—the finale of the Gospel.

Matthew 28.10. The women leave the tomb to announce the angel's message to the disciples in 28.8. Jesus meets them in 28.9 and reiterates the angel's instructions in 28.10. They continue on their way in 28.11, a transition to the story of the Jewish leaders' bribe of the guards (28.11-15). What is the significance of Jesus' appearance? The narrative would flow nicely without it: 'And going away quickly... they ran to announce to his disciples' (28.8). 'And as they were going, behold some of the guards coming...announced to the chief priests all the things that had happened' (28.11). Jesus' words even begin with a repetition of the angelic expression of reassurance, 'Fear not'. The content of Jesus' message is much the same (28.5-7 = 28.10, eight words in common including 'fear not').

Jesus' appearance confirms the angel's announcement that Jesus was raised.[1] It emphasizes the faith of the women as they approach and worship him.[2] It, along with the bribery incident, provides retardation before the final scene. It also emphasizes, through repetition, the importance and the certainty of the final reunion in Galilee. The slight variation is perhaps significant as well. Jesus tells the women not to announce to the disciples that he is going before you, but to 'announce to *my brothers* that *they* may go away into Galilee' and there will see him. Those who fled are to be restored as brothers and Jesus wants them to follow him to Galilee. Any doubt about the restoration of the disciples is crushed. They are returned to the special status of brothers.[3] When the women fulfill their mission, the disciples, like the

1. The women actually touch his feet. This is noted by Giblin 'Structural and Thematic Correlations', p. 410.

2. προσκυνεῖν, to worship, is a typical expression of the proper attitude toward Jesus. Falling (πεσὼν, πεσόντες) and worshipping appears in 2.11, 4.9, and 18.26.

3. Earlier references to brothers include 12.46-50, Jesus' indicating the disciples as his true brothers; 18.15-17, 21, 35; 23.8; and 25.40. Giblin notes the use of the phrase 'my brothers' ('Structural and Thematic Correlations', p. 409). He wants to make the additional point that this is a *gracious* act of Jesus on behalf of the disciples 'without reference to morally good deeds' on their part. Perhaps one should not try to stretch the point beyond saying that the phrase, my brothers, indicates the disciples are accepted once again by Jesus.

women, worship Jesus (28.9, 17). Some of the disciples, however, doubt. Nonetheless, the disciples as a character group resume the place that the women had taken in their absence.

6. *The Johannine Subplot*

In the last chapter the characterization of John the Baptist through repetition was discussed. There the many connections between John and Jesus were explored. These also have many implications for the plot of the Gospel. The episodes associated with John form a subplot which is related by analogy to the main plot. According to Abrams, a subplot is, 'a second story that is complete and interesting in its own right...when it is skillfully managed it serves to broaden our perspective on the main plot and to enhance rather than diffuse the overall effect'.[1] The Johannine subplot resembles the Gloucester subplot in *King Lear*. Gloucester's actions mirror those of Lear on a less 'cosmic and kingly' and more human level.[2] Gloucester also precedes Lear in a reconciliation with his true child and, like John, precedes his master in death.

John's message, pronouncements about the Jewish leaders, arrest, and execution foreshadow Jesus' message, pronouncements about the Jewish leaders, arrest, and execution. The reactions of the crowds and Jewish leaders to John foreshadow their reactions to Jesus. *John is the foreshadower as well as the forerunner of Jesus.* As noted in Chapter 3, these connections are established in large part by means of repetition. Thus each time an earlier phrase is repeated, not only is the character of John and his relationship to Jesus developed, but also suspense is created. Through repetition the implied reader links John and Jesus. What will the significance of the links be? Expectations about the future outcome of the plot are raised. By the time John's

1. Abrams, *Glossary*, 3rd edn, p. 129.

2. For a summary of the plot of *King Lear* and comments on the relationship of the Gloucester subplot and the main plot see E.E. Foster, 'King Lear', in F.N. Magill (ed.), *Masterplots* (Englewood Cliffs: Salem Press, rev. edn, 1976 [1949]), VI, p. 3151. Foster writes: 'The experience of Lear is mirrored in the Gloucester subplot on a more manageable human level.' Lear's failure and death is, however, cosmic and kingly and so 'brings down the whole political and social order with him.' In a similar vein see B.F. Kawin's discussion of *King Lear* in *Telling It Again and Again* (Ithaca, NY: Cornell University Press, 1971), pp. 51-59.

death is recounted so many repetitions have established parallels between John and Jesus, that the implied reader inevitably suspects that Jesus will meet the same fate. Just as the passion predictions lead the reader to anticipate Jesus' end, so too does the John subplot. This subplot contributes to the overall development of the story, adding information to sharpen the implied reader's response. The contribution, however, goes beyond merely helping the reader to predict Jesus' death. It also guides the implied reader's response in other ways. For example, the fact that the Jewish leaders are first portrayed as evil (subsequent to the birth story) in a confrontation with John leads the implied reader to view them as the plot's main antagonists and applaud Jesus in his later confrontations with them. Most of John's words to them in ch. 3 are repeated in later contexts by Jesus; some of them more than once. Another example already discussed in the chapter on character involving repetition is the common message of John, Jesus, and the disciples. Jesus tells the disciples to preach the same message that he and John have already preached (3.1-2 = 4.17 = 10.7). He also warns them that they may be 'delivered up' as John was, and as he will be (4.12; 10.17, 19; 17.22; 20.18, 19; 24.9, 10; 26.2, 15, 16, 21, 23, 24, 25, 45, 46, 48; 27.2, 3, 4, 18, 26). This establishes a pattern for the way in which God's messengers are received and links the disciples along with John and Jesus to the side of heaven.

A review of the passages and repetitions associated with John in the order they appear in the narrative shows how they contribute to the development of the plot as a whole. In ch. 3 John's identity is established by means of the label, 'the Baptist', scriptural quotation, and allusions to Elijah. He begins the proclamation of the kingdom of heaven and has the Gospel's first confrontation (subsequent to the birth story) with the Jewish leaders. In ch. 4 Jesus withdraws to Galilee after hearing that John has been delivered up (4.12). Jesus begins his ministry by proclaiming the same message with which John began his ministry (4.17). In 7.16-20 Jesus warns of those yielding bad fruit in the same terms that John used to condemn the Pharisees and Sadducees in ch. 3. In ch. 10 Jesus instructs the disciples to proclaim the same message (10.7). He warns that they may be persecuted and delivered up (10.16-23). In ch. 11 John's identity and significance are confirmed by Jesus who echoes the label, scriptural quotation, and allusion to Elijah of ch. 3. The crowds, however, do not understand John or the Son of Man (11.7-19). In 12.34 Jesus confronts the Jewish leaders with the same epithet John had used in 3.7. He also uses the same fruit imagery that John used to condemn them (3.8 = 12.33-35) in ch. 3 and which he himself used in the Sermon on the Mount (7.16-20). John's eschatological harvest imagery also appears on the lips of Jesus in 13.30, 42a, 50. Jesus uses the same words about the Son of Man that John had spoken concerning the coming one (3.12 = 13.30, seven words in common). Following 13.36, when Jesus turns from the crowds and begins to focus more and more on the disciples, the implied reader learns of John's death (14.1-12) and that Herod thinks Jesus is John *redivivus* (14.2). In the recounting of John's death the reader learns that Herod originally wanted to kill John, but 'he feared the crowd because they had him as a prophet'. When Jesus learns of John's death,[1] he withdraws as he did after John's arrest (4.12 = 14.13). In 16.14 the implied reader learns that some people think Jesus is John the Baptist or Elijah. In ch. 17, the questions of John's identity, significance, and fate are again raised by the Transfiguration appearance of Elijah. Jesus again affirms that Elijah has come. The disciples, and the implied reader, understand that Jesus is speaking of John the Baptist (17.13). They understand what the Jewish leaders and the crowds do not. Jesus also makes the parallel between the fate of John and the Son of Man explicit, 'they did not know him [John as Elijah] but did to him whatever they pleased. So also the Son of Man will suffer at their hands' (17.12). In ch. 21 Jesus confronts the chief priests and elders of the people with a question about John which they fear to answer for the very same reason Herod had feared to kill him: the crowd has John as a prophet (21.26). A short time later the priests and the Pharisees express the same sentiment about Jesus (21.46). In ch. 23 Jesus again reiterates John's epithet for the Jewish leaders, Brood of Vipers, and wonders, like John, how they will escape judgment (3.7 = 23.33). The plot is moving toward its inexorable climax. Jesus and John have preached the same message, been misunderstood, angered the same enemies. Inevitably they will meet the same fate. John has been delivered up and executed. Jesus will soon be delivered up and crucified. John is the foreshadower as well as the forerunner of Jesus.

1. Or to follow L. Cope's interpretation in 'The Death of John the Baptist in the Gospel of Matthew', *CBQ* 38 (1976), pp. 515-19, when Jesus learns Herod thinks of him as John *redivivus*.

7. *Double and Triple Stories*

As noted in the general description of the Matthean plot above, the plot moves forward as Jesus interacts with various character groups. These groups serve as foils for one another. Their attitudes toward Jesus and Jesus' attitudes toward them motivate the action. The sequence of episodes—the *sujet*—highlights the comparison and contrast between groups at the same time it moves the plot toward its climax and dénouement. Henry James's famous dictum is particularly relevant to the Gospel: 'What is character but the determination of incident? What is incident but the illustration of character?'[1] The form of verbal repetition which probably contributes the most to this process is the use of double and triple stories or doublets and triplets.[2]

Double and triple stories are stories which are essentially repeated two or three times with variations. They involve substantial verbal repetition. Some are almost carbon copies. Others are repeated with greater variation. Some episodes are reduplicated and then expanded. The placement and arrangement of these stories is crucial to the development of both plot and character in Matthew. The arrangement guides the implied reader's response. The first occurrence anticipates the second (and third), and the latter recalls the former. The implied reader reads each episode in the light of the other, in prospect and retrospect. This reading is affected by what has transpired between the episodes and the contexts in which they are found. Further, the overall arrangement of these episodes has a rhetorical effect on the implied reader. The *sujet* or the order in which the events of the story are told is important. Thus the temporal flow of the narrative, context, and variation are all important to creating an effect on the reader. Below two expanded double stories or doublets will be discussed first. Then the more nearly identical stories and their arrangement will be treated.

1. Abrams, *Glossary*, 3rd edn, pp. 127-28.

2. These terms will be reserved for entire stories rather than phrases as is sometimes done. Recently Fowler (*Let the Reader Understand*, pp. 140-41) has suggested that a better term for doublet in Mark would be '"matched pair" because these pairs of episodes work in tandem with each other'. He emphasizes the necessity of treating their role in the Gospel's rhetoric, rather than dismissing them as simply variants of oral tradition. He points to the variation in the second occurence as a means of incremental progression. His comments about Mark also apply to Matthew, although I retain the traditional term 'doublet'.

a. *Expanded Doublets*

The stilling of the storm episodes. Two examples of expanded doublets are the stilling of the storm incidents in 8.23-27 and 14.22-33 (seventeen words in common) and the healings of demoniacs in 9.32-34 and 12.22-37 (twenty-two words in common). The stilling of the storm episodes show the developing responses of the disciples to Jesus. The first stilling of a storm follows several teachings on the difficulty of discipleship. It precedes the exorcism of the Gadarene demoniacs.[1] It is a miracle, but as G. Bornkamm has put it, the focus is on discipleship.[2] On a boat journey, the disciples, frightened by wind and wave, wake Jesus, saying, 'Lord, save us, we are perishing.' Jesus responds: 'Why are you fearful, little-faiths?' Afterwards the men marvel, 'What sort of man is this that even the wind and sea obey him?'[3] They call Jesus 'Lord', a title used only by persons who have faith in Jesus. Yet they do not have enough faith to trust that they will be safe. Jesus, therefore, calls them little-faiths. This is an epithet he uses to label them in 6.30 and 16.8 as well as here and in the other stilling of the storm story. He also uses the closely related 'of little-faith' in 17.20.

The second stilling of a storm incident occurs later in the Gospel after the watershed of 13.35 when Jesus begins to devote more time to preparing the disciples for their future role. It follows the feeding of the 5,000, paralleling that story's emphasis on the faith *and* weakness of the disciples. Repetition links the two stories. When the implied reader reads the second story, he or she recalls the first and compares the two. The similarities and differences are highlighted. In the second story the fear and doubt of the disciples have not disappeared. They are still little-faiths. Nonetheless, as the plot moves forward they have made some progress. Again the disciples are at sea. But this time their fright is caused by the appearance of Jesus walking on the water. The doublet is expanded because this time Peter, exhibiting faith, walks on the water toward Jesus. His gaze falters, he fears the wind, and begins

1. 8.23-27 and 14.22-23 are discussed in terms of the characterization of Peter on pp. 93-94.

2. G. Bornkamm, 'The Stilling of the Storm in Matthew', in Bornkamm, Barth and Held, *Tradition and Interpretation in Matthew*, pp. 54-57.

3. Even though Bornkamm does not identify the men as the disciples, one wonders who else would be in a position to observe. The analogy with the second incident would also indicate that the disciples at least join in the question.

to sink. Just as the group cried out in the first incident, now Peter cries out, 'Lord, save me'. Jesus again responds, although in the singular, 'Little-faith, why did you doubt?' This time, however, the ones in the boat *worship* Jesus and make one of three human confessions of Jesus as Son of God in the Gospel.[1] All have grown in their understanding of Jesus' identity. The response of the men in the first episode was to wonder what sort of man Jesus might be. Now the disciples confess Jesus as Son of God. The first episode occurs before the watershed ch. 13 where Jesus contrasts those who see and hear, blessing the disciples, with those outside who do not. The second, with its focus on Peter and the disciples' closing confession appropriately follows ch. 13 where Jesus begins to focus more upon the disciples. The variations in the second story help to build the plot toward Peter's confession and rebuke in ch. 16.

The demoniac exorcisms. The second example of an expanded doublet is the exorcism of demoniacs in 9.32-34 and 12.22-37 (twenty-two words in common).[2] These episodes develop Jesus' conflict with the Pharisees and the struggle for the hearts of the crowd. In 9.32-34 Jesus exorcises a dumb demoniac. The crowd marvels, 'never was anything like this seen in Israel'. But the Pharisees respond, 'He casts out demons by the ruler of demons'. This is the first time that the Pharisees openly oppose Jesus.[3] With this open opposition a section of miracles and questions concerning Jesus' identity and activities is brought to a close. It also foreshadows events to come. It plants in the implied reader's mind seeds of a conflict which will come to flower later in the Gospel. Lest the reader forget, he or she is reminded of the conflict a few verses later. In 10.25 Jesus warns the disciples that opponents who identify him as 'Beelzeboul' will malign them as well. This also anticipates the second member of the doublet when the Jewish leaders again will charge Jesus with exorcising by the power of the ruler of demons. There they add the name Beelzeboul. The interpretation of 10.25 as retrospective as well as prospective assumes

1. The others are Peter's in 16.17 and the centurion's in 27.54.

2. This doublet is discussed in terms of the characterization of the Jewish leaders in Chapter 3.

3. Although in 9.3 the scribes claim he blasphemes and in 9.11 the Pharisees ask the disciples why he eats with tax collectors.

that the implied reader knows that Beelzeboul is the ruler of demons.[1] If he or she does not, the meaning of the term becomes a puzzle which will only be solved when the second story is read. It would then be an anticipation whose meaning only becomes clear in retrospect. This would draw even more attention to the stories and to 10.25. It would also highlight the controversy with the Jewish leaders over exorcism.

That controversy comes to a head in ch. 12. There, after two incidents of Sabbath breaking, the implied reader learns that the Pharisees are now plotting to destroy Jesus (12.14). Jesus withdraws. The narrator indicates that his withdrawal fulfills Isa. 42.1-4. This prophecy of the chosen servant echoes God's words in the baptism and foreshadows God's words in the transfiguration. The Pharisees plot against God's own son. The prophecy also offers hope to the Gentiles, who, unlike the Pharisees, accept the servant.

The stage is set for a replay of the demoniac incident with several significant variations. Jesus' healing in 12.22-37 is even more miraculous. This demoniac is blind as well as dumb. The crowd is not only amazed, but wonders if Jesus is the Son of David. They have grown in their openness and are willing to entertain the possibility.[2] This accords well with the fact that crowds follow Jesus, drawn by his healing and authority. The Pharisees, however, persist in their misunderstanding and opposition. Uniting the phraseology of 9.34 and 10.25 they claim, 'It is only by Beelzeboul, ruler of demons that this man casts out demons.' This time, instead of withdrawing, Jesus explodes in condemnation. The Pharisees have recognized neither the power of the Holy Spirit nor the dawn of the kingdom of God. They are enemies who will not be forgiven (12.30-32). Jesus castigates them in words which echo John's charges in 3.7-12 and his own warnings against false prophets in 7.15-20. The Pharisees are a brood of vipers, bad trees yielding evil fruit. Similar invective will reappear in chs. 15

1. The exact historical meaning of the term is uncertain, Allen, *St Matthew*, pp. 107-108 and McNeile, *St Matthew*, pp. 143-44.

2. Even if Kingsbury is right in asserting that the μήτι anticipates a negative answer. See 'Akolouthein and Matthew's View', *JBL* 97 (1978), p. 61. Dennis Duling notes that the *untrusting* statement of the Pharisees 'implies there could be a positive answer, at least for Matthew's reader', in 'The Therapeutic Son of David', *NTS* 24 (1978), p. 401. See also J.D. Kingsbury, 'The Title "Son of David" in Matthew's Gospel', *JBL* 95 (1976): 600 and J.M. Gibbs, 'Purpose and Pattern in Matthew's Use of the Title "Son of David"', *NTS* 10 (1963–64), p. 458.

and 23. The demoniac may have been physically blind, but the Pharisees are spiritually blind (15.14; 23.16-22, 26). The opposition of the Jewish leaders is emphasized by the repeated story. This brood of vipers blasphemed against the Holy Spirit, not once but twice. They twice claimed that Jesus' power to exorcize came from the ruler of demons. The implied reader sees Jesus' lengthy condemnation after the second story as warranted. The implied reader will also compare the similarities between the Jewish leaders' responses in both stories and the difference in the two responses of the crowds. The Jewish leaders persist in their opposition—indeed there are other indications between the first and second episodes (such as 12.14) that their opposition has grown. The crowd's openness has increased even though their sight is not clear as Jesus indicates in ch. 11 (see 11.7-24). The narrator uses the repetition with variation to develop the changing responses of the two groups as the plot develops.

b. *Nearly Identical Double Stories and a Triad*

Turning to more nearly identical doublets, similar contributions to the development of plot and character can be observed. A careful arrangement of these stories is also apparent. This arrangement allows the characters to be seen even more clearly as foils for one another, and moves the plot along.

If one simply lists the rest of the Gospel doublets as they appear in the narrative, a chiastic pattern emerges (or can be constructed by the reader). This pattern can be expanded by the inclusion of one further episode, the Canaanite woman (15.22-28):

- A Two blind men (9.27-31)
  - B Sign of Jonah (12.28-42)
    - C Feeding of 5,000 (14.13-21)
      - D Canaanite woman (15.22-28)
    - C′ Feeding of 4,000 (15.30-38)
  - B′ Sign of Jonah (16.1-4)
- A′ Two blind men (20.29-34)

The Canaanite woman episode follows the same pattern as the blind men doublets: cry for help (attempt to silence), renewed request—questioning by Jesus, healing on the basis of faith. It also contains the same request for help:

a. cried out saying: 'Have mercy on me Lord, Son of David'; (15.22),
b. cried out saying: 'Lord, have mercy on us, Son of David' (20.29),
c. cried out saying: 'Have mercy on us, Son of David' (9.27)', 'Yes, Lord' (9.28).[1]

Thus, the three healings form a triad. The Canaanite woman episode is the fulcrum of the chiastic pattern. The implied reader need not perceive that a chiastic pattern exists in order for it to affect him or her.

The pattern, encompassing a central section of the Gospel, highlights the contrasts between the five major character groups: the outcast supplicants, the Jewish leaders, the crowds, the disciples, and the Gentiles. The developing responses of the various groups to Jesus and contrasts between them, are a key engine of the Matthean plot. Although the same contrasts are made readily apparent in the rest of the narrative, repetition and the chiastic pattern make them quite crisp here. The stories move from a focus on (Jewish) supplicants, to the Jewish leaders, the disciples, a Gentile woman aligned with the other supplicants, back to the disciples, the Jewish leaders, and finally to the supplicants again. The linking of the blind men with the Gentile woman is particularly significant. It is they who exhibit the most faith, not the Pharisees who would reject contact with them both, nor the disciples whose faith and understanding waivers. One of the main themes of the Gospel is the extension of the mission to the Gentiles; what better way to justify that extension! Other functions of the pericopes included in the chiastic pattern can be seen in a detailed examination.

The triad: blind men and Canaanite woman. The chiastic pattern begins with the healing of two blind men in 9.27-31.[2] This episode occurs in a series of miracles preceding the missionary discourse. It immediately precedes the healing of the dumb demoniac. In the episode two blind men cry out, 'Have mercy on us, Son of David'. Jesus questions them, 'Do you believe that I am able to do this'. They answer yes, identifying Jesus as Lord, a title only those who have faith in him use. Their eyes are opened. Jesus charges them to remain silent,

1. There is a similar cry in 17.15, 'Lord, have mercy on my son…', but it lacks a reference to the Son of David.

2. See Gibbs, 'Purpose and Pattern', and Duling, 'Therapeutic Son of David', and Kingsbury, 'The Title Son of David' on all pericopes containing 'Son of David'.

but they spread his fame throughout the entire district. As they leave, the dumb demoniac (the second of the expanded doublets discussed above, 9.32-34) is brought to Jesus. The crowds marvel while the Pharisees charge him with exorcizing by the power of the ruler of demons.

The second episode in 20.29-34 follows the request of the mother of the sons of Zebedee for a place of honor for her sons. It occurs just prior to the entry into Jerusalem. The cry of the blind men is the same, but this time *the crowd* rebukes them. They cry out all the more repeating the same phrase, 'Lord, have mercy on us, Son of David' (20.29, 31). Jesus asks them what they want. They reply, 'Lord, let our eyes be opened'. This time, however, there is no injunction to silence and no disobedience. Instead they follow Jesus.

When the implied reader comes to the second member of the doublet, he or she reads it in the light of the first and vice versa. Verbal repetition draws the reader's attention to the similarities between the episodes, engaging the reader's memory. At the same time it also puts the variations in relief. The two major differences are the differing responses of the pairs of blind men to being healed and the role of the crowds which appears only in the second story.

In the first story the blind men exhibit faith but not enough. Jesus touched their eyes (οφθαλμῶν) and healed them according to their faith (9.29). Their eyes were opened, but unlike the second pair, they did not truly 'see' and failed in obedience. The second set was healed when Jesus touched their ὀμμάτων, a poetic word for eyes which often occurs in the phrase 'the eyes of the soul'.[1] The narrator explicitly states that they 'saw'. They then 'followed' Jesus. If the second pairs' 'following' indicates discipleship, they have made a transition that the first pair did not. At least nine actual reader-commentators have interpreted the stories in that way.[2] Other readers read 'following' as an indication that the men joined the group marching toward Jerusalem with Jesus, but not as a metaphor for discipleship.[3] In either case, the second pair of blind men are pictured

1. Gibbs, 'Purpose and Pattern', p. 459.

2. Kingsbury, 'Akolouthein', p. 57 lists eight; to which add Gibbs, 'Purpose and Pattern', pp. 454-55, 460.

3. Kingsbury is an important proponent of this reading. In 'Akolouthein' he argues that 'following' only indicates discipleship when Jesus and not the narrator speaks (pp. 58, 61). He also argues that two factors must be present, (A) 'personal

more favorably than the first who disobey.[1] The second major difference that emerges when each story is read in the light of the other is the role of the crowd. In the first episode the crowd is not present, but immediately following it the crowd is marveling at Jesus' ability to exorcize. In the second episode, the crowd rebukes the blind men. The repetition shows the development of the supplicants' and the crowds' responses as the plot nears its climax.

Both of the major differences, the response of the blind men to being healed and the role of the crowd, are related to where the stories are plotted in the narrative order. The first story is part of the series of miracles which precede the missionary discourse. These miracles emphasize Jesus' healing power and the spread of his fame, factors underscored by the encircling summaries of 4.23-25 and 9.35. They also highlight the faith of the supplicants. The faith of the blind men is seen in their request to Jesus as Lord and Son of David. The injunction to silence and their disobedience underlines the spread of Jesus' fame and the gathering of persons about him. The blind men are favorably contrasted with the Jewish leaders who attribute Jesus' power to the ruler of demons in the following episode. This pair and the second pair of blind men may be physically blind, but the Jewish leaders are spiritually blind (15.14; 23.16-22,26). The crowds, although not mentioned in the story, marvel at Jesus' power in the following story, 'Never has anything like this been seen in Israel' (9.33). The supplicants and the crowds gather about Jesus. The disciples are being groomed to serve them. In the missionary discourse Jesus commissions them to preach and heal as he has done. They are

commitment' where Jesus calls disciples or addresses those who are already disciples and (B) 'cost', which involves sacrifice or abandoning one's former life (p. 58). With the exception of 8.19 and 19.20-22 this limits him to contexts involving members of the character group, 'the disciples'.

1. Part of the difference in interpretation depends on whether discipleship is defined as becoming a member of the character group, 'the disciples' or as the response of faith. The blind men respond to Jesus, but do not appear in the narrative again as members of the character group. They are united with other supplicants and the narrator in calling Jesus 'Son of David', something the disciples never do. The disciples and supplicants do both call Jesus 'Lord'. Only members of 'the disciples' and the narrator call Jesus 'Christ' and along with the voice from heaven and the Roman centurion in 27.54, 'Son of God'. Perhaps most telling is that if the blind men became disciples, it would not be possible to contrast them (along with the Canaanite woman) with that character group.

warned that they also will be opposed by the Jewish leaders who have called their master Beelzeboul (see especially 10.17-25).

The second episode takes place immediately prior to Jesus' entry into Jerusalem. It follows the final passion and resurrection prediction, emphasizing the Jewish leaders' role in Jesus' death, and the squabble over places of honor initiated by the request of the mother of the sons of Zebedee. When Jesus enters Jerusalem and the temple, his healings and the cries 'Hosanna to the Son of David' (21.14-15) anger the Jewish leaders. The fact that the second pair of blind men follow Jesus rather than being enjoined to keep silence and disobeying as the first pair is appropriate since he is about to enter Jerusalem. The confrontation with the Jewish leaders about Jesus' identity is about to come to a climax. The differences between the first and second pairs also enhance the contrast between marginal characters and various character groups. As the close of the narrative draws near, marginal characters such as the blind men, women, and Gentiles like the Canaanite woman and Roman centurion of 27.54 respond more and more positively to Jesus. The Jewish leaders, on the other hand, grow more hostile; the crowd shifts from initial attraction to calling for Jesus' death; and the disciples' understanding and loyalty waivers. These three groups of characters all appear in an unfavorable light compared to the blind men in the immediate context. As noted above, the Jewish leaders' antagonism to Jesus is stressed in the passion and resurrection prediction which precedes the episode and their reaction to his entry into Jerusalem. The disciples do not fully understand the passion prediction and dispute among themselves about places of honor following the request of the mother of the sons of Zebedee. The crowds rebuke the blind men within the story itself. Shortly after the first member of the doublet they marveled at Jesus' ability to exorcize (9.33). Later, they wondered if he might be the Son of David (12.23).[1] Now their rebuke, which stands out in relief as a variation between the two blind men episodes, casts them in an unfavorable light. It foreshadows their eventual switch to the side of the Jewish leaders. They understand Jesus as a prophetic Son of David (21.9-11), not a lordly one. They do not treat the blind men with compassion (σπλαγχνισθεὶς, 20.34) as Jesus does—a compassion he had earlier shown toward them (9.36, 14.14, and 15.32).

1. See pp. 178-79.

The third episode which must be considered in tandem with the healings of the two blind men is that of the Canaanite woman (15.22-28). It forms the center of the chiastic pattern of double stories. It is sandwiched between the two feeding stories. It immediately follows the condemnation of the Pharisees' teaching on defilement and precedes the feeding of the 4,000. Linked to the healings in 9.27-31 and 20.29-34, this pericope also has ties to the healing of the centurion's slave in 8.5-13 ('Truly I say to you, not even in Israel have I found such faith') and Jesus' injunction to go only to the lost sheep of the house of Israel in the missionary discourse (10.6 = 15.24, six words in common). It gathers together many threads in the Gospel's plot, offering a particularly vivid justification for and anticipation of the extension of the mission to all the nations/Gentiles in 28.19. Jesus reiterates, at first, the limitation to Israel. He then breaks it because of the woman's great faith.

As noted above the repetitive triad creates several meaningful contrasts. The faith of the Jewish outcasts and Gentile woman can be seen synoptically and contrasted with that of the Jewish leaders, disciples, and crowds. It may be, however, that the implied reader is to see the faith of this Gentile woman as even greater than that of the blind Jews, especially that of the first pair who disobey Jesus. As a Gentile and a woman she has doubly marginal status. Yet, this Gentile woman recognizes Jesus as both Son of David and Lord. She calls Jesus Lord three times and *worships* him. She must overcome objections from the disciples (not just the crowds as in 20.31), and even Jesus himself ('I was sent only to the lost sheep of the house of Israel'). Her faith wins out and her daughter is healed *from that hour.* If the blind men pale by comparison, the Jewish leaders are hopeless. The context of the episode underlines this. Jesus' condemnation of the Jewish leaders' teaching on defilement (15.1-20) immediately precedes his approval of the woman's faith. Their second request for a sign follows shortly thereafter. It serves as a transition to Jesus' condemnation of their teaching on leaven in 16.5-12. Even the disciples cannot stand comparison. They attempt to silence her. Their little faith and difficulty in understanding in the feeding stories of 14.22-33 and 15.30-38, and in 16.5-12 are readily available for the implied reader to observe. She is willing to receive 'bread-crumbs' while the disciples do not understand about bread and the loaves of the 5,000 or the 4,000 (16.5-12). The motif of bread which ties these episodes together with that of the Canaanite woman and heightens the contrast will be discussed further below.

The sign of Jonah. The next doublet related in the chiastic pattern is the Pharisees' request for a sign (12.38-42 = 16.1-4, twenty-four words in common). This doublet has already been discussed in Chapter 3. Here several things should be reiterated. First, the initial request for a sign follows the second Beelzeboul episode and precedes Jesus' rejection of this mother and brothers, forming a climax to the rejection of Jesus' words and deeds prior to ch. 13. Secondly, in the second episode, the request of the Jewish leaders for a sign is identified as an effort to *test* or *tempt* Jesus. The implied reader, reading the second episode in the light of the first, sees the Jewish leaders becoming more perverse in the course of the narrative. The first request may have been genuine, the second is not. Thirdly, there is no interpretation of the sign of Jonah in the second episode. None is necessary. The implied reader learned its meaning from the first episode and is expected to recall it in retrospect. The Jewish leaders have not learned a thing. For the implied reader, suspense is created and sustained. When will the sign of Jonah appear, and exactly what will it be? As yet there have been no clear passion and resurrection predictions.[1] Yet both episodes tie the sign together with the opposition of the Jewish leaders. Fourthly, the second episode, preceded by the Canaanite woman (15.21-28), the healing of the dumb, maimed, lame and blind (15.29-31), and the feeding of the 4,000 (15.32-39), provides a contrast between the perversity of the Jewish leaders, the faith of the Gentile woman who called Jesus, 'Son of David' and 'Lord', and the amazement of the crowds who marvel at Jesus' power and glorify Israel's God. It also provides a bridge between the feeding of the 4,000 and Jesus' warnings about the leaven of the Pharisees and Sadducees (16.5-12). Reinforced by the echo of the first episode, the second request for a sign ensures that the implied reader will understand what the disciples initially do not, the meaning of the leaven. The implied reader has a superior perspective on the development of Jesus' conflict with the Jewish leaders.

1. For a special interpretation of the sign of Jonah doublet as an anticipation in relationship to the Jewish leaders see Giblin, 'Structural and Thematic Correlations', pp. 415-19.

The feeding stories. The final episodes to be considered are the feedings of the 5,000 and the 4,000 (14.13-21 = 15.29-38, fifty-six words in common) and the related question concerning the leaven of the Pharisees and Sadducees in 16.5-12.[1] The first feeding is preceded by Herod's belief that Jesus is John *redivivus*, the explanation of John's death, and Jesus' withdrawal.[2] A number of episodes intervene between it and the feeding of the 4,000: the second stilling of the storm episode (14.22-33); a summary of the healings in Gennesaret (14.34-35); the Jewish leaders' question about the tradition of the elders and Jesus' reply and teaching on defilement (15.10-11); the disciples' question whether Jesus knows he has offended the Jewish leaders and Jesus' reply labeling the Jewish leaders as blind guides and explanation (15.12-20); and the Canaanite woman near Tyre and Sidon (15.21-28). The second feeding is also followed by a sea journey: this one to the borders of Magadan (15.39). An incident which shows the Jewish leaders in a negative light—the second sign of Jonah request (16.14)—follows it as well.[3] Summaries of Jesus' healing activities (14.13-14 and 15.29-31) form the transition into each feeding proper.

There are many similarities between the stories. The site of the first incident is identified as a wilderness place (14.13) with a mountain nearby (14.23); the second, as a mountain near the Sea of Galilee

1. The parallel stories in Mark have been admirably treated by R.M. Fowler, *Loaves and Fishes* (SBLDS; Chico, CA: Scholars Press, 1981).

2. Whether Jesus withdraws because of John's death or because of Herod's reaction to Jesus. See Cope's argument that 14.3-12 is an explanatory aside ringed by γαρ (14.3) and δε (14.15) ('The Death of John the Baptist', pp. 517-18).

3. McNeile sees a pattern present in Mark as well, *St Matthew*, p. 237:

		Mt.	Mk.		Mt.	Mk.
(a)	xiv.	13-21	vi.31-44	Miraculous feeding of a multitude somewhere to the east of the lake	xv. 32-38	viii. 1-9
(b)		22-33	45-52	Crossing the lake	39a	10a
(c)		34-36	53-56	Arrival in the west of the lake	39b	10b
(d)	xv.	1-20	vii.1-23	Conflict with the authorities	xvi. 1-4a	11, 12
(e)		21-28	24-31	Avoidance of the dominion of Antipas	4b-12	13-21
(f)		29-31	32-37	Healing on the east of the lake	*vacat.*	22-26

(15.29). In both stories Jesus feeds large crowds with a few loaves and fishes. The disciples serve as mediators, giving the food to the crowd. The existence of the first story, however, affects the reading of its double. The implied reader asks why the disciples wonder where the loaves to feed the crowd will come from when they have participated in a similar situation so recently. The repetition underscores the wavering faith and understanding the disciples display in the intervening stories. Those stories include the second stilling of the storm episode and their lack of intelligence concerning the Pharisees and defilement in 15.12-20.

Differences between the two feeding episodes are also significant. There is repetition with variation. In the first story the disciples approach Jesus when evening falls, asking him to dismiss the crowds to go into the villages to buy food since 'the place is wilderness and the hour already passed' (14.15). In the second story Jesus speaks to the disciples first:

> And Jesus calling forward his disciples said: I am filled with tenderness over the crowd, because they remain with me now three days and do not have anything they may eat; and to dismiss them without food I am not willing lest they fall in the way (15.32).

In the first story, Jesus' reply to their request is to tell them to give the crowd something to eat. Their reaction is to say they have nothing except five loaves and two fishes. In the second story, the disciples' reaction to Jesus' statement that he is unwilling to dismiss the crowds is to ask: 'Whence, *to us* in a wilderness enough loaves to satisfy so great a crowd?' They seem to have at least learned that they are to provide the food, but do not know where to get enough. Jesus asks them how many loaves they have. They reply, 'Seven and a few fishes'.[1] The fact that Jesus expresses his concern for the crowd to the

1. The significance of the difference in numbers including 5,000 versus 4,000, 5 plus 2 versus 7 and a few, and 12 baskets and 7 baskets is not immediately apparent. It is sometimes argued with regard to Mark that the 12 baskets and 7 baskets represent Israel and the Gentiles, respectively. See W. Kelber, *Mark's Story of Jesus* (Philadelphia: Fortress Press, 1979), pp. 35 and 39, and H.C. Kee, 'The Gospel According to Matthew', in C. Laymon (ed.), *The Interpreter's One Volume Commentary on the Bible* (Nashville: Abingdon, 1971), p. 628. Another difference is the εὐλόγησενof 14.19 and the εὐχαριστήσας of 15:36. This has sometimes been explained historically as due to two different eucharistic traditions (Fowler, *Loaves and Fishes*, pp. 107-108).

disciples highlights their role as mediators. It also underscores their failure to understand fully what had occurred in the first story.

The disciples' wavering faith and understanding as the plot develops is driven home not only by the repetitive feeding stories, but also by the contexts in which they are found. The plotted order of episodes is significant. The second stilling of the storm episode where Peter walks on the water yet falters as a 'little-faith', the disciples' failure to understand Jesus' teaching on defilement, and the Canaanite woman episode intervene between the two stories. As noted above, the Canaanite woman's willingness to receive *bread*-crumbs is part of a motif of bread introduced in the first feeding story. This motif comes to a climax in 16.5-12. There the disciples do not understand why Jesus warns them of the *leaven* of the Pharisees and Sadducees. This warning is clear to the implied reader and ought to be clear to the disciples. The second request for a sign has just occurred, the only incident intervening between the second feeding and Jesus' warning. Jesus rebukes the disciples with a favorite Matthean label, 'O little faiths' (16.8 = 6.30 = 8.26 = 14.31, cf. 17.20). He asks, 'do you not yet perceive? Do you not remember the five *loaves* of the 5,000...? Or the seven *loaves* of the 4,000...?' Then, reminded by these echoes, they do understand. Immediately following, Peter is able to make the confession of Jesus as 'the Christ, the Son of the living God'. Even though Peter does not understand yet all that this entails, he and the other disciples are on the way to becoming the church with power to bind and loose (16.18-19 = 18.18-20). The implied author uses the doublet of the feeding and its sequel, the leaven of the Pharisees, to show the disciples in transit, in all their weakness, on the way to true discipleship.

Conclusion. In conclusion, we have seen that double and triple stories play an integral role in the development of plot and character in the Gospel of Matthew. The repetition of a similar episode is not merely an additional episode. It has a powerful rhetorical effect in which anticipation and retrospection and repetition with variation are involved. There is a complex texture of interlocking echoes forcing the implied reader to read one episode in the light of the other. The contexts in which the stories reverberate contributes to their effect.

The plotted order of the stories moves from marginal outsiders (the blind men) who respond to Jesus to enemies (the Jewish leaders) who as religious insiders should respond, to friends whose faith and understanding waivers, to a doubly marginal outsider (a Gentile woman) with great faith and outward again in reverse order. The final doublet shows outsiders who follow Jesus towards Jerusalem and the narrative's climax. The episodes characterize and move the plot forward as comparison and contrasts between the various character groups are made.

8. *Conclusion*

This chapter demonstrated the usefulness of 'plot' as a category for analyzing the Gospel of Matthew. It also showed the important role that verbal repetition plays in the Gospel's plot. Four plot devices involving verbal repetition were considered: (1) summary passages, (2) anticipation and retrospection, (3) the Johannine sub-plot, and (4) double and triple stories. Representative examples were treated in each category.

a. *Summary Passages*

The first category, summary passages, includes passages which compress a number of actions which normally would occur over an extended period of time. The repetitions associated with these passages emphasize the gathering of crowds and the healings which spread Jesus' fame as his ministry begins and moves forward. The summaries give through repetition a background and unifying texture to Jesus' movements. They lead up to the triumphal entry and healings in the temple. Two summary passages linked by twenty words, 4.23 = 9.36, also serve a more specific function. They form an inclusio around a section of the narrative. Each forms a bridge to what follows. Together they summarize activities which are illustrated by individual examples in the section they encircle.

b. *Anticipation and Retrospection*

Anticipation and retrospection form the second category. Anticipation or foreshadowing prepares the implied reader for events to come. Retrospection reviews events that have already occurred. They allow the implied author to guide the implied reader's response by engaging his or her memory—emphasizing, interpreting, and tying together certain events. Repetition aids in this process. The events involved may occur within the narrative itself or outside it in story time. The anticipations and retrospections discussed in this chapter appear in the voices of the narrator or reliable characters. They are provided to the implied reader and to privileged characters: the dreams of Joseph (and one to Pilate's wife); the passion–resurrection predictions to the disciples; and the predictions of an appearance in Galilee to the disciples and the women. The latter two anticipations are detailed and *repeated* so often that they create the suspense of anticipation, rather than the suspense of uncertainty. They build to the climax and denouement of the plot. Many of the anticipations discussed predict an event which is described in the same or nearly the same words when it occurs. The event itself then becomes retrospective. It confirms and points to the fulfillment of the prediction(s). Anticipation and retrospection underscore the temporal character of the process of reading. Repetition is particularly helpful when there are long gaps in reading time between an event and its anticipation or recall.

c. *The Johannine Subplot*

The Johannine subplot is a special plot device involving many anticipations and retrospections. It is a sub-plot by analogy to the main plot and largely created by means of repetition. It helps to sharpen and guide the implied reader's response. Through repetition John becomes the foreshadower as well as the forerunner of Jesus.

d. *Double and Triple Stories*

These stories are repetitions in which similarities and variations between nearly identical episodes are significant. The contexts and order in which they appear are also important. Their existence and arrangement in the narrative create comparisons and contrasts between various character groups and move the plot along. In a way they also function as anticipations and retrospections. The first episode anticipates the second (and third). The second (or third) episode recalls the first.

The similarities reinforced by verbal repetition between episodes engage the reader's memory requiring him or her to read each in the light of the other. The similarities may emphasize a character trait or provide motivation for the plot. How many times must Jesus perform miraculous feedings for the disciples truly to understand? How many times will the Jewish leaders seek a sign? Have they learned nothing in the course of the narrative?

e. Verbal Repetition: Variation, Context, and Order

Variations between verbal repetitions affect the implied reader's response. The variations are important in developing the plot. This is obviously true in the case of expanded doublets. The disciples' 'little faith' has continued as the narrative proceeds from the first storm scene to the second. However, Peter's walk on the water and the exclamation, 'Truly you are the Son of God', shows growth, and helps to prepare for Jesus' eventual reunion with the disciples and the great commission. In the immediate context it builds towards Peter's confession in ch. 16. The importance of variations in the more nearly identical doublets was also demonstrated in this chapter. The second pair of blind men are not told to remain silent. They do not disobey, but follow Jesus to Jerusalem as the passion approaches. Further the crowds do not appear in the first episode. In the second, nearer to their conversion to the side of the Jewish leaders as 'the people' (27.25), they rebuke the blind men.

Both examples offered above point to the importance of context. The contexts in which episodes are found affect their interpretation. The implied reader must not only attend to the differences and similarities between episodes, but also the contexts involved. The events which have intervened between episodes as well as the location of each in the overall narrative can be important.

Finally, the order in which repetitions appear is significant. The chiastic arrangement of the double and triple stories is an obvious example. It highlights the contrasts between supplicants, Jewish leaders, disciples, and crowd. It moves the plot forward as it develops the contrasting responses of these groups to Jesus. Thus it prepares the implied reader for the passion and the Great Commission.

Chapter 5

CONCLUSION: LITERARY ANALYSES OF REPETITION IN NARRATIVE, READER RESPONSE AND AURALITY

1. *Introduction*

In the previous chapters I intertwined the study of Matthew as narrative with a study of the functions of extended verbal repetition in the Gospel. From one perspective, I asked what verbal repetition does to the implied reader. From another, I asked how the reader creates—or what the reader does—with verbal repetition. In addition to showing the general functions of repetition outlined in Chapter 1, I explored the specific functions of verbal repetition that relate to the narrative categories of rhetoric, character, and plot. I showed that the temporal dimension of narrative, context, and repetition with variation are important throughout.

In the first chapter I noted that literary critics had applied the concept of redundancy, the availability of information from more than one source, to several types of narratives. Susan Wittig dealt with Middle English romances; Susan Rubin Suleiman with realistic narratives, particularly, the *roman à thèse*. Both emphasized expectations, predictability and persuasion. Both spoke of repeated phrases, scenes, and motives frequently reinforced by verbal repetition. These repetitions may occur within a single work or within a traditional corpus. Suleiman even came up with a sort of grammar of types of repetition including such items as the same event or sequence of events happens to a single character *n* times, several characters pronounce the same interpretive commentary, or the narrator pronounces *n* times the same commentary.[1] In this chapter I will extend the earlier discussion in two ways. First, I will compare my analysis of extended verbal repetition in Matthew with the work of two additional literary

1. Suleiman, 'Redundancy', pp. 127-29.

critics. Secondly, I will turn to a brief examination of verbal repetition, narrative criticism, and reader-response criticism in the light of recent discussions of orality, aurality, and literacy.

The two literary works I will explore are E.K. Brown's *Rhythm in the Novel* and C.S. Brown's *Repetition in Zola's Novels*.[1] I assure the reader that I have not chosen the two works because they repeat the name Brown. Rather I have chosen the first because it is the most well-known literary analysis of repetition in narrative. I have chosen the second, somewhat obscure monograph because it identifies in Zola's novels many of the very same types and functions of verbal repetition I found in Matthew. Thus, the nature of the types and functions of repetition outlined by these works can shed light on those found in Matthew through comparison and contrast. Some readers may find the choice of the Browns, who both deal primarily with modern novels, anachronistic. In the concluding discussion of orality and literacy I will explain why this view is both true in some ways and untrue in others.

2. *Literary Studies of Repetition in Narrative*

a. *E.K. Brown, Rhythm in the Novel*

Edward K. Brown's now classic *Rhythm in* the Novel was first published in 1950. There are four chapters, 'Phrase, Character, Incident'; 'Expanding Symbols'; 'Interweaving Themes'; and 'Rhythm in E.M. Forster's *A Passage to India*'. The first three deal with types of repetition; the fourth with the way these types function in a single novel. Brown is not concerned solely with verbal repetition, but with many forms of repetition with variation. He is careful to point out that it is variation that makes repetition most effective.

'Phrase, Character, Incident'. This is the title of the first chapter, and in it, Brown examines (a) the use of verbal repetition for comic effect

1. E.K. Brown, *Rhythm in the Novel* (Lincoln: University of Nebraska, Bison Books, 1978 [1950]). C.S. Brown, *Repetition in Zola's Novels* (University of Georgia Monographs, 1; Athens, GA: University of Georgia Press, 1952). Another literary critical work which deals with repetition, including verbal repetition is B.F. Kawin, *Telling It Again and Again: Repetition in Literature and Film* (Ithaca, NY: Cornell University Press, 1972) (discussed in Anderson, 'Over and Over and Over Again', 1985)

and reinforcement of the meaning of a plot; (b) repetition of incident depending on sequence in time; and (c) the reduplication of characters and situations. His treatment of verbal repetition is brief. He points first to the use of repetition in a character's speech for comic effect. This is associated with such characters as T.S. Eliot's Mr Brooke whose speech is full of 'well, now's', 'you know's', and 'will not do's' and Dickens's Mr Micawber.[1] Although Brown does not do so, this might be labeled characterization by means of speech habits. The repetition is what makes the characters comic. The second type of verbal repetition Brown treats is really a single example of repetition. He notes that the first paragraph of Moore's *Esther Waters* is repeated word for word with slight variations near the end of the novel. In the beginning Esther arrives at the great house of Woodview. She and everything around her are new and full of possibility. At the end she arrives again, but she and her surroundings are in decline with no future potential. Brown comments that the effect of this circularity is to supply 'a moving reinforcement of the meaning of his [Moore's] plot'.[2] Moore's use of verbal repetition is actually an example of the next type of repetition Brown treats—the repetition of incident depending on sequence in time. He seems to have treated it separately because it involved substantial verbal repetition.

The examples Brown gives of repetition of incident include Hardy's *The Well-Beloved*, Bennett's *The Old Wives' Tale*, and Thackeray's *Vanity Fair*. In Hardy's novel the protagonist falls in love with a nearly duplicate grandmother, mother, and daughter in turn. Although he has aged, each situation is much the same. In *Vanity Fair* the repeated situations are far less similar. Becky Sharp begins her life trying to escape the respectability of the Pinkerton's ladies' school. She attempts to marry Jos Sedley and his money. After ridding herself of Jos and gaining his money, she seeks respectability from a society of dowagers similar to the Pinkertons. Incident is repeated. Brown writes:

> She [Becky] needs nearly twenty years to learn that she cannot pay the cost of defying respectability. Her history has a beautiful circularity, which is the more satisfying since Becky at the end is exactly the same in impulse as she had been twenty years before.[3]

1. E.K. Brown, *Rhythm*, pp. 9-10.
2. E.K. Brown, *Rhythm*, p. 16.
3. E.K. Brown, *Rhythm*, pp. 19-20.

In this, as in Brown's two other examples, repetition depends for its effect on the passage of time between similar incidents.

From repetition depending on sequence in time Brown turns to a rhythmic process that does not so depend—the reduplication of character and situation. One example he offers is Balzac's *Le Père Goriot*. Père Goriot is 'a Lear without a Cordelia'.[1] His two daughters are different in superficial ways, but 'alike at the core, the very same indeed, because they are the products of the same circumstance, the deplorable upbringing their idolatrous father gave them'.[2] Only by repetition, Brown argues, can Balzac emphasize his theme and make sure the reader lays the guilt on the father. If there had been an unselfish daughter, the reader would have been tempted to lay the blame on nature rather than environment. In an examination of James' *The Ambassadors* Brown shows how James plays off the similarities and differences between Chad Newsome, Little Bilham, and Strether and the antitheses between Mrs Newsome and Madame de Vionnet, Waymarsh and Gloriani, Mamie Pocock and Jeanne de Vionnet.

Brown concludes the chapter with a brief discussion of why novelists use such devices.[3] The reasons he cites are:

1. To impose a unifying order on life.
2. To attain 'a greater force, more body'.[4] 'Repetition, expected and then presented, enforces the idea or feeling, makes it more emphatic in its resonance'.[5] However, repetition with subordinate variation is more effective than simple repetition.
3. To achieve other effects akin to Wagnerian motifs, effects which he discusses in the other chapters of the book.

1. E.K. Brown, *Rhythm*, p. 21.
2. E.K. Brown, *Rhythm*, p. 21.
3. He begins this discussion with a quote from Zola, the subject of the monograph discussed below:

> What you call repetitions occur in all my books. This is a literary device that I began by using with some timidity, but have since pushed perhaps to excess. In my view it gives more body to a work, and strengthens its unity. The device is somewhat akin to the motifs in Wagner, and if you will ask some musical friend of yours to explain his use of these, you will understand pretty well my use of the device in literature (p. 28).

In that book, *Repetition in Zola's Novels*, C.S. Brown argues that Zola did not derive his use of repetition from Wagner, citing the same passage and others (pp. 111-18).

4. E.K. Brown, *Rhythm*, p. 28.
5. E.K. Brown, *Rhythm*, p. 29.

To this might be added the following reasons which can be construed from the chapter:

4. To achieve comic effect.
5. To characterize by means of repeated speech.
6. To characterize and/or develop themes by showing the same character in similar situations over time, different characters confronted by the same situation, etc.

A summary of much of what Brown says about repetition in this chapter is found in a quotation he uses from Aldous Huxley's novel-writing character in *Point Counterpoint*:

> A novelist modulates by reduplicating situations and characters. He shows several people falling in love, or dying, or praying in different ways—dissimilars solving the same problem. Or *vice versa*, similar people confronted with dissimilar problems.[1]

Brown notes that in addition to these kinds of repetition, a third appears in *Point Counterpoint* itself: 'similar people confronted by the same problem'.[2] In the body of the chapter many of the repetitions discussed would fit one of these descriptions.

Although as Chapter One progresses Brown moves further from verbal repetition, the types and functions of repetition identified are similar to some characteristic of verbal repetition in Matthew. Both characterization through repeated speech (although not for comic effect) and the reduplication of phrases, characters, and situations occur in Matthew. All one has to do is to consider the double and triple stories to see that this is true. Many of the devices depend on the passage of narrative time for their effect and have an impact on plot. Anticipation and retrospection in particular create unity, force, and resonance. The Johannine sub-plot which draws out the similarities between John and Jesus through verbal repetition shows similar characters facing similar situations. It prepares the implied reader for the climax of the narrative. Perhaps Brown would especially appreciate the Johannine sub-plot because although analogies between Jesus and John are drawn, variations remain clear.

The main difference between Matthew and many of Brown's examples is the degree of repetition. Although variation is important,

1. E.K. Brown, *Rhythm*, p. 8.
2. E.K. Brown, *Rhythm*, p. 9.

Matthew's repetitions are reinforced with a greater degree of verbal similarity. It should be noted that Brown's judgment that a great deal of verbal similarity is mechanical depends on what effects are desired and modern canons of style and taste. He accepts the view that the artist should conceal artifice and strive for uniqueness and variation in expression.

Expanding symbols. Brown's second chapter concerns *expanding symbols*, symbols which grow as they gather meaning from a succession of contexts.[1] The temporal dimension of narrative plays an important role in this type of repetition. Brown takes his starting point from the discussion of rhythm in E.M. Forster's *Aspects of the Novel*. There Forster shows how a musical phrase composed by Vinteuil reverberates in different situations throughout Proust's *A la recherche du temps perdu*. Forster, then, contrasts expanding symbols with fixed symbols or banners which can only mechanically reappear. Brown approves of Forster's discussion of Proust, but disclaims his examples of banners in Meredith—'a double-blossomed cherry tree' for Clara Middleton and 'a yacht in smooth waters' for Cecilia Halkett—explaining how the symbol of the yacht, at least, expands. Instead, Brown offers as a fixed symbol, the thrice-put and thrice-answered question of accident or design in the cosmos posed by Wilder's *The Bridge of San Luis Rey*. Each traveler approaches the bridge 'at the same spiritual moment, after regeneration, and for each the regeneration has been in the same terms of a reappraisal of love'.[2] The distinction Brown and Forster make between fixed and expanding symbols is similar to Norman Perrin's description of Philip Wheelright's distinction between steno and tensive symbols, a single versus a range of possible referents.[3] Here, of course, the expanding

1. E.K. Brown, *Rhythm*, p. 9.
2. E.K. Brown, *Rhythm*, pp. 42-43.
3. N. Perrin, *Jesus and the Language of the Kingdom* (Philadelphia: Fortress Press, 1976), pp. 29-30. P. Wheelright discusses steno-symbols versus depth-symbols (expressive symbols) in *The Burning Fountain* (Bloomington: Indiana University Press, 1968), p. 15. Wheelright distinguishes between two uses of language with respect to what it means: 'to designate clearly for the sake of efficient and widespread communication, and to express with humanly significant fullness' (p. 14). See also Wheelright's *Metaphor and Reality* (Bloomington: Indiana University Press, 1962).

symbol accrues referents as it is repeated with variation in succeeding contexts.

After laying out the differences between fixed and expanding symbols, Brown returns to Forster's commentary on Proust quoting at length:

> A banner can only reappear, rhythm can develop, and the 'little phrase has a life of its own', unconnected with the lives of its auditors, as with the life of the man who composed it. It is almost an actor, but not quite, and that 'not quite' means that its power has gone towards stitching Proust's book together from the inside, and towards the establishment of beauty and the ravishing of the reader's memory. There are times when the little phrase—from its gloomy inception, through the sonata, into the sextet—means everything to the reader. There are times when it means nothing and is forgotten, and this seems to me the function of rhythm in fiction; not to be there all the time like a pattern, but by its lovely waxing and waning to fill us with surprise and freshness and hope.[1]

He then highlights three of Forster's points:

1. The importance of 'irregularity as essential to beauty in the use of this kind of rhythm'[2].
2. The stress on giving the reader time to forget, although Brown feels that Proust allows the reader to forget less than Forster thinks.
3. The fact that 'the little phrase has a life of its own'.[3] The music means different things to different characters and has a 'surplus of meaning', a depth which, Proust suggests, not even the narrator has plumbed.[4]

To illustrate further Brown offers an analysis of the expanding symbol of hay in Forster's *Howards End*. 'Like the little phrase [in Proust]', he writes, 'the hay has meaning only for a few of the characters; response to the hay, like response to the little phrase, is an index to value in a character'.[5] In both novels, characters who avoid analysis—Swann and Ruth Howard—are the first to respond deeply to the symbol. Later perceptive characters, Marcel and Margaret, help

1. E.K. Brown, *Rhythm*, p. 43.
2. E.K. Brown, *Rhythm*, p. 44.
3. E.K. Brown, *Rhythm*, p. 44.
4. E.K. Brown, *Rhythm*, p. 45.
5. E.K. Brown, *Rhythm*, p. 51.

the reader to penetrate further the expanding symbol. Brown contrasts, however, the degree to which the symbol is related to the plot in each novel. Forster's symbol has more to do with the plot and the ending of *Howards End* than Proust's with his story. Brown then speculates that the expanding symbol as a device was suggested to both Proust and Forster by music, especially Wagner.[1]

From a consideration of the source, Brown turns to 'the functions and effect of the device'.[2] He concludes the chapter by enumerating the following functions:

1. To render an elusive emotion or idea, 'that by its largeness or its subtlety cannot become wholly explicit. In contrast a fixed symbol is not as mysterious, more fully intelligible:

> The fixed symbol is almost entirely repetition; the expanding symbol is repetition balanced by variation, and that variation is in progressively deepening disclosure. By the slow uneven way in which it accretes meaning from the succession of contexts in which it occurs; by the mysterious life of its own it takes on and supports; by the part of its meaning that even on the last page of the novel it appears still to withhold—the expanding symbol responds to the impulses of the novelist who is aware that he cannot give us the core of his meaning, but strains to reveal now this aspect of it, now that aspect, in a sequence of sudden flashes.[3]

2. To direct the reader 'to something behind the story, the people, and the setting'; in 'prophetic' fiction, which has a bardic tone, which 'sing[s] in the hall of fiction'.[4] To warn 'the reader that he must look beyond the foreground where he can safely keep his eyes in a novel by Trollope or Thackeray'.[5]

3. To create order:

> By the use of an expanding symbol, the novelist persuades and impels his readers towards two beliefs. First, that beyond the verge of what he can express, there is an area which can be glimpsed, never surveyed. Second, that this area has an order of its own which we should greatly care to know—it is neither a chaos, nor something irrelevant to the clearly

1. He also notes Proust's comment that he found much the same pleasure in Ruskin's lectures *Sesame and Lilies* (E.K. Brown, *Rhythm*, p. 55).
2. E.K. Brown, *Rhythm*, p. 55.
3. E.K. Brown, *Rhythm*, p. 57.
4. E.K. Brown, *Rhythm*, pp. 57-8.
5. E.K. Brown, *Rhythm*, p. 58.

> expressed story, persons and settings that fill the foreground. The glimpses that are all the novelist can give us of this area do not suffice for our understanding how it is ordered, they merely assure us that it is ordered, and that this order is important to us. The use of expanding symbol is an expression of belief in things hoped for, an index if not an evidence of things not seen. It does not say what these things are like: it sings of their existence. To fall back on the words Elizabeth Brentano ascribed to Beethoven, by the expanding symbol we are permitted 'an incorporeal entrance into the higher world of knowledge which comprehends mankind, but which mankind cannot comprehend'.[1]

Brown's second chapter makes several important points that are echoed in the study of repetition in Matthew. The first is that certain kinds of repetition gather meaning from a succession of contexts while others always have the same meaning. Both kinds of repetition occur in Matthew. Labels such as 'Brood of Vipers' or 'Son of Man', for example, gather meaning from the various contexts in which they appear while 'the Baptist' remains a simple unchanging form of identification. Brown's point concerning expanding symbols and banners does not depend on a narrow definition of a symbol, a definition he never offers. Hay in *Howards End* and the repeated approach of regenerated travelers in *The Bridge of San Luis Rey* fit a rather broad description of a symbol as something that stands for a meaning beyond itself. If this is the case, then many kinds of Matthean repetitions are rhythmic. They depend for rhythmic effect on their appearance in successive contexts. However, the Matthean repetitions which most resemble Brown's poetic descriptions of expanding symbols were not discussed except in passing in this book. These would include symbols, images, and themes such as 'the kingdom of heaven', fruit imagery, harvest imagery, christological titles, and sensory images such as the oppositions between sight and blindness, hearing and deafness.

A second important point in Brown's second chapter is that expanding symbols wax and wane and depend on the memory of the reader. This is a clue to their ordering ability. It explains why they appear to have a life of their own and a surplus of meaning.[2] They call on the reader to participate strongly in the creation of meaning. They cause

1. E.K. Brown, *Rhythm*, p. 59.

2. Although Brown never quite makes clear why irregularity or recurrence is essential to the beauty of an expanding symbol.

him or her to draw associations, comparisons, and contrasts from memory of the narrative and personal experience. As we have noted, as the reader reads, his or her mind can be provoked to range backward or forward over the course of the narrative by the appearance of a repetition. Previous interpretations may be seen in a new light, new expectations created. Expanding symbols and many Matthean verbal repetitions in general draw on the reader's ability to order experience in temporal and non-temporal categories. Since an expanding symbol continues to evoke new associations in different contexts and, like metaphor, creates meaning through epiphor and diaphor, its meaning can never be completely stated in ordinary language. This view, of course, depends on the postulate that language can evoke or bear meaning as well as refer to it. Brown's prose in describing the functions of expanding symbols waxes romantic and seems to be striving for the same evocation of meaning 'beyond'.

Although I have discussed nothing quite like Forster's symbol of hay in *Howards End*, this book shares Brown's concern with repetition's demands on the reader's memory, its ordering possibilities, and its evocative power. The repetition of the label 'Hypocrites' is an example. Jesus does not associate the label with a specific group in his first use of the term (6.2, 5, 16). Its use, however, causes the implied reader to search for that group as he or she reads. It prepares the reader for Jesus application of the label to the Jewish leaders in 15.7; 22.18; and 23.13, 15, 23, 25, 27, 29. When it is applied to them, the reader's memory is engaged. The implied reader recalls the earlier description(s). Various behaviors are ordered under the title, 'Hypocrites' and focused as characteristic of the Jewish leaders. The use of the label builds to a crescendo in ch. 23. There many of the anti-Jewish leader threads of the Gospel are brought together in Jesus' diatribe against them. The previous associations of the label hypocrites (and the label blind guides) gathered from each context in which it (they) appeared are evoked. A small note is struck again when Jesus tells the parable of the slave whose master is delayed in ch. 22. He warns that a wicked slave will be cut off and find his place with the hypocrites, where there will be weeping and gnashing of teeth (24.48-51). The label appears irregularly, concentrated in chs. 6 and 23. The intermediate occurrences keep the reader's memory engaged. The associations in the various contexts affect one another. All of the impact of the label is not specified. The specific associations in the various contexts reverberate causing the reader to bring to the text associations from his or her own experience as well.

Interweaving themes. Brown's third chapter deals with what he calls *interweaving themes*, another of the rhythmic devices Forster described in *Aspects of the Novel.* Like the expanding symbol, the interweaving theme 'depends on repetition with variation and it too serves the novelist who would sing in the halls of fiction and invite the reader to attend to the knowledge which comprehends mankind but which mankind cannot comprehend'.[1] This device ties the larger parts of a novel together in the same way as the movements of a sonata or symphony. Brown offers three examples of this musical analogy: Woolf's *To the Lighthouse*, Cather's *The Professor's House*, and Tolstoy's *War and Peace.* The simplest and clearest of the three examples is *To the Lighthouse* which, like a sonata, contains three movements or books. These books are related as integration, disintegration of societal communion, and 'the splendor of life'.

Brown's most complex example is *War and Peace.* He sees it as a slow movement from separateness to union. In it, the world of war and the world of peace shift back and forth in the reader's view and then are violently brought together. In the later parts of the novel, the worlds of war and peace are 'interweaving more and more intimately, fusing with one another', as the love of Andrew Bolkonski and Natasha Rostov 'come[s] to the height'.[2] 'The movement from separateness to union is also expressed in political and intellectual terms', Brown writes.[3] Andrew and Pierre begin the novel separated from their fellow Russians by their admiration for Napoleon. As the novel progresses they turn from Napoleon and are reunited in spirit with their compatriots. They abandon Napoleon, who represents Reason, and turn to Kutuzov and Karataev who embody Wisdom and the Spirit of Russia. A third way in which the movement from separateness to union is expressed is 'in the rise of the Rostov family'.[4] The Rostovs are a force for union of human beings and eventually Andrew, Pierre, and Andrew's sister are drawn in.

In all three novels, *To the Lighthouse*, *The Professor's House*, and

1. E.K. Brown, *Rhythm*, p. 64.
2. E.K. Brown, *Rhythm*, p. 79.
3. E.K. Brown, *Rhythm*, p. 79.
4. E.K. Brown, *Rhythm*, p. 82.

War and Peace, Brown feels he has shown 'an interplay through the phases of the novel of two great forces, and a resolution in favor of one'.[1] Through this, unity is established. Interweaving themes, like the expanding symbol, demand that the reader attend to something beyond the foreground, to mystery. It 'is one of the most powerful, one of the most convincing and moving means for generalizing a novelist's effect'.[2]

Brown's description of interweaving themes, as also his description of expanding symbols, points to elements beyond individual verbal repetitions. Nonetheless, in Matthew verbal repetition contributes to the development of such themes. As noted in the chapter on character, for example, the contrast between the spiritual blindness of the Jewish leaders and the physical blindness of the outcasts is highlighted by repeated references to the Jewish leaders as 'Blind Guides'. This itself is part and parcel of the struggle in the Gospel between the forces arrayed on the side of God and the side of humanity. The struggle moves from Judea, where there is the initial threat of death; to Galilee, place of ministry and conflict; to Judea, where the forces of evil appear to have won; to Galilee, where God's ultimate victory is revealed. Various verbal repetitions occur within and interrelate each of these 'symphonic' movements, creating unity for the real reader who seeks (or uses the narrative elements to create) it.

Rhythm in A Passage to India. In the final chapter, Brown examines various uses of rhythm in Forster's *A Passage to India*. Here only the aspects most relevant to a study of verbal repetition in Matthew will be mentioned. The first example is the use of verbal repetition in a manner similar to that in *Esther Waters*. The phrase, 'Then you are an oriental', is repeated at the beginning and end of the novel. At the beginning, in the second chapter, Aziz, a Moslem doctor, discusses with friends whether 'it is possible to be friends with an Englishman'.[3] They conclude that in India it is impossible. This seems confirmed by a slight he receives soon after at the hands of two Englishwomen. However, retiring to a mosque, he meets an Englishwoman with whom he can be friends, Mrs Moore. She says, 'I don't think I understand people very well. I only know whether I like or dislike

1. E.K. Brown, *Rhythm*, p. 83.
2. E.K. Brown, *Rhythm*, p. 85.
3. E.K. Brown, *Rhythm*, p. 90, quoting Forster.

them.' Aziz responds, 'Then you are an oriental'.[1] At the end of the novel, after the trial precipitated by the Marabar caves, after Mrs Moore has died and Aziz has moved to a Hindu state to escape the English, he meets Mrs Moore's son Ralph. Ralph, an invader, stung by bees, is treated harshly by Aziz. Ralph responds by saying, 'Your hands are unkind.' Aziz remembers Mrs Moore. As they take leave of one another, Aziz asks, 'Can you always tell whether a stranger is your friend?' 'Yes', Ralph replies. 'Then you are an Oriental'—Aziz repeats the same words that had begun the cycle.[2] The cycle begins again with important variations. Ralph and his sister Stella, akin to their mother in spirit, are befriended by Aziz. He takes them on a trip to see a Hindu ceremony as he took Mrs Moore and Adela Quested to the Marabar Caves. Again disaster strikes. The two boats bearing Fielding and Stella and Ralph and Aziz collide with a raft carrying the Hindu god and overturn. However, this disaster is redeemed. The Hindu god and his retinue melt back to mud, floating ashore with letters from Adele and Ronnie Heaslop, and the Hindu Godpole smears the mud on his forehead. All is united. However, separation remains. At the very end of the book Aziz and Fielding go riding. As they move toward each other to embrace, their horses swerve apart. Subhuman India does not allow complete union between native and invader: 'They didn't want it, they said in their hundred voices (rocks, temples, jail, birds, etc.), "Not, not yet," and the sky said, "No, not there."'[3]

Although without cyclical implications, many phrases are repeated in Matthew by characters. Some even show the essential identity of character as does the phrase spoken by Aziz to both Ralph and Mrs Moore. As noted in Chapter 3, Jesus speaks the greatest majority of phrases repeated by one character. Jesus' granting of the authority to bind and loose to Peter and the disciples as a group (16.19 = 18.18-19, nineteen words in common) and the phrase, 'to the lost sheep of the house of Israel' (10.6 = 15.24, six words in common) are examples. The repetition of a vivid phrase such as 'Go [behind me] Satan' (4.10 = 16.23) provides the same kind of 'aha' experience for the reader as Forster's 'Then you are an oriental.' Each actual reader's response will differ, but there can be a mixture of surprise, recognition, and

1. E.K. Brown, *Rhythm*, p. 90, quoting Forster.
2. E.K. Brown, *Rhythm*, p. 91, quoting Forster.
3. E.K. Brown, *Rhythm*, p. 97, quoting Forster.

satisfaction—as when one finds a key piece of a jigsaw puzzle or hears a familiar, but strange snatch of a melody. The use of the same phrase by two different characters is also common in Matthew. The use of the same phrases by John and Jesus is particularly frequent. It is one link between the two.

The other use of repetition that is most directly relevant to Matthew is Brown's description of the rhythm achieved by Forster's division of his novel into three parts, 'Mosque', 'Caves', and 'Temple'. These are like the 'three big blocks of sound' in Beethoven's Fifth Symphony, a structure of 'rhythmic rise-fall-rise':

> Three big blocks of sound—that is what *A Passage to India* consists of. A first block in which evil creeps about weakly, and the secret understanding of the heart is easily dominant. A second block, very long, and very dark, in which evil streams forth from the caves and lays waste almost everything about, but yet meets an opposition, indecisive in some ways, but unyielding, in the contemplative insight of Professor Godpole, and the intuitive fidelity of Mrs. Moore. A third block in which evil is forced to recede, summarily, and spectacularly, not by the secret understanding of the heart, but by the strength on which the secret understanding of the heart depends, contemplative insight, intuitive fidelity. Then the final reminder, that good has merely obliged evil to recede as good receded before evil a little before.[1]

As noted above in the discussion of interweaving themes, this cannot help but remind one of the associations linked with the side of good and the side of evil and the geographical shifts of scene in Matthew: Judea associated with the power of enemies and death; Galilee associated with hope and life.

Conclusion. There are great differences between the novels E.K. Brown discusses and the Gospel of Matthew. Brown is also concerned with a broader definition of repetition. He tends to seek the poetic, the 'beyond'. Nevertheless, a number of the conclusions he reaches are similar to those reached in this book. These include the power of repetition to order, unify, reinforce, and to evoke associations not explicitly stated. Like Brown, previous chapters of this book also found that repetition with *variation*, the temporal dimension of narrative, the gathering of meaning from a succession of contexts, and the memory of the reader are important factors to consider. Many of

1. E.K. Brown, *Rhythm*, p. 113.

the types or categories of repetition treated by Brown are found in Matthew. Matching elements from Matthew to these categories is somewhat difficult because Brown does not offer clear and detailed criteria. Yet certainly repeated speech; reduplicated phrases, characters and incidents; banners, and elements similar to expanding symbols and interweaving themes are present. The categories I treated are concerned solely with verbal repetition and tend to be narrower than those he offers.

b. *Calvin S. Brown, Repetition in Zola's Novels*

The second literary study of repetition in narrative to be considered is Calvin S. Brown's *Repetition in Zola's Novels*. In this monograph Brown treats verbal repetition, ranging from 'significant single words to phrases, sentences, and occasionally passages of more than a page, repeated either identically or with variation'.[1] C.S. Brown's focus is more like that of this work in that he discusses *verbal* repetition in a single work and seeks to identify its functions. He believes he has discovered repetitions with 'a definite artistic purpose'. He feels that they can be identified as 'intentional with the author' and designed for the reader to recognize as repetitions.[2] C.S. Brown's procedure is to create a typology of Zola's verbal repetitions and treat each type in turn. Eleven types are classified by form, content, and function. A given verbal repetition may fall into more than one category, not only because there are multiple criteria, but also because 'at its best, Zola's repetition is a means of artistic economy designed to effect several different purposes simultaneously'.[3] As Brown treats each type of repetition he makes general comments about the functions of verbal repetition. He summarizes and expands these comments in chapters entitled 'Extension of Significance' and 'Conclusions'.

In many ways the task C.S. Brown assigns himself is similar to that of this book. The difference is that I treat verbal repetitions within the literary categories of direct commentary and point of view; character; and plot. Types of verbal repetitions are identified within each category. A single repetition may appear in more than one category. Neither Brown nor I develop a consistent, clear grid which is then applied to the texts concerned. Rather each examines the operation of

1. C.S. Brown, *Repetition*, p. 2.
2. C.S. Brown, *Repetition*, p. 2.
3. C.S. Brown, *Repetition*, p. 3.

verbal repetitions and begins to group repetitions according to patterns he or she sees emerging. A number of types identified are similar. Zola and the author of Matthew use some of the same techniques (whether the techniques are conscious or not). Below each of Brown's types similar to types of repetition in Matthew is discussed. Then Brown's general comments about verbal repetition in Zola's novels are compared and contrasted to my general conclusions.

Types. The first type of verbal repetition Brown treats is the *tag*: 'This is a word or phrase, usually brief, serving to describe or characterize a person or thing, or to represent a characteristic trait or habit'.[1] Examples are the titles used for the two central female characters in *Le Ventre de Paris*: 'Lisa is "la belle Lisa" (pp. 62, 84, 116, 126, 135) or "la belle charcutière" (pp. 116, 202, 207); and her rival in well-padded pulchritude is Louise, "la belle Normande" (pp. 84, 112, 114, 126, 127) or "la belle poissonnière" (p. 84)'.[2] These fixed epithets 'serve to point up an essential relationship of characters which is one of the principal structural features of the novel'.[3] Some tags are ironic.[4] Some are used by a single character and serve 'to summarize his attitude toward some other person'.[5] However, according to Brown, 'The most frequent function of the tag is to state or imply, with one or two brief strokes, the essentials of a person's character of function'.[6] Tags can also help the reader to keep characters straight when there is a large cast. In addition to characters, they may serve to identify and 'characterize' places, things or ideas.

Labels or epithets in Matthew would fall within Brown's category of the 'tag'. They briefly characterize, economically highlighting, identifying and fixing an important aspect of a character in the mind of the implied reader.[7] As with Brown's tags, some distinguish one character from another. Some are also used by a single character to

1. C.S. Brown, *Repetition*, p. 5.
2. C.S. Brown, *Repetition*, p. 6. Page numbers Brown gives are from *Les Oevres Complètes: Emile Zola* (Notes et Commentaires de Maurice Le Blond, Texte de l'édition Eugène Fasquelle, Paris: Typographic François Bernouard, n.d.).
3. C.S. Brown, *Repetition*, p. 7.
4. C.S. Brown, *Repetition*, pp. 7-9.
5. C.S. Brown, *Repetition*, p. 9.
6. C.S. Brown, *Repetition*, p. 9.
7. See Chapter 3, pp. 126-28.

capture an attitude toward another. Brown does not discuss the importance of the appearance of tags in various contexts as the narrative proceeds or the way in which each repetition can increase predictability and the assent of the implied reader. Brown's category is broader than the label since it includes repeated descriptions such as the emperor's watery eyes and the characterization of places, things or ideas. Examples of labels in Matthew are 'Brood of Vipers', 'the Baptist', 'the one betraying him', and, of course, the christological titles.

Brown's second type of repetition is the *frame*: 'its purpose is to set off an episode—usually a fairly brief one—by framing it between a statement of some sort and a repetition of that statement'. [1] Biblical scholars will recognize Brown's frame as an inclusio. One example he offers is the encircling of one of the fairy's speeches in *Contes* with the phrases: 'Aimez-vous, mes enfants. Laissez les souvenirs à l'austère vieillesse,...[and] Aimez-vous, mes enfants; laissez parler la vieillesse'.[2]

Brown points out that this frame not only gives a rounded-off effect, but also sets 'off the speeches of the fairy from everyday colloquial reality'.[3] Other frames in Zola also set off unusual incidents by framing them with repeated descriptions of the ordinary or the eternal with the transitory. A frame is also used to set off each of five chapters in *Fécondité*.[4] Although not one of my focii, inclusio is common as a concentrated form of repetition in Matthew. Examples are 7.16 = 7.20 and 19.30 = 20.16.[5] In Chapter 4 I discussed an inclusio in the extended repetition of the summary passages of 4.23 = 9.35.

Brown's third type of repetition is the *key-passage*: 'a relatively long repetition embodying, in a striking and memorable form, one of the fundamental ideas of a book, or sometimes, the single idea on which the entire work is based'. [6] One example is the death-bed

1. C.S. Brown, *Repetition*, p. 15.
2. Zola as quoted by C.S. Brown, *Repetition*, p. 15.
3. C.S. Brown, *Repetition*, p. 16.
4. This device is similar to the frames setting off the reign of each king in 2 Kings.
5. See J.C. Fenton, 'Inclusio and Chiasmus in Matthew', *SE* 1 (TU, 73; Berlin: Akademie-Verlag, 1959), pp. 174-79.
6. C.S. Brown, *Repetition*, p. 23.

instructions Blanche de Rionne gives to Daniel Raimbault in *Le Voeu d'une Morte*. These instructions recur throughout the narrative in echoed phrases and three sections are reproduced '*in extenso* at critical points of the story'.[1] Sometimes a key-passage is 'used to indicate a fixed idea or obsession in the mind of a character, like the corpse in *Thérèse Raquin*'.[2] Sometimes it is used as a 'means of establishing a general background and tone for the action'.[3] In *Le Rêve*, for example, the Saints, 'their lives, attributes and miracles', recur 'constantly as a background for the world of wonder, primitive faith, and miracle in which the heroine lives'.[4] Many key-passages are metaphoric and underscore the basic theme of a novel. In several of Zola's series of novels key-passages recur from novel to novel. There is no exact parallel to this device in Matthew. However, many phrases embodying key ideas do recur. An example is the proclamation, 'Repent the Kingdom of Heaven is at hand' in 3.1-2 = 4.17 = 10.7.

Brown's fourth type of repetition is the *hammer*: 'It consists of a short passage, usually itself repetitious, which is used intensively throughout a relatively short scene in order to emphasize an action or situation, driving it home by repeated blows'.[5] There are thirty-eight uses of the hammer in Zola's novels. Several times 'a person suffering a great emotional shock reacts by mechanically repeating the first exclamation which it provokes'.[6] For example, Eve cries, 'Tu mens, tu mens!' five times in two pages in *Paris*.[7] Another use of the hammer is 'to indicate a string or exclusive preoccupation with any single idea'.[8] For example, in *La Débâcle* the question, 'Où est-ce?' is in Silvine's mind as she searches for her fiancé's body, five times in six pages.[9] The hammer also appears in the shouts of a crowd. Another usage is the repetition of a phrase as a 'formula for an act or situation' repeated 'with each repetition of the act, or as a means of

1. C.S. Brown, *Repetition*, p. 23.
2. C.S. Brown, *Repetition*, p. 26.
3. C.S. Brown, *Repetition*, p. 27.
4. C.S. Brown, *Repetition*, p. 28.
5. C.S. Brown, *Repetition*, p. 33.
6. C.S. Brown, *Repetition*, p. 34.
7. C.S. Brown, *Repetition*, p. 34.
8. C.S. Brown, *Repetition*, p. 34.
9. C.S. Brown, *Repetition*, p. 35.

keeping the situation before the reader'.[1] One example is Gervaise's use of the phrase, 'Monsieur, écoutez donc...' six times as she attempts to solicit in *L'Assommoir*.[2] The above examples are repeated phrases spoken by a character. Some hammer phrases appear in the narrator's voice. The narrator, for example, uses the 'rouler, rouler' formula for the train to and from Lourdes in *Lourdes*. 'In two cases, hammer repetitions are used to create a backdrop for the grand finale of a novel'.[3] In *Nana*, for example, as the lovers and courtesans reminisce about Nana as she lies dead, the crowds shout, 'À Berlin! à Berlin! à Berlin!'[4] Finally, in two cases Zola uses the hammer with variation. In *Paris* Salvat's flight from the police is 'dominated by a pairing of some form of the verb *galoper*'.[5]

Concentrated repetition was not treated in my discussion of Matthew. However, Matthew does contain concentrated repetition similar to the hammer. Allen lists sixteen examples of the 'editor's' repetition of 'a phrase or construction two or three times at short intervals'.[6] C.H. Lohr offers over twenty examples of what he calls the repetition of *key-words*.[7] The repetition of key-words unifies 'the individual sections of a composition' and develops 'a leading idea by putting stress on certain salient words'.[8] Brown stresses the importance of the hammer as emphasizing an action or situation or a person's preoccupation with a single idea. Concentrated key-words or phrases in Matthew may have these functions, but they have others as well. In many cases they stress a theme. In addition to emphasizing an idea, others also have a structuring function as with 'you have heard that it was said...' (5.21, 27, 33, 38, 43).

The fifth type of repetition is the *quotation*. This occurs when the

1. C.S. Brown, *Repetition*, p. 36.
2. C.S. Brown, *Repetition*, p. 36.
3. C.S. Brown, *Repetition*, p. 37.
4. C.S. Brown, *Repetition*, p. 38.
5. C.S. Brown, *Repetition*, p. 38.
6. Allen, *S. Matthew*, pp. lxxvi-lxxxvii.
7. Lohr, 'Oral Techniques', pp. 422-24. The examples include '*genea* (11.16; 12.39, 41, 42, 45), *dynameis* (11.20, 21, 23), *sēmeion* (12.38, 39 *ter*), and *krisis* (11.22, 24; 12.18, 20, 36, 41, 42)' (p. 422). To his examples add ἀργύρια (27.3, 5, 6, 9) and phrases like 'your Father who sees in secret will reward you' (6.4, 6, 18) and 'you have heard that it was said (to men of old)' (5.21, 27, 33, 38, 43) which have a structural function within a brief section of the Gospel.
8. Lohr, 'Oral Techniques', p. 422.

narrator or a character quotes him or herself or another character and the quotation is identified as a quotation. One example is Mlle. Saget's comment on Florent's arrival in *Ventre*. 'Je ne sais quel micmac il y a chez eux...mais ça ne sent pas bon', repeated when awaiting Florent's arrest at the end of the novel, 'Je vous le disais, vous vous rappelez: "Il y a un micmac chez les Quenu qui ne sent pas bon."'[1] Frequently, the narrator borrows phrases from his own characters. Again in *Ventre*, Claude describes Claire as 'une vierge de Murillo'. Zola (i.e. the narrator) uses this epithet later, 'crediting it to Claude...'[2] Some quotations dominate a work in the same way as a key passage.

Matthew contains many quotations. Chapter 2 noted that the narrator and Jesus frequently quote Scripture. The repetitions involved, however, are the introductory formulas. In most cases the quotation is not a repetition of a section of Scripture already used in the Gospel.[3] In 28.6 an angel tells the women at the tomb that Jesus 'was raised as he said', but does not repeat an entire passion-resurrection prediction. Most of the exact repetitions of previous dialogue—and there are many—are not identified as quotations. Examples are 'Repent for the kingdom of heaven is at hand' (3.1-2 = 4.17 = 10.7); 'there will be weeping and the gnashing of teeth' (8.12 = 13.42 = 13.50 = 22.13 = 24.51 = 25.30); and 'If you are the Son of God...' (4.3 = 4.6 = 27.40). In Chapter 3 the characterizing functions of repeated dialogue of a single character and dialogue of one character repeated by another were discussed. Brown does not discuss such functions.

Brown's sixth type of repetition is that of repeated *metaphor and symbol*. This category is defined by content rather than use. It overlaps a great deal with other types. Sometimes a work of art or music is used symbolically. In *Madeleine* a song from Madeleine's Paris days is repeated by Vert-de-Gris twice as a 'symbol of an inescapable past', for example.[4] This reminds one of an expanding symbol discussed by E.K. Brown, Proust's use of Vinteuil's music. C.S. Brown offers several other examples of repeated symbols and metaphors, but does not discuss any typical functions. Repeated symbol and imagery were not discussed in this dissertation. They are, however, present in Matthew, as noted above in the discussion of E.K. Brown. Imagery of

1. C.S. Brown, *Repetition*, citing Zola, p. 41.
2. C.S. Brown, *Repetition*, p. 42.
3. An exception is Jesus' use of Hos. 6.6 in 9.13 and 12.7.
4. C.S. Brown, *Repetition*, p. 42.

fruit and harvest for example, recurs throughout the Gospel. The characterizing functions of this imagery applied by John and Jesus to the Jewish leaders is treated in Chapter 3.

Brown's seventh type of repetition is the use of *parallels*, identical or similar language used by the author to report similar situations. This would fall within E.K. Brown's category of the reduplication of incident. Parallels, according to C.S. Brown, have a dual function: to 'demonstrate the sensitivity and objectivity of the writer as a recording apparatus', and to 'bring the identity or similarity forcibly to the reader's attention'.[1] The objectivity of the author is demonstrated, according to Brown because he or she reports 'identical or similar happenings in identical or similar words'.[2] Parallels have different purposes depending on their subject. If the subjects are identical the accounts will emphasize this. If there is: 'a basic similarity with significant differences—usually due to intervening developments—both aspects will be reflected, the identity by identical language, and the differences by variations which by virtue of their setting in repetitions, will stand out sharply'.[3]

Both Browns emphasize the importance of repetition with variation. C.S. Brown notes that Zola often shortened the second of a pair of parallels. This is the case in the description of Lisa and Quenu's work in a *charcuterie* before and after their marriage in *Ventre*.[4] Another example emphasizing determinism is the repeated description of abortion employed when Valerie and Reine each die in *Fécondité*.[5] According to Brown, the repetition shows that the same false values lead to the same disastrous results. Sometimes when the reader begins reading the second of the pair of parallels, he or she realizes the same circumstances are to be repeated. In the case of Valerie and Reine, this leads the reader to foresee and accept Reine's death as inevitable. Brown cites 'cases where an event comes to pass according to dreams or expectations' as a variation of this type of parallel.[6] In effect, Brown is saying that parallels can serve as anticipations and retrospections. Brown's examples of parallels emphasized by repetition for

1. C.S. Brown, *Repetition*, p. 53.
2. C.S. Brown, *Repetition*, p. 53.
3. C.S. Brown, *Repetition*, p. 53.
4. C.S. Brown, *Repetition*, pp. 53-54.
5. C.S. Brown, *Repetition*, p. 56.
6. C.S. Brown, *Repetition*, p. 59. This occurs in the Matthean birth story.

the sake of differences make clear that difference in context is important. One example occurs in *Le Docteur Pascal.* After Clotilde first gives herself to Pascal she murmurs in his ear: '—Maître, oh! maître, maître...' Later, when she finds him dead, she poignantly again cries, '—Oh! maître, maître, maître...'[1]

C.S. Brown's 'parallels' sound very much like the Matthean double and triple stories as well as the Matthean anticipations such as the dreams and passion-resurrection predictions. As Brown, I noted the use of repetition to bring the similarities between situations to the reader's attention, the importance of variations, and of differing contexts in the course of the narrative. Zola's use of parallels to 'demonstrate the sensitivity and objectivity of the writer as a recording apparatus'[2] is a function I did not contemplate. Whether parallels achieve that purpose seems to depend more on explicit literary conventions than the others. Zola breaks with the modern convention that variation is artistic in order to pursue and convey 'realism'. It is not at all clear that verbal repetition in similar situations in and of itself conveys objectivity.

Brown's eighth type of repetition is the *slogan*, 'a catch-word or short phrase designed to promote some idea or attitude by incessant reiteration'.[3] Some appear in only one novel. Others are repeated in several. The 'most obvious and persistent of all the slogans is "vérité et justice."'[4] A slogan is usually placed 'in emphatic positions, where its impact on the reader will be the greatest'.[5] This category is defined by use and so may overlap other categories such as the tag and metaphor. Matthean repetitions similar to the tag and metaphor were discussed previously.

Brown's tenth type of repetition is the *focus*. The focus gathers together in a fairly small space 'a number of passages originally much more widely distributed'.[6] The 'general purpose of the focus is to serve as a summary, either in Zola's own narrative or, even more often, in the mind of one of his characters'.[7] One example occurs in

1. Quotations from Zola in C.S. Brown, *Repetitions*, p. 61.
2. C.S. Brown, *Repetition*, p. 53.
3. C.S. Brown, *Repetition*, p. 67.
4. C.S. Brown, *Repetition*, p. 67.
5. C.S. Brown, *Repetition*, p. 68.
6. C.S. Brown, *Repetition*, p. 79.
7. C.S. Brown, *Repetition*, p. 79.

La Faute de l'Abbé Mouret. The novel begins with the description of Serge's day. At the end of the day, Serge reviews the day and earlier descriptions and metaphors are echoed. It is a recapitulation containing 'quotations and echoes from the earlier accounts'.[1] Focal repetitions result in 'flashes of association' and give 'the whole passage an air of familiarity...'[2] In the above cited example the repeated phrases also serve to put the reader in Serge's place. 'It is also characteristic that many of the phrases used in such focal repetitions are motives with an independent existence of their own.'[3] Also, focal repetition may be used to recreate an elaborately described background in a relatively short space...Finally...it can be turned to the ends of propaganda'.[4]

The Matthean summaries, discussed in Chapter 4, are similar to the focus. They summarize in a few sentences actions which occurred over an extended period of time. They often indicate that Jesus continued to pursue activities such as proclaiming and healing, examples of which have already been given in scene form. Key words and phrases do connect many of the passages to scenes. Repetition also links several of the summaries to one another and one set forms an inclusio. Brown does not mention the latter forms of repetition in Zola's novels.

General comments. In addition to describing types of verbal repetition, C.S. Brown makes a number of general comments about its use and significance in Zola's novels.[5] One important observation is the distinction between static and dynamic repetitions: 'Though many of the repetitions are fixed formulae which are given static associations or significance and are used to recall these when it seems desirable, others are dynamic, and take on a wider or different range of meaning in the course of their use'.[6] This distinction is much the same as the one E.K. Brown makes between fixed and expanding symbols.

1. C.S. Brown, *Repetition*, p. 80.
2. C.S. Brown, *Repetition*, p. 81.
3. C.S. Brown, *Repetition*, p. 82.
4. C.S. Brown, *Repetition*, p. 84.
5. Not discussed are Brown's chapters devoted to repetition in Zola's novel cycles and a consideration of conscious and unconscious repetitions. Brown documents many of the conscious repetitions with Zola's own notes.
6. C.S. Brown, *Repetition*, p. 87.

The extension of the word 'ignoble' 'from the description of a putrified and swollen corpse to all the consequences of a murder' in *Thérèse Raquin* is an example of dynamic repetition.[1] There are other subtler examples comparable to Forster's use of hay in *Howards End.*

In addition to the gathering of meaning in a succession of contexts, C.S. Brown notes several of the same functions as E.K. Brown: the creation of order or structure, the achievement of a lyric ('singing in the halls of fiction') tone, increase in intensity or force, and implicitly the engagement of the reader's memory.[2] In terms of order, C.S. Brown argues that Zola 'groped his way' to a solution of the problem of the naturalistic writer in imposing form, particularly in terms of selection from the real world and arrangement of time. Repetition allowed him to shape his material without violating the impression of a cross-section of life.

Brown also argues that Zola's use of repetition was 'influenced by both the scope and the tone of a novel'.[3] The 'larger the list of characters and the more complicated their relationships'[4] and/or the more 'lyrical' the tone, the more extensive the use of repetition. Repetition's effect upon the memory of the reader is implied in his comments about complexity. The role of the reader is also important in terms of a 'lyrical' or 'poetic' tone.

Finally, in explaining the significance of repetition in Zola's novels Brown emphasizes the ability of repetition to achieve striking effects. He argues that 'the importance of Zola's repetition is perhaps best shown by the fact that striking or memorable passages...owe some of their effectiveness to this device'.[5] He attributes the power of repetition, as in the use of dynamic symbols, to the increase of intensity gained by the building up of associations and the very fact of repetition itself:

1. C.S. Brown, *Repetition*, p. 87.

2. Brown notes that the effect of a repetition depends on the reader's perception of it: 'The effect of a repetition lies in the mind of the reader, and the use of 'ignoble' which secures a definite effect in *Thérèse Raquin* would be entirely lost in the verbal and repetitious exuberance of *Fécondité*', p. 118. He also notes how certain phrases 'remind the reader' of earlier events, p. 120.

3. C.S. Brown, *Repetition*, p. 119.

4. C.S. Brown, *Repetition*, p. 119.

5. C.S. Brown, *Repetition*, p. 119.

> The secret of the power of repetition to achieve such striking results seems to lie in a constant increase of tension which it can produce when skillfully and moderately used. A phrase or passage selected as a repeated motive must be striking to begin with, or it will not be remembered on its subsequent appearance. But in each of the later recurrences it gains added intensity both from the building up of further associations and from the very fact of its repetition. Thus it is that Zola can use repetition both as one of the primary structural devices in the working out of his novels and as a means of creating memorably effective individual scenes.[1]

Conclusion. In addition to similar types of repetition, a comparison of C.S. Brown's work and that of the previous chapters concerning Matthew revealed a number of similar conclusions about the use and functions of repetition. These include the importance of repetition with *variation*; the accretion of meaning as a word, phrase, or symbol is repeated in successive contexts; repetition's power to emphasize, order and unify; and the importance of the reader's memory, especially involving anticipation and retrospection. All of these points involve repetition as a means of communication between implied author and implied reader, something implicit in Brown's book and explicit here. C.S. Brown identified two purposes of verbal repetition in Zola that were not proposed as purposes of Matthean repetition. The first is the power of repetition to shape a narrative while maintaining the impression of a cross-section of life. The shaping power of repetition in Matthew was noted and is similar in many respects to that in Zola's novels. The goal of a 'realistic' novel, however, is something Brown gleans from Zola's comments on his own work. Zola replaces ordering conventions which he feels his audience will perceive as 'fiction' with repetition. Without specifying the expectations of a particular group of actual readers—whether the original authorial audience or a contemporary audience—it is impossible to say whether repetition in Matthew will create the impression of a slice of life or seem stilted and artificial. When the chapter and verse divisions that appear in modern texts of Matthew are absent, however, one can appreciate how much repetition shapes and orders the narrative. This would be the experience of readers reading a manuscript without chapter and verses as well as that of ancient or modern auditors. Such ordering repetition ranges from the

1. C.S. Brown, *Repetition*, p. 121.

concentrated inclusio, 'From their fruits you will know them', in 7.16 = 7.20 which encircles a warning about producing good fruits to the chiastic extended repetitions of the double and triple stories. In Matthew, picking a passage at random, the reader or hearer finds a series of interlocking echoes that bind it to what has gone before and to what follows. The section enclosed by 7.16-20, for example, echoes 3.8, 10 and anticipates 12.33; 21.41b, 43 which all have to do with producing fruit (3.10b = 7.19, eleven words in common; 7.16-20 = 12.33, eleven words in common). The metaphor of interweaving themes or repeated musical phrases strikes a chord with reference to Proust, Zola, or Matthew.[1]

The second purpose of verbal repetition noted by C.S. Brown, but not stressed in this book, is the creation of a lyric tone. Both Browns argue that repetition in certain novels creates a lyric or bardic ('singing in the halls of fiction') tone. This is perhaps the most slippery of their conclusions. There are no criteria given for defining such a tone or determining when one exists. In his description E.K. Brown merely echoes the murky emotional tone he attempts to describe, arguing that repetition evokes, the depths, things that cannot be said. One suspects that what the Browns are pointing to is (1) the resemblance between ancient epics containing a great deal of repetition and modern novels which utilize repetition and (2) the way in which many narrative repetitions require the actual reader to supply associations from the various appearances of a repetition and from personal experience as he or she reads. Certain repetitions create meaning, but remain elusive since they do not spell it out in detail. They evoke and require the reader to fill (or leave unfilled) the gaps. This may account for the Browns' sense of the 'poetic' or 'emotive' or 'deep' character of certain novels employing repetition. The multiple levels on which repetition occurs including semantic, syntactic, as well as visual and/or aural creates a resonance that is simple and complex at the same time.

Examination of the work of the Browns reveals that several literary critics have made observations about the types and uses of repetition in modern narratives that hold true for Matthew. Whether this is due to compositional conventions common to all narratives, the similar reading conventions of myself and the Browns, or the nature of

1. Or for that matter with Mark, according to Joanna Dewey ('Oral Methods', p. 40) who points out the structural interlocking of that Gospel.

repetition itself in a temporal medium can be debated. What is unlikely to be said about repetition in the works the Browns describe is that repetition is artless, merely due to orally influenced composition or editing of sources, and irrelevant to understanding how the texts convey their messages. This suggests that my consideration of repetition as a Matthean narrative device with effects upon readers is not something that should be dismissed out of hand, whatever the explanation of its origins. The rhetorical effects described could occur whatever the genesis of the repetitions. Repetition can impact readers and, as I will suggest below, hearers of the Gospel whether they come from the first or the twenty-first century.

3. *Orality, Aurality, Narrative, and Reader-Response*

Even granting all that I have said about the similarities between the functions of repetition in Matthew and those identified by modern literary critics, some readers will question comparison to novels as anachronistic. They may also reject the use of literary methods such as narrative and reader-response criticisms, largely developed in conjunction with modern novels. Why not turn to Homer and the Parry-Lord oral-formulaic theory instead, especially since it was used so fruitfully by C.H. Lohr in his article, 'Oral Techniques in the Gospel of Matthew'?[1]

My first answer goes to the purpose of my work. My goal was to examine Matthew in terms of narrative categories rather than to explain its genesis or to recreate the response of the first century audience. Verbal repetition is a feature of the text that is part of the

1. C.H. Lohr's article is discussed at length in Chapters 1 and 4 above. Important works in the development of oral-formulaic theory include Milman Parry, 'Studies in the Epic Technique of Oral Verse-Making I: Homer and Homeric Style', *Harvard Studies in Classical Philology* 41 (1930), pp. 73-197; *idem*, 'Studies in the Epic Technique of Oral Verse-Making II: The Homeric Language as the Language of Oral Poetry', *Harvard Studies in Classical Philology* 43 (1932), pp. 1-50 and the work of Parry's student A.B. Lord, *The Singer of Tales* (Cambridge, MA: Harvard University Press, 1960; repr. edn, New York: Atheneum, 1974). For the most helpful review and bibliography of works using this theory see J.M. Foley, *The Theory of Oral Composition: History and Methodology* (Bloomington: Indiana University Press, 1988). For an earlier review of the Parry–Lord theory, its application to Homer, and criticism by Homeric scholars see H. Clarke, *Homer's Readers* (Newark: University of Delaware Press, 1981), pp. 263-81.

communication between implied author and implied reader. Any actual reader or hearer must respond to that feature whatever the century. Particular reading or hearing conventions may alter actual readers' responses. The work of the Browns suggests that repetition is a literary device that modern readers find meaningful. The similarity in types of repetition between certain modern novels and Matthew suggests that some types of repetition are common to a variety of narratives. Modern readers, however, may view a great deal of verbal repetition as 'redundant' in the pejorative sense of the term. Susan Rubin Suleiman suggests that readers dislike the amount of redundancy in some modern *romans à thèse* because it leads to excessive predictability, leaving little work for the reader.[1] Some contemporary readers may find the Gospels excessively redundant. It has been my experience, however, that most modern readers find the Gospels rather enigmatic. They seek to explain the exact verbal repetition they find, often in terms of its compositional origin. It is often in this vein that appeals to Homer and the oral-formulaic theory are made.

It is certainly true that Matthew has many of the features characteristic of orally composed narratives or narratives with a strong oral legacy or residue.[2] If the difference between poetry with its need to meet metrical requirements and prose is kept in mind, the oral-formulaic theory and study of oral traditional narrative in general can greatly contribute to an understanding of the oral tradition lying behind the Gospels as Werner Kelber has so aptly demonstrated in *Orality and Literacy*.[3] However, the oral-formulaic theory

1. 'Redundancy', pp. 139-40.

2. These include its formulaic, additive, aggregative, and redundant style; its episodic structures and its 'flat' or heavy characters. See W.J. Ong, *Orality and Literacy: The Technologizing of the Word* (London and New York: Methuen, 1982), pp. 3-41, 141-55 for a discussion of these characteristics. Although Matthew certainly seems to be more plotted than Ong would argue that oral literature is. Matthew shares many of the characteristics Werner Kelber describes as marks of Mark's oral legacy in *The Oral and the Written Gospel* (Philadelphia: Fortress Press, 1983), pp. 44-89 and those which Joanna Dewey describes in 'Oral Methods of Structuring Narrative in Mark', *Int* 43 (1989), pp. 32-44.

3. Parry and Lord argue that repetition arises out of the need for the oral bard to fill slots—to fill metrical lines and construct scenes rapidly as he or she sings. The key unit on the level of phrases is the formula; on the level of the narrative it is the theme. Parry defined a *formula* as 'a group of words which is regularly employed under the same metrical conditions to express a given essential idea' (*Studies in the*

has focused primarily on the genesis or composition of narratives, rather than the interrelations of narrative elements and reception which are my central concerns. I have focused on the rhetorical effects of repetition rather than its origin. My emphasis on narrative rhetoric is not unique. Even in Homeric studies which are deeply influenced by the oral-formulaic theory, scholars are increasingly concerned to study the narrative significance of repeated formulas and

Epic Technique, I, p. 272). Formulas were part of a formulaic system and did not have any particular stylistic functions. In 'Perspectives on Recent Work on the Oral Traditional Formula' (*Oral Tradition*, I (1986), pp. 491-92) Lord, Parry's student, distinguished between a formula and a repetition. A formula is repeated because it helps the oral poet in verse-making. '*Formulas do not point to other uses of themselves; they do not recall other occurrences*' (emphasis is Lord's, p. 492). Repetitions 'are repeated for aesthetic or referential reasons rather than ease in verse-making' (p. 492). In transitional texts lying between oral and written, formulas give way to true repetitions according to Lord. Lord defined *themes* as 'the groups of ideas regularly used in telling a tale in the formulaic style of traditional song' (*Singer of Tales*, p. 68). In 'Perspectives on Recent Work on Oral Literature' *FMLS* 10 (1974), p. 20 he added that these narrative elements must have a strong component of verbal repetition. Lord's views on the distinction between formula and repetition are similar to those expressed by Meier Sternberg with regard to the Hebrew Scriptures in the *Poetics of Biblical Narrative: Ideological Literature and the Drama of Reading* (Bloomington: Indiana University Press, 1987): 'The comparison with the ancient tradition that produced a *Gilgamesh* and on the other hand with modern literature turns out especially enlightening. In the very frequency of repetition and its objective control, biblical narrative is of its time and place. Yet in the flexibility of form and operation, it not only anticipates but often surpasses the achievements of modernism. Such is the range of variables endowed with distinctive force—the type of member, the nature of the object, the source of presentation, the degree of specificity and redundancy, the kind of correspondence effected, the order of serialization, or the motivational logic—as to do more than invalidate any formulaic approach. None of the possibilities of repetition—neither verbatim nor variant nor telescoped, for example—is allowed to assume control as the general norm against the background of which any departure gains its perceptibility and meaning' (pp. 436-37). My view is that a modified form of the theory of oral composition is extremely helpful in understanding the traditions lying behind the Gospels. The Gospels themselves are not oral compositions, but rather lie somewhere between orality and modern literacy. I argue in Chapter 3, for example, that epithets such as Blind Guides or Brood of Vipers do not simply fill slots, but have important effects on the reader's or hearer's response to the story. They are not simply part of a formulaic storehouse, but have specific rhetorical effects in this single text.

typical scenes.[1] Further, the only form in which we have Matthew is as a handwritten manuscript or printed text. Recent work in the field of orality and literacy in New Testament and other fields has shown the complex interplay between orality and textuality in the composition and reception of texts like the Gospels or the Middle English romances discussed by Wittig.[2] In the Hellenistic period, as Mary Ann Tolbert has pointed out, the predominance of rhetorical concerns in both oral performance and handwritten texts most often read aloud particularly blurs the lines between orality and textuality.[3] Many of the features used to identify oral narratives such as repeated phrases and episodes; 'flat', stereotyped characters; and significant foreshadowing are also characteristics of handwritten narratives in the ancient Mediterranean world. They are common rhetorical conventions that would shape the response of the first-century audience. What orally composed and handwritten Greek narratives probably had in

1. Examples are I.J.F. de Jong, *Narrators and Focalizers: The Presentation of the Story in the Iliad* (Amsterdam: Grüner, 1987); S. Richardson, *The Homeric Narrator* (Nashville: Vanderbilt University Press, 1990); J.M. Brenner, I.J.F. de Jong, and J. Kalff, *Homer: Beyond Oral Poetry. Recent Trends in Homeric Interpretation* (Amsterdam: Grüner, 1987); and I.J.F. de Jong, 'Narratology and Oral Poetry: The Case of Homer', *Poetics Today* 12 (1991), pp. 405-24. J.M. Foley, editor of the journal *Oral Tradition* has indicated that study of the aesthetics of oral or oral-derived texts will be an increasing scholarly focus in coming years. He writes, 'Characters' special, repetitive designations are not simply convenient line-fillers or generic labels; rather, according to the traditional "shorthand", they reference the person's or the god's entire traditional identity. Likewise, a typical scene is neither a narrative stopgap nor a generically appropriate description, but a commonplace that reverberates with the associative meaning derived *pars pro toto* from its other uses in the continuing tradition' (*The Theory of Oral Composition*, p. 111). In these comments, however, Foley is focusing on the aesthetics of an oral tradition as a whole, rather than the aesthetics of a particular oral performance or orally influenced text. Foley has indicated that in order to do cross-cultural comparisons one must consider tradition-dependence including natural language characteristics, genre-dependence, and text-dependence (pp. 109-10).

2. See for example the articles found in *Semeia* 39 (1987): 'Orality, Aurality and Biblical Narrative', and B.M. Stock, *The Implications of Literacy: Written Language and Models of Interpretation in the Eleventh and Twelfth Centuries* (Princeton: Princeton University Press, 1983). J. Dewey points out the cross-influences of orality and literacy in relation to Mark in 'Oral Methods', pp. 33-34.

3. See *Sowing the Gospel: Mark's World in Literary-Historical Perspective* (Minneapolis: Fortress Press, 1989), especially pp. 41-47.

common in the first century was aural reception.

In a recent review of literary approaches to Matthew, Graham N. Stanton suggests that the evangelist Matthew used verbal repetition including inclusio, chiasmus, foreshadowing, etc. because he intended the Gospel to be read aloud.[1] Given the evidence supplied by Moses Hadas in *Ancilla to Classical Reading*[2] the authors of the essays

1. G.N. Stanton, 'Literary Criticism: Ancient and Modern', in *A Gospel for a New People: Studies in Matthew* (Edinburgh: T. & T. Clark, 1992), pp. 54-84. Stanton also suggests that relative scholarly agreement about the structure of short sections and disagreement about the overall structure of Matthew is due to the exigencies of reading the Gospel aloud. This, he argues, is due to the fact that reading the entire Gospel would take about three hours. Thus, the Gospel 'was probably read in shorter sections, the length of which varied from time to time' (p. 75). Thus, hearers could appreciate structural markers in shorter sections, but would not be aware of (or need) overall markers. Listeners would have knowledge of the overall story line. Thus, readings could begin at various points. Given this, Stanton argues, reader-response critics who seek to recreate the response of a first-time reader of the Gospel as a whole are misguided. Stanton's comments challenge narrative criticism since such criticism focuses on the interrelations of the elements of a Gospel taken as a whole. They also challenge most forms of reader-response criticism since they, too, treat the Gospel as a whole, usually recreating a reader's response as he or she progresses through the narrative. Stanton is also challenging the notion that Matthew is addressing *virginal* readers who are educated by the text, who can be surprised by each twist and turn of the narrative. He is suggesting that listeners familiar with the outline of the story rather than readers should be paradigmatic tools used to interpret the text. Stanton explains the genesis of repetition in terms of the author's intent, the author's need to communicate with the first-century audience. Although I agree that Matthew was likely read aloud in the first century, I disagree with Stanton on a number of points. The examples in Hadas' *Ancilla* and elsewhere suggest that it is quite possible that first-century listeners would listen to an entire Gospel. Even today's antsy, impatient audiences sit through two-hour movies or plays. Further, the predictions of the passion and Peter's denial, the Johannine subplot, and other devices depend in large part upon hearing or reading the Gospel as a whole. Although creating a reading that emphasizes *surprise* may be anachronistic in terms of a first century audience—especially given the heavy doses of foreshadowing we find in Matthew—these techniques do indicate that a hearers or readers will ask 'how' the events expected will come to pass. This is supported by Duckworth, *Foreshadowing* and Hägg, *Narrative Techniques*. Joanna Dewey has argued that the reason scholars have failed to reach an agreement on the structure of Mark is because 'the structure consists of overlapping repetitive sequences' ('Oral Methods', p. 40). In addition, it must be stressed that not all interpreters have the goal of reading Matthew as a first-century audience might.

2. New York: Columbia University Press, 1954.

collected in *Semeia* 39, 'Orality, Aurality and Biblical Narrative', (1987), Mary Ann Tolbert in *Sowing the Gospel: Mark's World in Literary-Historical Perspective*[1] , and Paul J. Achtemeier in '*Omne verbum sonat*: The New Testament and the Oral Environment of Late Western Antiquity',[2] Stanton is very likely correct.[3] Although what I have done in the previous chapters is to examine the use of verbal repetition as a narrative device in terms of communication between the implied author and implied reader, my work could support a reconstruction of the Gospel's reception in the first century. If Matthew is read aloud, verbal repetitions help listeners to follow the story. They help listeners to overcome 'noise' in the communication channel due to the length of the reading, a growling stomach, or even noisy animals or people nearby. Aural, syntactic, and semantic factors involved in sounded verbal repetition create redundancy that hearers often need. If particular forms of verbal repetition in a text such as chiasm, doublets, or well-known proverbs are part of a traditional aural repertoire, then the redundancy increases. Whether reading is silent or aural, verbal repetition within a text increases predictability and can have rhetorical power. Because of the demands and conventions of the aural medium, verbal repetition is not as likely to appear as superfluous to a hearer as it might to a silent reader. Verbal repetition is particularly important for hearers because the hearer cannot page backwards and forwards, but is dependent on the memory of previous words through the temporal flow of the narration. General functions of repetition I have outlined such as emphasis and creating unifying patterns would be very effective in an aural context. Specific types of repetition such as labels or epithets for characterization, repeated speech characteristics common to the narrator and reliable main character, double stories with variations that develop characters and carry forward the plot, and the like make perfect sense in terms of an aural rhetoric.

1. Minneapolis: Fortress Press, 1989.
2. *JBL* 109 (1990), pp. 3-27.
3. Boomershine's ('Peter's Denial as Polemic or Confession', *Semeia* 39 [1987], p. 53) citation of the Ethiopian eunuch reading aloud in Acts 8 and the instructions for reading Revelation aloud in Rev. 1.1 are particularly persuasive in terms of New Testament tradition. Caution must be exercised, however, about saying that *all* reading was done aloud as B.M.W. Knox points out in 'Silent Reading in Antiquity', *Greek, Roman, and Byzantine Studies* 9 (1968), pp. 421-35.

However, even in aural narratives verbal repetition is not always completely exact. It depends for its effectiveness on variation. Even violation of expectations created by verbal repetition is significant. There can be no violation if a pattern has not been previously established. The importance of repetition with variation is not only supported by modern critics like myself and the Browns, but also by the ancient *Rhetorica ad Herennium* (c. first century BCE): 'We shall not repeat the same thing precisely—for that, to be sure, would weary the hearer and not elaborate the idea—but with changes' (4.42.54).[1] Repetition with variation also plays an important role in the Tanach as Sternberg has shown.[2] Experience with repetition with variation would have been common to those among the Gospel's first-century audience who listened to readings from the Hebrew Bible or the Septuagint.

As in Matthew, in addition to repetition with variation, context is also important in the narrative rhetoric of other ancient aural narratives. Irene de Jong has shown, for example, that even in Homer traditional repeated epithets and formulas vary with context *and* that this variation can have important narrative functions.[3] In the *Odyssey* the suitors, for example, never refer to Odysseus as ' much enduring' or 'cunning', while the narrator frequently does. In the *Iliad* the Trojans call the Greek hero Diamedes 'forceful creator of panic' twice (6.97, 278). Later in the narrative (12.39), the narrator calls Hector 'forceful creator of panic' just as Hector is about to break through the wall around the Greek camp. The repeated phrase, according to de Jong, 'signals the reversal of fortunes: due to Zeus's support, it is now the Trojans who have the upper hand'.[4]

Thus, comparison with the conventions of ancient aural narratives supports the conclusions I reached in previous chapters. It also shows important areas of continuity between the use of repetition in ancient and modern narratives. In addition, examining Matthew and other Gospels in terms of first-century aural conventions also offers support for the use of narrative and reader-response criticisms even by critics whose primary concern is historical. This is especially true of one of

1. I owe this reference to Tolbert, *Sowing the Gospel*, pp. 43 n. 31.

2. *The Poetics of Biblical Narrative*, pp. 390-400.

3. 'Narratology and Oral Poetry', pp. 417-20. The examples are taken from pp. 418-19.

4. De Jong, 'Narratology and Oral Poetry', p. 419.

the key tenets of narrative criticism: viewing the Gospels as wholes. Narrative criticism, taking its cue from American New Criticism, began by challenging what it saw as a disintegrating historical criticism. Repetitive devices characteristic of ancient first-century narratives often depend for their full effect on reading or listening to the whole narrative. This is certainly true of the predictions and occurrence of Peter's denial and the passion; of the Johannine subplot; of the epithets and repeated actions used to characterize the Jewish leaders; and of other occurrences of extended verbal repetition in Matthew. Matthew consists of a series of interlocking echoes that run throughout the narrative. Likewise, paradoxically, as Stephen Moore has pointed out, *reader*-response criticism with its emphasis on the temporal, sequential flow of the narrative 'has clear affinities with the syllable-by-syllable experience of hearing a text read, an experience that makes all the difference for one's conceptualization of the text'.[1] Ironically, narrative and reader-response criticism which originally developed as literary methods in opposition to historical criticism may offer important keys to reconstructing the response of the first-century audience. Although they cannot recreate the intonation and interpretation of those who first read the Gospel out loud, these approaches draw modern readers closer to first-century hearers' reception of Matthew. They draw them to listen for repeated words. They draw them to the anticipation and retrospection of a dream and its fulfillment, to a striking epithet which engages the memory when repeated, to the comparison and contrast of characters aroused by a double story, to the persuasive force of a phrase used repeatedly by the narrator and the Gospel's most reliable character, Jesus. Whether one seeks to reconstruct the first-century reception of Matthew, understand a sixteenth-century exegesis, or create an entirely new interpretation, narrative and reader-response criticisms along with the communication model draw the reader into a narrative web spun with the threads of verbal repetition.

1. *Literary Criticism of the Gospels*, pp. 87-88.

Appendix A

EXTENDED VERBAL REPETITION IN THE GOSPEL OF MATTHEW

Phrases of three words or less or of particular interest are listed in Greek. They are cited according to the Greek of the first passage in which they appear. The equal signs indicate parallels. The number of words in parentheses indicates the number of words each passage shares in common.

Chapter 1

1.1 = 1.20 = 9.27 = 12.23 = 15.22 = 20.30-31 = 21.9 = 21.15 = 22.41 (5 words)
1.2 = 8.11 = 22.32 (3 words) Ἀβραάμ, Ἰσαακ, Ἰακὰβ
1.16 = 27.17 (4 words)
1.20 = 1.24 = 2.13 = 2.19 = 28.2 (2 words) ἄγγελος κυρίου
1.30 = 2.13 = 2.19 (7 words)
1.20 = 2.12 = 2.13 = 2.19 = 2.22 = 27.19 (2 words) κατ' ὄναρ
1.22 = 2.15 = 2.17 = 2.23 = 3.3 = 4.14 = 8.17 = 12.17 = 13.25 = 21.4 = 26.56 = 27.9 (2–11 words)

Chapter 2

2.2 = 2.8 = 2.11 = 4.9 = 4.10 = 8.2 = 9.18 = 14.33 = 15.25 = 18.26 = 20.20 = 28.9 =28.17 (1 word) προσκυνῆσαι
2.2 = 2.8 = 9.18 = 15.25 (3 words) ἤλθομεν προσκυνῆσαι αὐτῷ
2.11 = 4.9 = 18.26 (3 words) πεσόντες προσεκύνησεν αὐτῷ
8.2 = 9.18 = 20.20 = 28.9 (3 words) προσελθῶν προσκύνει αυτῷ
8.2 = 9.18 (4 words) προσελθὼν προσκύνει αὐτῷ λέγων
14.33 = 28.17 (2 words) προσελθὼν αὐτῷ (All of the above except 4.10 include these two words.)
2.8, see 2.2
2.11, see 2.2
2.12 = 2.22 (6 words)
2.12, see 1.20
2.13, see 1.20
2.14 = 2.21 (10 words)
2.15, see 1.22
2.17, see 1.22
2.19, see 1.20
2.22, see 2.12; also 1.20

Chapter 3

3.1-2 = 4.17 = 4.23 = 9.35 = 10.7 = 24.14 (3 words) κηρύσσων ἡ βασιλεία
 3.1-2 = 4.17 = 10.7 (7 words)
 3.1-2 = 4.17 (9 words)
3.3, see 1.22
3.3 = 11.10 (4 words)
3.7 = 12.34 = 23.33 (2 words) γεννήματα ἐχιδνῶν
3.8, 10 = 7.16-20 = 12.33 = 21.41b, 43 (2–11 words)
 3.10b = 7.19 (11 words)
 7.16-20 = 12.33 (11 words)
 7.16 = 7.20 (6 words) concentrated repetition
3.10 = 13.42a = 13.50 (3 words) εἰς πῦρ βάλλεται
3.12 = 13.30 (6 words)
3.17 = 12.18 = 17.5 (3–15 words)
 3.17 = 12.18 (5 words)
 3.17 = 17.5 (15 words)
 12.18 = 17.5 (3 words) ἰδοὺ ὁ ἀγαπητός

Chapter 4

4.1 = 16.1 = 19.3 (1 word) πειρασθῆναι
 16.1 = 19.3 (5 words)
4.3 = 8.19 = 13.10 (4 words) = 18.21 (3 words) (καὶ) προσελθὼν εἶπεν αὐτῷ
4.3 = 4.6 = 27.40 (5 words)
4.5 = 27.53 (4 words)
4.6 = 11.10 = 13.41 = 16.27 = 18.10 = 24.31 = 25.41 (3 words) τοῖς ἀγγέλοις αὐτοῦ (μου)
 13.41 = 16.27 (7 words)
 11.10 = 13.41 = 24.31 (4 words) ἀποστέλλω τὸν ἄγγελόν μου (αὐτοῦ)
4.6 = 17.25 = 19.18 = 19.20 = 20.21 = 26.35 = 26.71 = 27.13 = 27.22 (1 word) λέγει used as an historical present with someone other than Jesus as the subject, see also 4.10
 27.13 = 27.22a (4 words) concentrated repetition, λέγει αὐτῷ ὁ Πιλάτος
 4.6 = 19.18 = 19.20 = 20.21 = 26.35 = 27.13 (2-3 words) (καὶ/τότε) λέγει αὐτῷ
4.8 = 5.1 = 14.23 = 15.29-30 = 17.1 = 28.16 (2 words) εἰς ὄρος, see 5.1,
4.9, see 2.2
4.10, see 2.2
4.10 = 4.19 = 8.4 = 8.7 = 8.20 = 8.22 = 8.26 = 9.6 = 9.9 = 9.28 = 9.37 = 12.13 = 14.31 = 15.34 = 16.15 = 17.20 = 18.22 = 19.8 = 20.23 = 21.13 = 21.16 = 21.19 = 21.31c = 21.42 = 21.45 = 22.20 = 22.21b = 22.43 = 26.25b = 26.31 = 26.26 = 26.38 = 26.40 = 26.45 = 26.52 = 26.64 = 28.10 (1 word) λέγει, used as an historical present with *Jesus* as the *subject*; see also 4.6
 4.19 = 8.26 = 9.9 = 21.13 = 21.19 = 22.20 = 26.38 = 26.45 (3 words) καὶ λέγει αὐτοῖς (αὐτῷ) (αὐτὴ)
 8.7 = 16.15 = 19.8 = 20.23 = 22.43 = 26.25b (2 words) λέγει αὐτῷ (αὐτοῖς)
 14.31 = 18.22 = 21.31c = 21.42 = 26.64 (4 words) λέγει αὐτῷ (αὐτοῖς) ὁ Ιησοῦς
 4.10 = 26.31 = 26.52 = 28.10 (5 words) τότε λέγει αὐτῷ (αὐτοῖς) ὁ Ιησοῦς
 8.4 = 8.20 = 9.28 = 15.34 (5 words)καὶ λέγει αὐτῳ (αὐτοῖς) ὁ Ιησοῦς
 8.22 = 17.20 = 21.16 (4-5 words) ὁ δὲ ('Ιησοῦς) λέγει αὐτῷ (αὐτοῖς)
 22.21b = 26.38 (3 words) τότε λέγει αὐτοῖς
 9.6 = 9.37 = 12.13 = 26.36 τότε λέγει τῷ (τοῖς)
 9.37 = 26.36 (3 words) λέγει τοῖς μαθηταῖς

4.10 = 16.23 (2 words) ὕπαγε σατανᾶ
4.14, see 1.22
4.15 = 4.25 = 19.1 (3 words) πέραν τοῦ Ἰορδάνου
4.17, see 3.1-2
4.17 = 16.21 (4 words)
4.17 = 16.21 = 26.16 (2 words) ἀπὸ τότε
4.19, see 4.10
4.20 = 4.22 (6 words) concentrated repetition
4.20 = 4.22 = 20.34 (3 words) εὐθέως ἠκολούθησαν αὐτῷ
4.23 = 9.35 = 10.1 (7 words)
4.23 = 9.35 = 24.14 = 26.13 (5-20 words)
   4.23 = 9.35 (20 words)
4.24 = 8.16 (8 words)
4.25 = 19.16 (8 words)
4.25 = 8.1 = 12.15 = 14.13 = 19.2 = 20.29 (3-4 words) (καὶ) ἠκολούθησαν αὐτῷ (οχλοι) (πολλοὶ)

Chapter 5

5.1 = 8.5-6 = 9.14 = 13.10 = 13.36b = 14.15 = 15.1 = 15.12 = 18.1 = 22.23 = 24.1 = 24.3 = 26.17a, 26.69, see also 4.3 (2-8 words)
   5.1 = 24.3 (8 words)
   5.1 = 13.36b = 14.15 = 15.12 = 18.1 = 24.1 = 24.3 = 26.17a (4-6 words) (και) (τὸτε) προσῆλθαν αὐτῷ οἱ μαθηταὶ (αὐτοῦ)
      = 9.14 τὸτε προσέρχονται αὐτῷ οἱ μαθηταὶ Ἰωάννου λέγοντες
      15.1 = 18.1 = 26.17a (4 words) προσέρχονται τῷ Ἰησου λέγοντες
5.1 = 14.23 (6 words)
5.1 = 15.29-30 (7 words)
   5.1 = 14.23 = 15.29 (4 words; 14.23 = 15.29, 5 words)
   4.8 = 5.1 = 14.23 = 15.29-30 = 17.1 = 28.16 (2 words) εἰς ὄρος
   5.1 = 14.23 = 15.29-30 = 21.1 (of olives) = 24.16 = 26.30 (of olives) 28.16 (3 words) εἰς τὸ ὄρος
5.11 = 10.18 = 10.39 = 16.25 = 19.29 = 24.1 (2 words) ἕνεκεν ἐμοῦ
5.16 = 6.1 = 10.32-33 (10 words)
   5.16 = 5.45 = 6.1 = 7.11 = 7.21 = 10.32 = 10.33 = 12.50 = 16.17 = 18.10 = 18.14 = 18.19 (6-7 words) τὸν πατέρα ὑμῶν τὸν ἐν (τοῖς) οὐρανοῖς or τὸν πατέρα μου τοῦ ἐν (τοῖς) οὐρανοῖς
   5.16 = 6.9 (6 words) πάτηρ ὑμῶν (ἡμῶν) ὁ ἐν τοῖς οὐρανοῖς
   5.48 = 6.14 = 6.26 = 6.32 = 15.13 = 18.35 = 23.9 (5 words) ὁ πατὴρ ὑμῶν ὁ οὐράνιος or ὁ πατὴρ μου ὁ οὐράνιος
   5.16 = 6.8 = 6.15 = 10.20 = 10.29 (3 words) ὁ πατὴρ ὑμῶν
5.17 = 7.12 = 11.13 = 22.40 (4 words)
5.17 = 10.34 (7 words)
5.18 = 24.34-35 (16 words)
5.18 = 11.25 = 24.35 (5 words)
5.19-20 = 18.1, 3 (14 words)
5.21 = 19.18 (2 words + sense) οὐ φονεύσεις
5.27 = 19.18 (2 words + sense) οὐ μοιχεύσεις
5.29-30 = 18.8-9 (30 words)
5.31-32 = 19.3-9 (15 words)
5.34-36 = 23.22 (7 words)

5.43 = 19.19 = 22.39 (4 words) ἀγαπήσεις τὸν πλησίον σου
5.48, see 5.16
5.48 = 19.21 (2 words) Ἔσεσθε... τέλειοι

Chapter 6

6.1, see 5.16
6.1-2 = 23.5-7 (10 words)
6.4 = 6.6 = 6.18 (14 words) concentrated repetition
6.6 = 6.18 concentrated repetition
6.8 = 6.32 (6 words)
6.10 = 6.19-20 = 9.6 = 10.29 = 10.34 = 13.8 = 13.28 = 14.34 = 15.35 = 16.19 = 18.18 = 18.19 = 23.9a = 23.35 = 27.45 = 28.18 (2-3 words) ἐπὶ γῆς or ἐπὶ τῆς γῆς
    6.10 = 6.19-20 = 18.18 (5 words)
    See also 5.18
6.14 = 6.15 (8 words) concentrated repetition
6.14 = 18.35 (7 words)
6.15 = 18.35 (6 words)
6.15 = 6.26 = 10.20 = 10.29 (3 words) ὁ πατήρ ὑμῶν; see also 5.16
6.19 = 6.20 (12 words) concentrated repetition
6.20 = 19.21 (3 words) θησαυροὺς ἐν οὐρανῷ
6.23 = 20.15 (5 words)

Chapter 7

7.7 = 18.19-20 = 21.22 (1 word) αἰτεῖτε
7.11, see 5.16
7.12, see 5.17
7.15 = 24.11 = 24.24 (1 word) ψευδοπροφητῶν
7.16 = 7.20 (6 words) concentrated repetition
7.16-20, see 3.8, 7.19 = 3.10b (11 words)
7.21b = 12.50 (9 words) = 18.14 (7 words) = 21.31 (4 words)
7.22-23 = 25.11-12 (5 words)
7.24 = 7.26 (18 words) concentrated repetition
7.24-26 = 25.2 = 25.3-4 = 25.8 (2 words) φρονίμῳ, μωρῷ
7.25 = 7.27 (18 words) concentrated repetition
7.28-29 = 11.1 = 13.53 = 19.1 = 26.1 (6–9 words) see also 9.10; transitional formula closing discourses
7.28 = 22.23 (7 words)

Chapter 8

8.1, see 4.25
8.1 = 17.9 (4 words)
8.2, see 2.2
8.3 = 12.49 = 14.31 (3–4 words) (καὶ) ἐκτείνας τὴν χεῖρα
    8.3 = 14.31 (5 words)
8.4, see 4.10
8.4 = 9.30 = 16.20 = 17.9 (1 word) μηδενὶ
    8.4 = 9.30 = 17.9 (4 words) αὐτῷ ὁ Ἰησοῦς· μηδενὶ
    8.4 = 9.30 (7 words) καὶ λέγει αὐτῷ ὁ Ἰησοῦς· ὅρα μηδενὶ

8.4 = 17.9 (5 words) αὐτῷ ὁ Ἰησοῦς· μηδενὶ εἴπῃς
8.4 = 16.20 = 17.9 (2 words) μηδενὶ εἴπῃς
8.7, see 4.10
8.11 = 22.32 (5 words) Ἀβραάμ καὶ Ἰσαὰκ καὶ Ἰακὼβ; see also 1.2
8.12 = 13.42 = 13.50 = 22.13 = 24.51 = 25.30 (9–17 words)
8.12 = 22.13 = 25.30 (15 words)
13.42 = 13.50 (17 words)
8.12 = 13.38 (4 words)
8.13 = 15.28 (10 words)
8.14 = 9.23 (8 words)
8.16, see 4.24
8.17, see 1.22
8.18 = 8.28 = 14.22 = 16.5 (3 words) εἰς τὸ πέσαν
8.19, see 4.3
8.19 = 8.22 = 9.9 = 16.24 = 19.21 = 19.27 = 19.28 (2 words) ἀκολουθήσω σοι (μοι)
8.22 = 9.9 (4 words) λέγει αὐτῷ ἀκολούθει μοι
8.20, see 4.10
8.20 = 9.6 = 10.23 = 11.19 = 12.8 = 12.32 = 12.40 = 13.37 = 13.41 = 16.13 = 16.27 = 16.28 = 17.9 = 17.12 = 17.22-23 = 19.28 = 20.17-19 = 20.28 = 24.27 = 24.30a = 24.30b = 24.37 = 24.39 = 24.44 = 25.31 = 26.2 = 26.24a = 26.24b = 26.45 = 26.64 (4 words) ὁ υἱὸς τοῦ ἀνθρώπου
24.20 = 26.64 (12 words)
10.23 = 16.28 (9 words)
13.41 = 16.27 (7 words)
13.41 = 16.28 (7 words)
17.22-23a = 26.45b (7 words)
9.6 = 12.40 (6 words)
16.28 = 24.30 = 26.64 (6 words)
17.22-23a = 26.2 (6 words)
20.17-19 = 26.2 (6 words)
26.2 = 26.45b (6 words)
10.23 = 11.19 = 16.27 = 16.28 = 19.28 = 20.28 = 24.30b = 24.44 (5 words) ἔλθῃ ὁ υἱὸς τοῦ ἀνθρώπου
17.9b = 17.22-23a = 20.18-19 (5 words) ὁ υἱὸς τοῦ ἀνθρώπου ἐγερθῇ
17.12d = 17.22-23a - 20.17-19 (5 words) ὁ υἱὸς τοῦ ἀνθρώπου μέλλει
17.22 = 20.18 = 26.2 = 26.24a = 26.24b = 26.45 (5 words) ὁ υἱὸς τοῦ ἀνθρώπου παραδίδοται
19.28 = 25.31 = 26.64 (5 words) ὁ υἱὸς τοῦ ἀνθρώπου καθίσῃ
8.22, see 4.10
8.22 = 9.9 = 19.21 (6 words)
8.23-27 = 14.22-33 (17 words)
8.26, see 6.30
8.34 = 14.36 (3 words) καὶ αὐτὸν παρεκάλεσαν

Chapter 9

9.2 = 9.22 = 9.29 = 15.28 (3 words) τὴν πίστιν αὐτῶν
9.2 = 9.22 (7 words) concentrated repetition
9.2 = 15.28 (5 words)
9.4 = 12.25 (5 words) εἰδὼς [ἰδων UBS + Nestlé's 26th edn] τάς ἐνθυμήσεις αὐτῶν εἶπεν
9.6, see 4.10

9.6, see 8.20
9.6 = 28.18 (3–4 words) εξουσίαν ἐπὶ [τῆς] γῆς
9.9, see 4.10
9.9, see 8.19
9.9, see 8.22
9.13 = 12.7 (7 words)
9.14, see 5.1
19.14-15 = 15.1-3 (9 words)
19.18, see 2.2
9.20-21 = 14.36 (9 words)
9.26 = 9.31 (5 words) concentrated repetition
9.27-31 = 20.29-34 (20 words)
    9.27 = 15.22 (6 words)
    9.27 = 17.15 = 20.30 = 20.31 (3 words) λέγοντες· ἐλέησον ἡμᾶς (μου)
    15.22 = 17.15 (4 words)
    15.22 = 20.30 = 20.31 (7 words)
9.28, see 4.10
9.28 = 13.51 = 14.17 = 15.12 = 15.33 = 19.7 = 19.10 = 20.22 = 20.33 = 21.31b = 21.41 = 22.21a = 22.42 = 27.22 (1 word) λέγουσιν used in the historical present
    9.28 = 13.51 = 14.17 = 15.12 = 15.33 = 19.7 = 19.10 = 20.22 = 20.33 = 21.41 = 22.42 (2 words) λέγουσιν αὐτῷ
    15.12 = 15.33 = 19.10 (4 words) οἱ μαθηταὶ λέγουσιν αὐτῷ
9.30, see 8.4
9.32-34 = 12.22-27 (22 words)
9.35, see 4.23
9.36 = 14.14 = 15.32 = 18.27 = 20.34 (1 to 4 words) ἐσπλαγχνίσθη
9.36 = 26.31 (2 words) πρόβατα, ποιμένα
9.37, see 4.10

Chapter 10

10.1, see 4.23
10.1 = 9.35 (7 words)
10.4 = 26.25 = 26.46 = 26.48 = 27.3 (3–4 words) (Ἰσούδας) ὁ παραδοὺς (παραδιδοὺς) αὐτόν
10.6 = 15.24 (6 words)
10.7, see 3.1-2
10.8 = 11.5 (4 words) νεκροὺς ἐγείρετε, λεπροὺς καθαρίζετε
10.15 = 11.24 (11 words) = 11.22 (8 words)
10.17, 23 = 23.34, 36 (13 words)
10.17-22 = 24.9-14 (18 words)
    10.22a = 24.9 (9 words)
10.18, see 5.11
10.20, see 5.16
10.23, see 8.20; esp. 10.23 = 16.28 (9 words)
10.29, see 5.16
10.29-31, see 6.26
10.32 = 10.33 (15 words) concentrated repetition
10.32, see 5.16
10.33, see 5.16 and 10.32
10.32, see 5.17
10.34, see 5.17

10.37-39 = 19.24 (4 words)
10.38-39 = 16.24-25 (18 words)
10.38 = 16.24 = 27.32 (3 words) τὸν σταυρὸν αὐτοῦ
10.40-42 = 18.5-6 (7 words)
    10.42 = 18.6, 10, 14 (4 words) ἕνα τῶν μικρῶν τούτων

Chapter 11

11.1, see 7.28-29
11.4 = 13.13, 17 (3 words) ἀκούετε καὶ βλέπετε
11.5, see 10.8
11.5 = 15.31 (5 words)
11.10, see 3.3
11.10, see 4.6
11.10 = 13.41 = 24.31 (4 words)
11.13, see 5.17
11.14 = 17.10 = 17.11 = 17.12 (2 words) Ἠλίας ἔρχεσθαι
11.15 = 13.9, 43 (4 words) ὁ ἔχων ὦτα ἀκουέτω
11.19, see 8.20
11.21, 22 = 15.21 (3 words) Τύρῳ καὶ Σιδῶνι
11.22, see 10.15
11.22 = 11.24 (9 words) concentrated repetition
11.24, see 10.5
11.24, see 11.22
11.25 = 12.1 = 14.1 (4 words) Ἐν ἐκείνῳ τῷ καιρῷ

Chapter 12

12.1, see 11.25
12.7, see 9.13
12.8, see 8.20
12.13, see 4.10
12.14 = 22.15 = 27.1 = 27.7 = 28.12 (2 words) συμβούλιον ἔλαβον
    12.14 = 22.15 (6 words)
    27.1 = 28.12 (4 words) συμβούλιον ἔλαβον οἱ πρεσβύτεροι
    See also 26.3-4 συνεβουλεύσαντο
12.15, see 4.25
12.17, see 1.22
12.18, see 3.17
12.22-27, see 9.32-34
12.24 = 12.27 (5 words) concentrated repetition
12.25, see 9.4
12.32, see 8.20
12.33, see 3.8, 10
12.34, see 3.7
12.35 = 13.52 (4 words)
12.38-42 = 16.1-4 (24 words)
12.40, see 8.20
12.40 = 16.21 = 17.22-23 = 20.17-19 = 26.61 = 27.40 = 27.63 = 27.64 (2 words) τρεῖς ἡμέρας or τῇ τρίτῃ ἡμέρα

16.21 = 17.22-23 = 20.19 = 27.63 (3 words) τρίτῃ ἡμέρα ἐγερθῆναι
16.21 = 17.22-23 (7 words)
26.61 = 27.40 (6 words)
12.41 = 12.42 (15 words) concentrated repetition
12.46 = 12.48 = 12.49 = 12.50 = 13.55 (6 words)
12.49, see 8.3
12.50, see 5.16
12.50, see 7.21b

Chapter 13

13.3 = 13.10b = 13.13a = 22.1 (4 words) = 13.35 (2 words) (ἐλάλησεν αὐτοῖς) ἐν παραβολαῖς
13.9, see 11.15
13.10, see 5.1
13.10 = 13.36, see 4.3
13.12 = 25.29 (13 words)
13.24a = 13.31a = 13.33a = 21.28 = 21.33 (2 words)
13.24b = 13.31b = 13.33b = 13.44 = 13.45 = 13.47 = 18.23 = 20.1 = 22.2 = 25.1 (5-6 words)
13.30, see 3.12
13.31 = 17.20 (2 words) κόκκῳ σινάπεως
13.35, see 1.22
13.36 = 15.15 (4 words)
13.36b, see 5.1
13.37, see 8.20
13.38, see 8.12
13.39 = 13.40 = 13.49 = 24.3 = 28.20 (2–5 words) συντέλεια αἰῶνος
13.40-42 = 13.47-50 (26 words) concentrated repetition
13.41, see 4.6
13.41, see 8.20
13.41 = 16.27 = 16.28 (7 words)
13.42, see 8.12
13.43 = 17.2 (4 words) (ἐκ)λάμψουσιν ὡς ὁ ἥλιος
13.50, see 8.12
13.51, see 9.28
13.53, see 7.28

Chapter 14

14.1, see 11.25
14.5 = 21.26 = 21.46 (6 words)
14.13, see 4.25
14.13-23 = 15.29-39 (82 words)
14.14, see 9.36
14.15, see 5.1
14.17, see 9.28
14.19-21 = 16.9 (4 words)
14.19b = 15.36 = 26.26-27 (7 words)
14.19b = 26.26 (7 words)
15.36 = 26.26-27 (7 words)
14.19b = 15.36 (15 words)

14.22-32, see 8.23-27
14.23, see 5.1
14.31, see 4.10
14.31, see 6.30
14.31, see 8.3
14.33, see 2.2
14.33 = 27.54 (5 words)
14.36, see 8.34
14.36, see 9.20-21

Chapter 15

15.1, see 5.1
15.1-3, see 9.14-15
15.4 = 19.19 (6 words)
15.10-11 = 15.17-18 (12 words) concentrated repetition
15.12, see 5.1
15.12, see 9.28
15.13, see 5.16
15.14 = 23.16, 24 (2 words) ὁδηγοὶ τυφλῶν
15.15, see 13.36
15.17 = 16.11 (3 words) οὐ νοεῖτε ὅτι
15.22, see 9.27
15.24, see 10.6
15.25, see 2.2
15.28, see 9.2
15.29-30, see 5.1
15.29-39, see 14.13-23
15.30 = 21.14 (8 words)
15.31, see 11.5
15.32, see 9.36
15.33, see 9.28
15.34, see 8.4
15.34-38 = 16.10 (4 words)
15.36, see 14.19b

Chapter 16

16.1, see 4.1
16.1-4, see 12.38-42
16.6 = 16.11 = 16.12 (8 words) concentrated repetition
16.8, see 6.30
16.9, see 14.19-21
16.10, see 15.34-38
16.11, see 15.17
16.11, see 16.6
16.12, see 16.6
16.12 = 17.13 (4 words)
16.13, see 8.20
16.15, see 4.10
16.16 = 26.63 (10 words)

16.17, see 5.16
16.19 = 18.18 (21 words)
16.20, see 8.4
16.21, see 4.17
16.21, see 8.20; esp. 16.21 = 20.17-19 (10 words)
16.23, see 4.10
16.24, see 8.19
16.24-25, see 10.38-39
16.24 = 27.32 (4 words)
16.27, see 4.6
16.27, see 8.30
16.27, see 13.41
16.28, see 8.20
16.28, see 10.23
16.28, see 13.41
16.28 = 24.30 = 26.64 (6 words)
24.30 = 26.64 (12 words)

Chapter 17

17.1, see 5.1
17.1 = 26.37 (4 words)
17.2, see 13.43
17.5, see 3.17
17.6 = 27.54 (2 words) ἐφοβήθησαν σφόδρα
17.7 = 28.5 (3 words) εἶπεν· μὴ φοβεῖσθε
17.9, see 8.1
17.9, see 8.4
17.9, see 8.20
17.12, see 8.20
17.13, see 16.12
17.15, see 9.27
17.19, see 8.4
17.20, see 4.10
17.20, see 6.30
17.20, see 13.31
17.20 = 21.21 (12 words)
17.22-23, see 8.20
17.25, see 4.6

Chapter 18

18.2-3 = 19.13-15 (8 words)
18.4 = 23.12 (3 words) ὅστις ταπεινώσει ἑαυτὸν
18.5-6, see 10.40-42
18.8-9, see 5.29-30
18.10, see 4.6
18.10, see 5.16
18.10 = 18.14 (10 words) concentrated repetition
18.14, see 5.16
18.14, see 18.10

18.18, see 6.19, 20
18.18, see 16.19
18.19, see 5.16
18.19-20, see 7.7
18.22, see 4.10
18.23, see 13.24b
18.26, see 2.2
18.35, see 5.16
18.35, see 6.14
18.35, see 6.15

Chapter 19

19.1, see 7.28-29
19.3, see 4.1
19.3-9, see 5.31-32
19.3 = 19.9 (4 words) concentrated repetition
19.7, see 9.28
19.8, see 4.10
19.10, see 9.28
19.13-15, see 18.2-3
19.13 = 19.15 (4 words) concentrated repetition

Chapter 20

20.1, see 13.24b
20.15, see 6.23
20.16, see 19.30
20.17 = 26.2 (5 words)
20.17-19, see 8.20; esp. 16.21 = 20.17-19 (10 words)
20.17-19, see 12.40
20.20, see 2.2
20.21, see 4.6
20.22, see 9.28
20.23, see 4.10
20.22-23 = 23.25 = 23.26 = 26.39b (2 words) τὸ ποτήριον; see also 10.42
20.26 = 23.11 (5 words)
20.28, see 8.20
20.29-34, see 9.27-31
20.33, see 9.28

Chapter 21

21.1 = 24.3 = 26.30 (4–5 words) (εἰς) τὸ ὄρος τῶν ἐλαιῶν
21.4, see 1.22
21.6 = 26.19 (8 words)
21.9, see 1.1
21.9 = 21.15 (6 words) concentrated repetition
21.9 = 23.39b (6 words)
21.13, see 4.10
21.14, see 15.30

21.16, see 4.10
21.21, see 17.20
21.22, see 7.7
21.23 = 21.27 (5 words) concentrated repetition
21.23 = 26.3 = 26.47 = 27.1 = 27.3 = 27.12 = 27.20 = 28.11-12 (4–7 words)
    21.23 = 26.3 = 26.47 = 27.1 (6–7 words)
21.26, see 14.5
21.28, see 13.24a
21.31, see 7.21
21.31c, see 4.10
21.33, see 13.24a
21.34 = 22.3 (4 words)
21.35 = 22.6 (4 words)
21.36 = 22.4 (4 words)
21.41, see 9.28
21.41b = 21.43, see 3.8, 10
21.42, see 4.10
21.45, see 4.10
21.45 = 27.62 (5 words)

Chapter 22

22.1, see 13.3
22.2, see 13.24b
22.3, see 21.34
22.4, see 21.36
22.6, see 21.35
22.13, see 8.12
22.15, see 12.14
22.20, see 4.10
22.21b, see 4.10
22.21c, see 9.28
22.23, see 5.1
22.32, see 8.11
22.33, see 7.28
22.39, see 5.43
22.40, see 5.17
22.42, see 9.28
22.43, see 4.10
22.43 = 22.45 (4 words) concentrated repetition

Chapter 23

23.5, see 6.14, 15
23.5-7, see 6.1-2
23.9, see 6.10
23.11, see 20.26
23.13 = 23.15 = 23.23 = 23.25 = 23.27 = 23.29 (7 words)
23.16, see 15.14
23.22, see 5.34-36
23.25, see 20.22-23

23.26, see 20.22-23
23.33, see 3.7
23.34, 36, see 10.17, 23
23.35, see 6.10
23.36 = 24.34 (8 words)
23.39, see 21.9

Chapter 24

24.1, see 5.1
24.3, see 5.1
24.3, see 21.1
24.3, see 13.39
24.4 = 24.5 = 24.11 = 24.24 (1-4 words) πλανήσῃ concentrated repetition
24.5, see 24.4
24.9-14, see 10.17-22, esp. 10.22a = 24.9 (9 words)
24.11, see 7.15
24.24, see 7.15
24.27, see 8.20
24.30, see 8.20, esp. 24.30 = 26.24 (12 words)
24.31, see 4.6
24.34-35, see 5.18
24.34, see 23.36
24.36 = 24.42 = 25.13 (2–6 words) ἡμέρας οἶδεν
    24.42 = 25.13 (6 words)
24.37, see 8.20
24.39, see 8.20
24.42, see 24.36
24.44, see 8.20
24.51, see 8.12

Chapter 25

25.1, see 13.24b
25.2-4, see 7.24, 26
25.11-12, see 7.22-23
25.13, see 24.36
25.16 = 25.27 (4 words) concentrated repetition
25.19, see 13.24b
25.20 = 25.22 (14 words) = 25.24 (7 words) concentrated repetition
25.21 = 25.23 (25 words) concentrated repetition
25.24 = 25.26 (11 words) concentrated repetition
25.29, see 13.12
25.30, see 8.12
25.31, see 8.20
25.34 = 25.41 (4 words) concentrated repetition
25.35-36 = 25.42-43 (24 words) concentrated repetition
25.37-39 = 25.44 (15 words) concentrated repetition
24.40 = 25.45 (15 words) concentrated repetition
25.41, see 4.6
25.41, see 25.34

25.42-43, see 25.35-36
25.44, see 25.37-39
25.45, see 25.40

Chapter 26

26.1, see 7.28-29
26.2, see 8.20
26.3, see 21.23
26.3-4, see 12.14
26.16, see 4.17
26.17a, see 5.1
26.24a, see 8.20
26.24b, see 8.20
26.25, see 10.4
26.26-27, see 14.19b
26.30, see 21.1
26.31-32 = 28.5-7 = 28.10 (6-8 words) = 28.16 (3 words) εἰς τὴν Γαλιλαίαν
26.31-32 = 28.10 (8 words)
28.5-7 = 28.10 (8 words)
26.32 = 28.7 (6 words)
26.34 = 26.75 (7 words)
26.35, see 4.6
26.36, see 4.10
26.38, see 4.10
26.39b, see 20.22-23
26.40, see 4.10
26.42, see 5.16
26.45, see 4.10
26.45, see 8.20
26.46, see 10.4
26.47, see 21.23
26.49, see 10.4
26.52, see 4.10
26.54 = 26.56 (4 words) concentrated repetition
26.56, see 26.54
26.61, see 12.40
26.61 = 27.40 (8 words)
26.62 = 27.13 (3 words) εἶπεν αὐτῷ· μαρτυροῦσιν
26.63, see 16.17
26.64, see 4.10
26.64, see 8.20
26.69, see 5.1

Chapter 27

27.1, see 21.23
27.3, see 21.23
27.11 = 27.37 (4 words)
27.12, see 21.23
27.13, see 4.6

27.13, see 26.62
27.22, see 9.28
27.40, see 12.40
27.40, see 26.61
27.54, see 14.33
27.54, see 17.6
27.56 = 27.61 = 28.1b (5–7 words)
27.63, see 12.40
27.64, see 12.40
27.64 = 28.13 (5 words)

Chapter 28

28.1b, see 27.56
28.5, see 17.7
28.5-7, see 26.31-32
28.9, see 2.2
28.10, see 4.10
28.10, see 26.31-32
28.11-12, see 21.23
28.12, see 12.14
28.13, see 27.64
28.16, see 26.31-32
28.16, see 5.1
28.20, see 13.39

Appendix B

Extended Repetitions of Nine Words or More

Repetitions are listed once at the first passage. The equal signs indicate parallels. The number of words in parentheses indicates the number of words each passage shares in common.

1.22 = 2.16, 17, 23 = 3.3 = 4.14 = 8.17 = 12.17 = 13.35 = 21.4 = 26.56 = 27.0 (= 26.54) (2–11 words)—fulfillment of Scripture.

2.13 = 2.19-20 (18 words) = 1.20 (7 words) = 2.12, 22 = 27.19 (2 words, κατ' ὄναρ)—dreams.

2.14 = 2.21 (10 words)—so rising took the child.

3.1-2 = 4.17 (9 words) = 10.7 (7 words)—Repent the Kingdom of Heaven has drawn near.

3.8, 10 = 7.16-20 = 12.33—fruit imagery (3 to 11 words) 3.10b = 7.19 (11 words); 7.16-20 = 12.33 (11 words); see also 21.41b, 43.

3.17 = 17.5 (15 words)—voice at baptism and transfiguration = 12.18 (5 words).

4.23 = 9.35 (20 words)—summary of teaching, proclaiming and healing = 10.1 (6 words).

5.16 = 6.1 = 10.32-33 (10 words)—(being seen) before men—Father in Heaven.

5.18 = 24.34-35 (16 words)—heaven and earth pass away.

5.19-20 = 18.1, 3 (14 words)—great in Kingdom of Heaven, except... by no means enter.

5.29-30 = 18.8-9 (30 words)—eye, hand, etc. cause to sin.

5.31-32 = 19.3-9 (15 words)—divorce.

6.1-2 = 23.5-7 (10 words)—doing things to be seen by men.

7.21b = 12.50 (9 words) = 18.14 (7 words) = 21.31 (4 words)—(the one doing) the will of the Father.

7.28-29 = 11.1 = 13.53 = 19.1 = 26.1 (6–9 words)—transitional formula closing discourses; see also 9.10.

8.12 = 13.42, 50 = 22.13 = 24.51 = 25.30 (9–17 words)—weeping and gnashing of teeth; 8.12 = 22.13 = 25.30 (15 words).

8.13 = 15.28 (10 words)—Jesus said: let it be... and was healed that hour.

8.23-27 = 14.22-33 (17 words)—storm double stories.

9.14-15 = 15.1-3 (9 words)—Then approach to Jesus (him) saying, 'Why your disciples...?'

9.20-21 = 14.36 (9 words)—touching the fringe of his garment.

9.27-31 = 20.29-34 (20 words)—blind men double stories.

  9.27 = 15.22 (6 words)—crying out (cried out) saying, 'Have mercy Son of David.'

  9.27 = 17.15 = 20.30 = 20.31 (2 words) saying, 'Have mercy...'

  15.22 = 17.15 (4 words)—saying, 'Have mercy, Lord.'

  15.22 = 20.30 = 20.31 (7 words)—cried out saying, 'Lord have mercy Son of David.'

9.32-34 = 12.22-27 (22 words)—ruler of demons double stories.

10.15 = 11.24 (11 words) I say to you, day of judgement, more tolerable = 11.22 (8 words).

10.17, 23 = 23.34, 36 (13 words)—and in their synagogues, scourge, persecute... city.

10.17-22 = 24.9-14 (18 words)—deliver, hated because of my name, testimony to the nations. 10.22a = 24.9 (9 words).

10.23 = 16.28 (9 words)—Amen I say to you...until comes the Son of Man.
10.38-39 = 16.24-25 (18 words)—take cross...lose life will find it; 10.38 = 16.24 = 27.32 (3 words)—the cross of him.
12.38-42 = 16.1-4 (24 words)—sign of Jonah double stories.
13.12 = 25.29 (13 words)—he who has more be given.
14.31-21 = 15.29-38 (56 words)—Feeding double stories.
16.17 = 26.63 (10 words)—You are the Christ.
16.19 = 18.18 (21 words)—binding and loosing.
16.21 = 20.17-19 (10 words)—Passion prediction.
16.27 = 25.31 (10 words)—Son of Man with angels.
17.20 = 21.21 (12 words)—faith move mountains.
19.28 = 25.31 (10 words)—Son of Man sits on the throne.
24.30 = 26.64 (12 words)—Son of Man coming on clouds.

BIBLIOGRAPHY

Abrams, M.H., *A Glossary of Literary Terms* (New York: Holt, Rinehart & Winston, 3rd edn, 1971, 5th edn, 1988).

—*The Mirror and the Lamp* (London: Oxford University Press, 1953).

Achtemeier, P.J., '*Omne verbum sonat*: The New Testament and the Oral Environment of Late Western Antiquity', *JBL* 109 (1990), pp. 3-27.

Allen, W.C., *A Critical and Exegetical Commentary on the Gospel According to S. Matthew* (ICC; Edinburgh: T. & T. Clark, 3rd edn, 1977).

Anderson, B.W., 'The New Frontier of Rhetorical Criticism: A Tribute to James Muilenburg', *Rhetorical Criticism* (ed. J.J. Jackson and M. Kessler; PTMS, 1; Pittsburgh: Pickwick Press, 1974), pp. ix-xviii.

Anderson, J.C., 'Double and Triple Stories, the Implied Reader, and Redundancy in Matthew', *Semeia* 31 (1985), pp. 71-90.

—'Matthew: Gender and Reading', *Semeia* 28 (1983), pp. 3-27.

—'Point of View in Matthew: Evidence' (Symposium on the Literary Analysis of the Gospels and Acts, SBL Annual Meeting, 1981, unpublished paper).

Anderson, J.C., and S.D. Moore (eds.), *Mark and Method: New Approaches in Biblical Studies* (Minneapolis: Fortress Press, 1992).

Bal, M., *Narratology* (trans. C. van Boheemen; Toronto: University of Toronto Press, 1985).

Barth, G., 'Matthew's Understanding of the Law', in G. Bornkamm, G. Barth and H.J. Held (eds.), *Tradition and Interpretation in Matthew* (trans. P. Scott; Philadelphia: Westminster Press, 1963), pp. 58-159.

Bauer, D.R., *The Structure of Matthew's Gospel: A Study in Literary Design* (BLS, 15; JSNTSup, 31; Sheffield: Almond Press, 1988).

Benson, L.D., 'The Literary Character of Anglo-Saxon Formulaic Poetry', *PMLA* 81 (1966), pp. 334-41.

Blass, F., and A. Debrunner, *A Greek Grammar of the New Testament and Other Early Christian Literature* (trans. and rev. R.W. Funk, Chicago: University of Chicago Press, 1961).

Book, C.L., and T.L. Albrecht *et al.*, *Human Communication: Principles, Contexts and Skills* (New York: St Martin's Press, 1980).

Boomershine, T.L., 'Peter's Denial as Polemic or Confession', *Semeia* 39 (1987), pp. 47-68.

Booth, W., *Critical Understanding* (Chicago: University of Chicago Press, 1979.

—*The Rhetoric of Fiction* (Chicago: University of Chicago Press, 1961).

Bornkamm, G., 'The Authority to "Bind" and "Loose" in the Church in Matthew's Gospel: The Problem of Sources in Matthew's Gospel', in D.G. Miller and

D. Hadidian (eds.), *Jesus and Man's Hope* (Pittsburgh: Pittsburgh Theological Seminary, 1970), I, pp. 37-50.

—'The Stilling of the Storm in Matthew', in Bornkamm, Barth and Held (eds.), *Tradition and Interpretation in Matthew*, pp. 52-57.

Bornkamm, G., G. Barth and H.J. Held (eds.), *Tradition and Interpretation in Matthew* (trans. P. Scott; Philadelphia: Westminster Press, 1963).

Borsck, F.H., 'Matthew's Intricate Fabric' (includes review of *Matthew: Structure, Christology, Kingdom* by Jack D. Kingsbury), *Int* 31 (1977), pp. 73-76.

Brenner, J.M., I.J.F. de Jong and J. Kalff, *Homer: Beyond Oral Poetry. Recent Trends in Homeric Interpretation* (Amsterdam: Grüner, 1987).

Brown, C.S., *Repetition in Zola's Novels* (University of Georgia Monographs, 1; Athens: University of Georgia Press, 1952).

Brown, E.K., *Rhythm in the Novel* (Lincoln: University of Nebraska, Bison Book, repr. 1978 [1950]).

Brown, R.E., *The Birth of the Messiah* (Garden City: Doubleday, 1977).

—'Review of *Matthew: Structure, Christology, Kingdom* by Jack D. Kingsbury', *Union Seminary Quarterly Review* 31 (1976), pp. 299-300.

Brown, R.E., K.P. Donfried and J. Reumann, *Peter in the New Testament* (Minneapolis: Augsburg, 1973).

Burnett, F.W., 'Prolegomenon to Reading Matthew's Eschatological Discourse: Redundancy and the Education of the Reader', *Semeia* 31 (1985), pp. 91-110.

Butler, B.C., *The Originality of St Matthew: A Critique of the Two Document Hypothesis* (Cambridge: Cambridge University Press, 1951).

Carpenter, R.H., 'Stylistic Redundancy and Function in Discourse', *Language and Style* 3 (1970), pp. 62-68.

Chatman, S., *Story and Discourse* (Ithaca, NY: Cornell University Press, 1978).

Cherry, C., *On Human Communication* (Cambridge: MIT Press, 1957).

Clarke, H., *Homer's Readers* (Newark: University of Delaware Press, 1981).

Cope, L., 'The Death of John the Baptist in the Gospel of Matthew', *CBQ* 38 (1976), pp. 515-19.

Crane, R.S., 'The Concept of Plot and the Plot of Tom Jones', in R.S. Crane (ed.), *Critics and Criticism* (Chicago: University of Chicago Press, 1952; abridged edn 1957), pp. 62-93.

Culler, J.D., *On Deconstruction: Theory and Criticism after Structuralism* (Ithaca, NY: Cornell University Press, 1982).

Culpepper, R.A., *Anatomy of the Fourth Gospel* (Philadelphia: Fortress Press, 1983).

Danker, F.W., 'Review of *Matthew: Structure, Christology, Kingdom* by Jack D. Kingsbury', *Dialog* 16 (1977), pp. 64-65.

Davies, W.D., *The Setting of the Sermon on the Mount* (London/New York: Cambridge University Press, 1966).

Davies, W.D., and D.C. Allison, *A Critical and Exegetical Commentary on the Gospel According to Matthew* (ICC; Edinburgh: T. & T. Clark, 1988), vol. I and (1991), vol. II.

Dewey, J., *Markan Public Debate, Literary Technique, Concentric Structure, and Theology in Mark 2.1-3.6* (SBLDS, 48, Chico, CA: Scholars Press, 1980).

—'Oral Methods of Structuring Narrative in Mark', *Int* 43 (1989), pp. 32-44.

de Jong, I.J.F., *Narrators and Focalizers: The Presentation of the Story in the Illiad* (Amsterdam: Grüner, 1987)

—'Narratology and Oral Poetry: The Case of Homer', *Poetics Today* 12 (1991), pp. 405-24.

Dowling, W.C., *The Critic's Hornbook* (New York: Thomas Y. Crowell, 1977).

Duckworth, G.E., 'Foreshadowing and Suspense in the Epics of Homer, Apollonius, and Vergil' (PhD dissertation, Princeton University 1933; Princeton: Princeton University Press, 1933).

Duling, D., 'The Therapeutic Son of David', *NTS* 24(1978), pp. 392-410.

Eco, U., *A Theory of Semiotics* (Bloomington: Indiana University Press, 1976).

Edwards, R.A., *Matthew's Story of Jesus* (Philadelphia: Fortress Press, 1985).

Ellis, P.F., *Matthew: His Mind and Message* (Collegeville, Minnesota: Liturgical Press, 1974).

Fenton, J.C., *The Gospel of Matthew* (Pelican Gospel Commentaries; Harmondsworth: Penguin Books, 1963).

—'Inclusio and Chiasmus in Matthew', *SE I* (= *Texte und Untersuchungen*, 73; Berlin: Akademie-Verlag, 1959), pp. 174-79.

Fiorenza, E.S. (ed.), *Searching the Scriptures. Volume 1: A Feminist Introduction* (New York: Crossroad, 1993).

Fish, S., 'Why No One's Afraid of Wolfgang Iser', *Diacritics* 11 (1981), pp. 2-13.

Foley, J.M., *The Theory of Oral Composition: History and Methodology* (Bloomington: Indiana University Press, 1988).

Forter, E.E., 'King Lear', in F.N. Magill (ed.), *Masterplots* (Englewood Cliffs: Salem Press; rev. edn, 1976 [1949]), VI, pp. 3148-52.

Forster, E.M., *Aspects of the Novel* (New York: Harcourt Brace, 1927).

Fowler, R.M., *Let the Reader Understand: Reader-Response Criticism and the Gospel of Mark* (Minneapolis: Fortress Press, 1991).

—'Reader-Response Criticism: Figuring Mark's Reader', in J.C. Anderson and S.D. Moore (eds.), *Mark and Method* (Minneapolis: Fortress Press, 1992).

—*Loaves and Fishes* (SBLDS, 54; Chico: Scholars Press, 1981).

Frye, F.M., 'A Literary Perspective for the Criticism of the Gospels', in D.G. Miller and D. Hadidian (eds.), *Jesus and Man's Hope* (Pittsburgh: Pittsburgh Theological Seminary, 1971), II, pp. 193-221.

Genette, G., *Narrative Discourse: An Essay in Method* (Ithaca, NY: Cornell University Press, 1975).

Gibbs, J.M., 'Purpose and Pattern in Matthew's Use of the Title "Son of David" ', *NTS* 10 (1963–64), pp. 446-64.

Giblin, C.H., 'Structural and Thematic Correlations in the Matthean Burial—Resurrection Narrative (Matt. 27.57–28.20)', *NTS* 21 (1975), pp. 406-20.

Gibson, W., 'Authors, Speakers, Readers, and Mock Readers', in J.P. Tompkins, *Reader-Response Criticism* (Baltimore: Johns Hopkins University Press, 1980), pp. 1-6.

Goulder, M.D., *Midrash and Lection in Matthew* (London: SPCK, 1974).

—'Review of *Matthew: Structure, Christology, Kingdom* by Jack D. Kingsbury', *JTS* 28 (1977), p. 145.

Gray, B., 'Repetition in Oral Literature', *JAF* 84 (1971), pp. 289-92.

Hadas, M., *Ancilla to Classical Reading* (New York: Columbia University Press, 1954).

Hägg, T., *Narrative Techniques in Ancient Greek Romances* (Skrifter Utgivna av Svenska Institutet: Athen, 8; VIII Acta Institutet Athiensis Regni Seuciae; Stockholm: Svenska Institutet i Athen, 1971).

Hare, D.R.A., 'Review of *Matthew: Structure, Christology, Kingdom* by Jack D. Kingsbury', *JBL* 96 (1977), pp. 307-308.

Hare, D.R.A. and D.J. Harrington, 'Make Disciples of All the Gentiles', *CBQ* 37 (1975), pp. 359-69.

Hawkins, J.C., *Horae Synopticae: Contributions to the Study of the Synoptic Problem* (Oxford: Clarendon Press, reprint edn, 1968).

Held, H.J., 'Matthew as Interpreter of the Miracle Stories', in Bornkamm, Barth and Held (eds.), *Tradition and Interpretation in Matthew*, pp. 165-299.

Hernandi, P., 'Literary Theory: A Compass for Critics', *CI* 3 (1976), pp. 369-86.

Hirsch, E.D., Jr, *Validity in Interpretation* (New Haven: Yale University Press, 1967).

Howell, D.B., *Matthew's Inclusive Story: A Study in the Narrative Rhetoric of the First Gospel* (JSNTSup, 42; Sheffield: JSOT Press, 1990).

Iser, W., *The Act of Reading* (Baltimore: Johns Hopkins University Press, 1978).

—*The Implied Reader* (Baltimore: Johns Hopkins University Press, 1974).

—'Talk Like Whales', *Diacritics* 11 (1981), pp. 82-87.

Jackson, J.J., and M. Kessler (eds.), *Rhetorical Criticism* (PTMS, 1; Pittsburgh: Pickwick Press, 1974), pp. ix-xvii.

Jakobson, R., 'Closing Statement: Linguistics and Poetics', in T.A. Sebeok, *Style in Language* (Cambridge: MIT Press, 1960), pp. 350-77.

Johnson, M.D., *The Purpose of the Biblical Genealogies* (SNTSMS, 8; London/New York: Cambridge University Press, 1969).

Kawin, B.F., *Telling It Again and Again: Repetition in Literature and Film* (Ithaca, NY: Cornell University Press, 1972).

Kee, H.C., 'The Gospel According to Matthew', in C. Laymon, *The Interpreter's One Volume Commentary on the Bible* (Nashville: Abingdon Press, 1971), pp. 609-43.

Kelber, W., 'Biblical Hermeneutics and the Ancient Art of Communication', *Semeia* 39 (1987), pp. 97-106.

—*The Oral and the Written Gospel* (Philadelphia: Fortress Press, 1983).

—*Mark's Story of Jesus* (Philadelphia: Fortress Press, 1979).

Kilpatrick, G.D., *The Origins of the Gospel According to St Matthew* (Oxford: Clarendon Press, repr., 1950 [1946]).

Kingsbury, J.D., 'The Figure of Peter in Matthew's Gospel as a Theological Problem', *JBL* 98 (1979), pp. 67-83.

—*Matthew As Story* (Minneapolis: Fortress Press, 2nd edn, 1988 [1986]).

—*Matthew: Structure, Christology, Kingdom* (Philadelphia: Fortress Press, 1975).

—'The "Miracle Chapters" of Matthew 8-9', *CBQ* 40 (1978), pp. 559-73.

—'The Plot of Matthew's Story', *Int* 46 (1992), pp. 347-56.

—'The Title Son of David in Matthew's Gospel', *JBL* 95 (1976), pp. 591-602.

—'The Verb *Akolouthein* ("To Follow") as an Index to Matthew's View of his Community', *JBL* 97 (1978), pp. 56-73.

Knox, B.M.W., 'Silent Reading in Antiquity', *Greek, Roman, and Byzantine Studies* 9 (1968), pp. 421-35.

Lagrange, M.J., *L'Évangile selon S. Matthieu* (Paris: Gabalda, 1948).

Lanser, S.S., *The Narrative Act: Point of View in Prose Fiction* (Princeton: Princeton University Press, 1981).

Lattimore, R., *The Four Gospels and Revelation* (New York: Farrar, Straus, & Giroux, 1962).

Laymon, C. (ed.), *The Interpreter's One Volume Commentary on the Bible* (Nashville: Abingdon Press, 1971).

Levine, A.J., *The Social and Ethnic Dimensions of Matthean Salvation History* (New York: Edwin Mellen, 1988).

Lohr, C.H., 'Oral Techniques in the Gospel of Matthew', *CBQ* 23 (1961), pp. 403-35.

Lohse, E. (ed.), *Der Rut Jesu und die Antwort des Gemeinde* (Göttingen: Vandenhoeck & Ruprecht, 1970).

Lord, A.B., 'Perspectives on Recent Work on Oral Literature', *FMLS* 10 (1974), pp. 187-210.

—'Perspectives on Recent Work on the Oral Traditional Formula', *Oral Tradition* I (1986), pp. 467-503.

—*The Singer of Tales* (New York: Atheneum, repr. 1974 [1960]).

Lotman, J.M., 'Point of View in a Text', *NLH* 6 (1975), pp. 339-52.

Luz, U., 'Die Jünger im Matthäusevengelium', *ZNW* 62 (1971), pp. 141-71.

—*Matthew 1–7: A Commentary* (trans. W.C. Linss, Minneapolis: Augsburg, 1989).

Macauley, R., and G. Lanning, *Technique in Fiction* (New York: Harper & Row, 1964).

Machen, J.G., *New Testament Greek for Beginners* (New York/Toronto: Macmillan, 1923).

Malbon, E.S., 'Narrative Criticism: How Does the Story Mean?', in Anderson and Moore (eds.), *Mark and Method: New Approaches in Biblical Studies*, pp. 23-49.

Malbon, E.S., and J.C. Anderson, 'Literary Critical Methods', in Fiorenza (ed.), *Searching the Scriptures*, I (New York: Crossroad, 1993), pp. 241-54.

Malina, B.J. and J.H. Neyrey, *Calling Jesus Names: The Social Value of Labels in Matthew* (Sonoma, CA: Polebridge Press, 1988).

Matera, F.J., 'The Plot of Matthew's Gospel', *CBQ* 49 (1987), pp. 233-53.

McNeile, A.H., *The Gospel According to St Matthew* (Grand Rapids: Baker Book House, repr. 1980 [1915]).

Meier, J.P., 'John the Baptist in Matthew's Gospel', *JBL* 99 (1980), pp. 383-405.

—'Review of *Matthew: Structure, Christology, Kingdom* by Jack D. Kingsbury' (CBA Task Force on Matthew, unpublished paper, n.d.).

Mendilow, A.A., *Time and the Novel* (New York: Humanities Press, 1965).

Minear, P.S., 'The Disciples and the Crowds in the Gospel of Matthew', *ATR*, sup. series, 3 (1974), pp. 28-44.

Moore, S.D., *Literary Criticism and the Gospels: The Theoretical Challenge* (New Haven: Yale University Press, 1989).

Morgan, R., *The Interpretation of Matthew* (ed. G. Stanton; Philadelphia: Fortress Press and London: SPCK, 1983).

Muilenburg, J., 'Form Criticism and Beyond', *JBL* 88 (1969), pp. 1-18.

Nolan, B.M., *The Royal Son of God* (Gottingen: Vandenhoeck & Ruprecht, 1979).

Notopoulos, J.A., 'Continuity and Interconnection in Homeric Composition', *TAPA* 82 (1951), pp. 81-101.

Ong, W.J., *Orality and Literacy: The Technologizing of the Word* (London and New York: Methuen, 1982).

Parry, M., 'Studies in the Epic Technique of Oral Verse-Making I: Homer and Homeric Style', *HSCP* 41 (1930), pp. 73-197.

—'Studies in the Epic Technique of Oral Verse-Making II: The Homeric Language as the Language of Oral Poetry', *HSCP* 43 (1932), pp. 1-50.

Perrin, N., 'The Evangelist as Author: Reflections on Method in the Study and Interpretation of the Synoptic Gospels and Acts', *BR* 17 (1972), pp. 5-18.

—'The Interpretation of the Gospel of Mark', *Int* 30 (1976), pp. 115-24.

—*Jesus and the Language of the Kingdom* (Philadelphia: Fortress Press, 1976).

—*The New Testament: An Introduction* (New York: Harcourt, Brace, Jovanovich, 1974).

—'The Use of *(para)didonai* in Connection with the Passion of Jesus in the New Testament', in E. Lohse (ed.), *Der Ruf Jesu und die Antwort des Gemeinde* (Göttingen: Vandenhoeck & Ruprecht, 1970), pp. 204-12.

Petersen, N., *Literary Criticism for New Testament Critics* (GBS; Philadelphia: Fortress Press, 1978).

—' "Point of View" in Mark's Narrative', *Semeia* 12 (1978), pp. 97-122.

Pierce, J.P., *Symbols, Signals and Noise: The Nature and Process of Communication* (New York: Harper & Row, 1961).

Powell, M.A., 'Direct and Indirect Phraseology in the Gospel of Matthew', in *Society of Biblical Literature 1991 Seminar Papers* (Atlanta: Scholars Press, 1991), pp. 405-17.

—'The Plot and Subplots of Matthew's Gospel', *NTS* 38 (1992), pp. 187-204.

—*What is Narrative Criticism?* (GBS; Minneapolis: Fortress Press, 1990).

Prince, G., 'Introduction to the Study of the Narratee', in J.P. Tompkins (ed.), *Reader-Response Criticism* (Baltimore: Johns Hopkins University Press, 1980), pp. 7-25.

Ressequie, J.L., 'Reader-Response Criticism and the Synoptic Gospels', *JAAR* 52 (1984), pp. 307-24.

Rhoads, D., and D. Michie, *Mark as Story: An Introduction to the Narrative of a Gospel* (Philadelphia: Fortress Press, 1982).

Richardson, S., *The Homeric Narrator* (Nashville: Vanderbilt University Press, 1990).

Ricoeur, P., *Interpretation Theory* (Fort Worth: Texas Christian University Press, 1976).

Rimmon-Kenan, S., *Narrative Fiction: Contemporary Poetics* (London and New York: Methuen, 1983).

Ruland, V., *Horizons of Criticism* (Chicago: American Library Association, 1975).

Schaberg, J., *The Illegitimacy of Jesus: A Feminist Theological Interpretation of the Infancy Narratives* (San Francisco: Harper & Row, 1987).

Scholes, R., and Kellogg, R., *The Nature of Narrative* (London/New York: Oxford University Press, paper 1968; original 1966).

Sebeok, T.A. (ed.), *Style in Language* (Cambridge: MIT Press, 1960).

Seesemann, H., 'πειράζν', *TDNT*.

Silberman, L. (ed.), 'Orality, Aurality and Biblical Narrative', *Semeia* 39 (1987).

Schenk, W., 'Das Präsens Historicum als makrosyntaktische Gliederungssignal im Mattäusevangelium', *NTS* 22 (1976), pp. 464-74.

Sheridan, M., 'Disciples and Discipleship in Matthew and Luke', *BTB* 3 (1973), pp. 235-55.

Smith, F., *Understanding Reading: A Psycholinguistic Analysis of Reading and Learning to Read* (Hillsdale, NJ: Lawrence Erlbaum Associates, 4th edn 1988).

Souvage, J., *An Introduction to the Study of the Novel* (Gent: E. Story-Scientia PVBA, 1965).

Staley, J., *The Prints First Kiss: A Rhetorical Investigation of the Implied Reader in the Fourth Gospel* (SBLDS, 82; Atlanta: Scholars Press, 1988).

Stanton, G.N., *A Gospel for a New People* (Edinburgh: T. & T. Clark, 1992).

—(ed.), *The Interpretation of Matthew* (IRT, 3; Philadelphia: Fortress Press, 1983).

Sternberg, M., *The Poetics of Biblical Narrative: Ideological Literature and the Drama of Reading* (Bloomington: Indiana University Press, 1988).

Stock, B.M., *The Implications of Literacy: Written Language and Models of Interpretation in the Eleventh and Twelfth Centuries* (Princeton: Princeton University Press, 1983).

Studing, R., 'Review of *Telling It Again and Again* by Bruce F. Kawin', *JAAC* 31 (1972), p. 277.

Suleiman, S.R., 'Introduction', in S. Suleiman and I. Crossman (ed.), *The Reader in the Text* (Princeton: Princeton University Press, 1980), pp. 3-45.

—'Redundancy and the "Readable" Text', *Poetics Today* 1 (1980), pp. 119-42.

Tannehill, R.C., 'The Disciples in Mark: The Function of a Narrative Role', *JR* 57 (1977), pp. 386-405.

—*The Narrative Unity of Luke-Acts* (Minneapolis: Fortress Press, vol. I, 1986 and vol. II, 1990).

Thompson, W.G., *Matthew's Advice to a Divided Community: Mt. 17, 22-18, 35* (Analecta Biblica, 44; Rome: Pontifical Biblical Institute, 1970).

—'Reflections on the Composition of Mt. 8:1–9:34', *CBQ* 33 (1971), pp. 365-88.

Tompkins, J.P. (ed.), *Reader-Response Criticism* (Baltimore: Johns Hopkins University Press, 1980).

Tolbert, M.A., '1978 Markan Seminar: Response to Robert Tannehill', paper discussed at the 1978 annual meeting of the Society of Biblical Literature, private circulation.

—*Perspectives on the Parables* (Philadelphia: Fortress Press, 1979).

—*Sowing the Gospel: Mark's World in Literary-Historical Perspective* (Minneapolis: Fortress Press, 1989), esp. pp. 41-47.

Uspensky, B., *A Poetics of Composition* (trans. V. Zavarin and S. Wittig; Berkeley: University of California Press, 1973).

Van Tilborg, Sjef, *The Jewish Leaders in Matthew* (Leiden: Brill, 1972).

von Dobschütz, E., 'Matthäus als Rabbi und Katechet', *ZNW* 27 (1928), pp. 338-48.

Waetjen, H.C., 'The Genealogy as the Key to the Gospel According to Matthew', *JBL* 95 (1976), pp. 205-30.

Wainwright, E.M., *Towards a Feminist Critical Reading of the Gospel according to Matthew* (Berlin: de Gruyter, 1991).

Weaver, D.J., *Matthew's Missionary Discourse: A Literary Critical Analysis* (JSNTSup, 38; Sheffield: JSOT Press, 1990).

Wellek, R., and A. Warren, *Theory of Literature* (New York: Harcourt, Brace & World, 3rd edn, 1962).

Wheelright, P., *The Burning Fountain* (Bloomington: Indiana University Press, 1968).

—*Metaphor and Reality* (Bloomington: Indiana University Press, 1962).

White, E.B., *Charlotte's Web* (New York: Harper Trophy, 1952).

Wimsatt, W.K., *The Verbal Icon* (Lexington: University of Kentucky Press, 1954).

Witherup, R.D., 'Cornelius Over and Over and Over Again: "Functional Redundancy" in the Acts of the Apostles', *JSNT* 49 (1993), pp. 44-66.

—'Functional Redundancy in the Acts of the Apostles: A Case Study', *JSNT* 48 (1992), pp. 67-86.

Wittig, S., 'Formulaic Style and the Problem of Redundancy', *Centrum* 1 (1973), pp. 123-36.

—*Stylistic and Narrative Structures in the Middle English Romances* (Austin: University of Texas Press, 1978).
—'A Theory of Polyvalent Reading', in *SBL Seminar Papers* (ed. G. MacRae; Missoula: Scholars Press, 1975), II, pp. 169-84.

INDEXES

Index of References

Old Testament

New Testament

CLASSICAL AUTHORS

Index of Authors

JOURNAL FOR THE STUDY OF THE NEW TESTAMENT

Supplement Series

45 THE RHETORIC OF ROMANS:
ARGUMENTATIVE CONSTRAINT AND STRATEGY AND PAUL'S DIALOGUE WITH JUDAISM
Neil Elliott

46 THE LAST SHALL BE FIRST:
THE RHETORIC OF REVERSAL IN LUKE
John O. York

47 JAMES AND THE Q SAYINGS OF JESUS
Patrick J. Hartin

48 TEMPLUM AMICITIAE:
ESSAYS ON THE SECOND TEMPLE PRESENTED TO ERNST BAMMEL
Edited by William Horbury

49 PROLEPTIC PRIESTS
PRIESTHOOD IN THE EPISTLE TO THE HEBREWS
John M. Scholer

50 PERSUASIVE ARTISTRY:
STUDIES IN NEW TESTAMENT RHETORIC IN HONOR OF GEORGE A. KENNEDY
Edited by Duane F. Watson

51 THE AGENCY OF THE APOSTLE: A DRAMATISTIC ANALYSIS OF PAUL'S RESPONSES TO CONFLICT IN 2 CORINTHIANS
Jeffrey A. Crafton

52 REFLECTIONS OF GLORY:
PAUL'S POLEMICAL USE OF THE MOSES–DOXA TRADITION IN 2 CORINTHIANS 3.12-18
Linda L. Belleville

53 REVELATION AND REDEMPTION AT COLOSSAE
Thomas J. Sappington

54 THE DEVELOPMENT OF EARLY CHRISTIAN PNEUMATOLOGY WITH SPECIAL REFERENCE TO LUKE–ACTS
Robert P. Menzies

55 THE PURPOSE OF ROMANS:
A COMPARATIVE LETTER STRUCTURE INVESTIGATION
L. Ann Jervis

56 THE SON OF THE MAN IN THE GOSPEL OF JOHN
Delbert Burkett

57 ESCHATOLOGY AND THE COVENANT:
A COMPARISON OF 4 EZRA AND ROMANS 1–11
Bruce W. Longenecker

58 NONE BUT THE SINNERS:
RELIGIOUS CATEGORIES IN THE GOSPEL OF LUKE
David A. Neale

59 CLOTHED WITH CHRIST:
THE EXAMPLE AND TEACHING OF JESUS IN ROMANS 12.1–15.13
Michael Thompson

60 THE LANGUAGE OF THE NEW TESTAMENT:
CLASSIC ESSAYS
Edited by Stanley E. Porter

61 FOOTWASHING IN JOHN 13 AND THE JOHANNINE COMMUNITY
John Christopher Thomas

62 JOHN THE BAPTIZER AND PROPHET:
A SOCIO-HISTORICAL STUDY
Robert L. Webb

63 POWER AND POLITICS IN PALESTINE:
THE JEWS AND THE GOVERNING OF THEIR LAND 100 BC–AD 70
James S. McLaren

64 JESUS AND THE ORAL GOSPEL TRADITION
Edited by Henry Wansbrough

65 THE RHETORIC OF RIGHTEOUSNESS IN ROMANS 3.21-26
Douglas A. Campbell

66 PAUL, ANTIOCH AND JERUSALEM:
A STUDY IN RELATIONSHIPS AND AUTHORITY IN EARLIEST CHRISTIANITY
Nicholas Taylor

67 THE PORTRAIT OF PHILIP IN ACTS:
A STUDY OF ROLES AND RELATIONS
F. Scott Spencer

68 JEREMIAH IN MATTHEW'S GOSPEL:
THE REJECTED-PROPHET MOTIF IN MATTHAEAN REDACTION
Michael P. Knowles

69 RHETORIC AND REFERENCE IN THE FOURTH GOSPEL
Margaret Davies

70 AFTER THE THOUSAND YEARS:
RESURRECTION AND JUDGMENT IN REVELATION 20
J. Webb Mealy

71 SOPHIA AND THE JOHANNINE JESUS
Martin Scott

72 NARRATIVE ASIDES IN LUKE–ACTS
Steven M. Sheeley

73 SACRED SPACE
AN APPROACH TO THE THEOLOGY OF THE EPISTLE TO THE HEBREWS
Marie E. Isaacs

74 TEACHING WITH AUTHORITY:
MIRACLES AND CHRISTOLOGY IN THE GOSPEL OF MARK
Edwin K. Broadhead

75 PATRONAGE AND POWER:
A STUDY OF SOCIAL NETWORKS IN CORINTH
John Kin-Man Chow

76 THE NEW TESTAMENT AS CANON:
A READER IN CANONICAL CRITICISM
Robert Wall and Eugene Lemcio

77 REDEMPTIVE ALMSGIVING IN EARLY CHRISTIANITY
Roman Garrison

78 THE FUNCTION OF SUFFERING IN PHILIPPIANS
L. Gregory Bloomquist

79 THE THEME OF RECOMPENSE IN MATTHEW'S GOSPEL
Blaine Charette

80 BIBLICAL GREEK LANGUAGE AND LINGUISTICS: OPEN QUESTIONS IN CURRENT RESEARCH
Stanley E. Porter and D.A. Carson

81 THE LAW IN GALATIANS
In-Gyu Hong

82 ORAL TRADITION AND THE GOSPELS: THE PROBLEM OF MARK 4
Barry W. Henaut

83 PAUL AND THE SCRIPTURES OF ISRAEL
Craig A. Evans and James A. Sanders

84 FROM JESUS TO JOHN: ESSAYS ON JESUS AND NEW TESTAMENT CHRISTOLOGY IN HONOUR OF MARINUS DE JONGE
Edited by Martinus C. De Boer

85 RETURNING HOME: NEW COVENANT AND SECOND EXODUS AS THE CONTEXT FOR 2 CORINTHIANS 6.14–7.1
William J. Webb

86 ORIGINS OF METHOD: TOWARDS A NEW UNDERSTANDING OF JUDAISM AND CHRISTIANITY—ESSAYS IN HONOUR OF JOHN C. HURD
Bradley H. McLean

87 WORSHIP, THEOLOGY AND MINISTRY IN THE EARLY CHURCH: ESSAYS IN HONOUR OF RALPH P. MARTIN
Edited by Michael Wilkins and Terence Paige

88 THE BIRTH OF THE LUKAN NARRATIVE
M. Coleridge

89 WORD AND GLORY: ON THE EXEGETICAL AND THEOLOGICAL BACKGROUND OF JOHN'S PROLOGUE
Craig A. Evans

90 RHETORIC IN THE NEW TESTAMENT
ESSAYS FROM THE 1992 HEIDELBERG CONFERENCE
Edited by Stanley E. Porter and Thomas H. Olbricht

91 MATTHEW'S NARRATIVE WEB: OVER, AND OVER AND OVER AGAIN
J.C. Anderson